Reading Reminders

Tools, Tips, and Techniques

JIM BURKE

BOYNTON/COOK PUBLISHERS
Heinemann
Portsmouth, NH

Boynton/Cook Publishers, Inc.
361 Hanover Street
Portsmouth, NH 03801–3912
www.boyntoncook.com

Offices and agents throughout the world

© 2000 by Jim Burke

The author and publisher wish to thank those who have generously given permission to reprint borrowed material:

"Ten Principles for Looking at Reading/Language Arts Lessons in Your Classroom" by Richard L. Allington, University of Florida. Reprinted by permission of the author.

"Traits of an Effective Reader Reading an Informational Text Scoring Guide" and "Traits of an Effective Reader Reading a Literary Text Scoring Guide" by Northwest Regional Educational Laboratory. Copyright by Northwest Regional Educational Laboratory, Portland, OR. Reprinted by permission. The Northwest Regional Educational Laboratory grants permission for school personnel to reproduce these two scoring guides for use in their own schools and districts for instructional development purposes.

"Independent Reading Follow-Up Essay Assignment," "Rhetorical Modes," "A Concise Glossary of Literary Terms," "103 Things to Do Before/During/After Reading," and text excerpts from *The English Teacher's Companion: A Complete Guide to Classroom, Curriculum, and the Profession* by Jim Burke. Copyright © 1999 by Jim Burke. Published by Boynton/Cook Publishers, Inc., a subsidiary of Reed Elsevier Inc., Portsmouth, NH. Reprinted by permission of the author and publisher.

Library of Congress Cataloging-in-Publication Data
Burke, Jim, 1961–
   Reading reminders : tools, tips, and techniques / Jim Burke
      p.   cm.
   Includes bibliographical references and index.
   ISBN 0-86709-500-8
      1. Reading (Secondary).   2. High school students—Books and reading.
   3. Teenagers—Books and reading.   I. Title.

   LB1632 .B84 2000
   428.4'071'2—dc21   00-057526

Editor: Lois Bridges
Production: Abigail M. Heim
Interior design: Joni Doherty Design
Cover design: Judy Arisman
Cover photograph: Julie Nelson
Manufacturing: Louise Richardson

Printed in the United States of America on acid-free paper

11 12 13 14 15   09 10 11

This book is
dedicated
to all 150
of my sophomores,
who taught me
so much
about reading
during our semester
together.

It is also dedicated
to my editor
and friend,
Lois Bridges.

Finally,
it is dedicated
to my wife, Susan,
who makes
everything seem
possible for me
and our three
wonderful children.

Contents

· ·

Evaluate Your Own Teaching   83

Evaluate Your Students   103

WHAT STUDENTS MUST BE ABLE TO DO

Read a Variety of Texts for Different Purposes   127

Use Various Strategies   173

Evaluate and Monitor Their Understanding, Performance, and Progress   313

Appendices   328

Introduction

. . . .

Throughout the semester during which I wrote this book, I had posted on my wall one reminder: "Write the book you wish you had." I teach full time, and thus am constantly challenged to remember all that I must or should help my students to master during their time with me. This book addresses only what we must help them accomplish as readers—never mind what they must learn to do as writers, speakers, and thinkers!

I expect that you know much if not all of what is contained here; indeed, as I wrote, I often envisioned my readers saying, "I forgot all about that strategy! That will be perfect for what I am doing tomorrow!" As the title indicates, this book is made up of reminders—my intention in writing it was to help you realize and remember all that you already know.

Like most of us in the classroom, I received little specific training in how to teach reading. Now I tend to think of it in much the same way Frank Smith (1995) does when he writes that "the prime value of reading and writing is the *experience* they provide through which we may constantly and unobtrusively learn." Thus is reading similar to a conversation—with the author; with the past, the present, or the future; with an aspect of ourselves that is called into existence through the words we read. Reading is a physical as well as intellectual experience, one that becomes more complex as technology spawns new, more interactive types of texts. To these experiences, these textual encounters, we each bring our own set of talents, strategies, cultures, and perspectives, all of which inevitably color our reading of any text.

Nothing helped me write this book more than my students: 150 sophomores at Burlingame High School, each of whom brought to the class their own experiences with school, with reading, and with life. With their differences and difficulties, their enthusiastic support and equally entrenched resistance, they were my teachers as I tried to help them become the readers we want all our students to be. This book grows out of that intense collaboration, a period of time during which I watched my students improve as I never had before. These gains in performance, confidence, and engagement were all the more important to me because the class makeup was so diverse. More than twenty students

I figured out you need to use different imaginations for different kinds of books.

ANNIE AU-YEUNG, SOPHOMORE AT BURLINGAME HIGH SCHOOL

had identified learning difficulties and many had gone through or were enrolled in our ESL program. Whenever possible in the book I use examples from these students or others who face particular challenges when it comes to reading. Most students in these classes summed up their progress in June using words similar to Alex Dove's:

> In the last few months I have learned how to enjoy reading. I have learned how much better reading a book can be rather than watching a movie. I never used to want to read, because any time I had to, it was usually for school, and in school I didn't get to read what I wanted to. I have just recently discovered that reading can actually be fun, interesting, entertaining, and very enjoyable. I have discovered that because Mr. Burke allows us to pick our own books, with no guidelines to follow. Without this class I never would have read *Hoop Dreams*. If I never read that book, I would maybe never want to read like I want to now.

The examples warrant one additional explanation. I wrote this book during the spring semester, having just returned from sabbatical (during which I was working on *Illuminating Texts*). Many of the examples come from our study of Shakespeare's *Macbeth*. While I would have liked to make use of a wider range of texts, these examples effectively illustrate the challenges kids face in reading difficult material. Most of the other examples I include are from equally difficult texts, my point being that kids can read these texts if we support their reading development using the ideas in this book.

Writing this book and using the techniques described in it have reminded me how complex reading is, especially when one is trying to guide thirty-five kids from diverse backgrounds and reading levels toward mastery despite the time limits, interruptions, and general distractions of a typical fifty-minute period.

Writing this book helped me become a better teacher—and reader—and, more importantly, helped my students become better readers. My sincere hope is that it will do the same for you and yours.

Jim Burke

How to Use This Book

. . . .

I designed this book to support both working teachers who are trying to help their students read better and professors who are preparing future teachers. I wanted to create a book that would enable you through a two-minute read—between periods, while planning, even while teaching—to be more successful. I also tried to write a book that would make sense to and help teachers in any subject area.

The book is organized as follows:

• *Reminder*. Each reminder is summed up by its title. I wanted you to be able to scan the table of contents and get an idea in thirty seconds or less that will help you in your classroom practice. If you then want more information you can go to the appropriate place in the text for instructions or to view examples of student work or read about actual activities.

• *Rationale*. Each reminder begins with a brief explanation of why the specified idea or activity is important. These rationales are based on my own experiences in the classroom, on research, or both.

• *"What to Do."* Suggestions for classroom practice comprise the bulk of each reminder. Here you will find examples of student work, questions to ask, activities to try, and strategies to use. On occasion, I include actual sample assignments, complete with student work examples that you could use as exemplars for your own students. These exemplars make a big difference. In my own classroom, for example, I might copy entries from a student's reading journal onto a transparency, put them on the overhead, then discuss their merits with the whole class, in order to help students improve their own reading, writing, and thinking. In some cases I included several examples, to show you a range of possible responses or approaches.

• *Graphic Organizers.* A number of forms, located in the appendices, have been provided for you to reproduce and use in the classroom. (These graphic organizers, and various other forms also included in the appendices, are intended to be enlarged to 125% or more during photocopying.) Additional forms, materials, and ideas also can be found at my website: <www.englishcompanion.com>.

Have you a place where, when the world ends, you want to be? Have you a person who will be there when you put out a hand? When the sky weeps, whose fall will you weep? Look steadily into the fire— what face or sign do you see? If a fault is yours, what forgiveness? Who will understand?

WILLIAM STAFFORD, "SOME QUESTIONS TO ASK DURING YOUR READING," FROM HIS DEDICATION TO HIS BOOK, *HOLDING ONTO THE GRASS*

My goal was to create a book that you could use in your own way to meet your own needs, regardless of what grade level, ability level, or subject you teach. In short, I tried to structure this book so that you can get the information you seek as easily and quickly as possible.

Reading Reminders has a final, more ambitious objective. Schools need to develop and use a common set of strategies, habits, and terms to help students become better readers in all subject areas. As I mentioned before, the reminder in my office was to "write the book I wish I had," but in the end I was trying to write the book our schools need, a book that will help you and your colleagues become confident, effective teachers of reading who work together to ensure that all students inherit a lifelong passion for reading.

Establish a

Reading Culture

My daughter is seven, and some of the other second-grade parents complain that their children don't read for pleasure. When I visit their homes, the children's rooms are crammed with expensive books, but the parents' rooms are empty. Those children do not see their parents reading, as I did every day of my childhood. By contrast when I walk into an apartment with books on the shelves, books on the bedside tables, books on the floor, and books on the toilet tank, then I know what I would see if I opened the door that says PRIVATE—GROWNUPS KEEP OUT: a child sprawled on the bed, reading.

—ANNE FADIMAN, FROM EX LIBRIS: CONFESSIONS OF A COMMON READER

Marc Sutter during sustained silent reading time.

When you walk into a class that honors reading, you know it. The evidence is contained not only in the conversations but on the walls, on the shelves, and on the tables. Like any fertile garden, such environments are the result of careful attention to many needs and interests; they are also, like gardens, the result of trial and error.

Edwin Schlossburg, in *Interactive Excellence: Defining and Developing New Standards for the Twenty-First Century* (1998), writes that his first question when designing any museum exhibit or interactive experience is, "Who do I expect this person to be when they enter the door?" My students learn upon entering my room that I expect them to be readers, and that I will go the distance to support that expectation. This might mean bringing in books or magazines I think they will like. It might mean asking someone who is reading a book to tell another person with common interests about it.

It means, to borrow Frank Smith's idea, that I must foster a sense of community or "club" that enables every student to give themselves permission to be a reader, to take themselves and their interests as readers seriously. Nothing has helped me achieve this more than sustained silent reading (SSR).

SSR demanded that I make a commitment of time I had never given reading before, but the results were obvious and impressive. It provided me with an important opportunity to model for my students how I read; indeed, I found out early on that if I did not read with them, I was often the cause of their distraction. During SSR, anyone not reading violated the culture we worked so hard to establish.

Kids need time to be quiet and reflect on what they want, who they are (and are not); SSR, if done regularly and dependably, supports that need. The SSR culture allows students the opportunity to read what will benefit them as individuals. Sophomore Erica Goodspeed illustrates this idea best in her response to Piri Thomas's *Down These Mean Streets*, a book she picked up one day during SSR when she forgot to bring the book she had been reading to class:

> Some people believe that they can't be touched by a book. For a long time I was one of those people, until I read *Down These Mean Streets*, by Piri Thomas. I was so shocked that somebody would write an autobiography about a life that was so realistic.
>
> I read this book every day. I got more and more wrapped up in Piri's life. One day I realized why this man's life was so interesting and so familiar. It was my family he was describing. A family with lots of kids, a deadbeat father, and a mother as strong as a brick wall holding everything together. A family of color barely making it on that small paycheck every week. Most of all this man was my brother. I have seen and I am still seeing

my brother live this life on the mean streets, trying to find himself, tempted by women, sex, drugs, and easy street, trapped by confusion, hatred, jail, crime, and life.

This book was so good. I would recommend it to anybody. It captures people's lives in a mere three hundred and some odd pages. This book's message is amazing, heartbreaking, and so very true. It also teaches a lesson in a very understanding way. In reality it would take a lifetime to comprehend.

Erica's comments offer powerful evidence of the power of books. She was able to find her way to this book because of the culture of reading we achieved, an idea that student Justin McGovern later reinforced. Justin had not come into the class initially describing or identifying himself as a reader, but neither had he found books about the things that mattered most to him. Waiting for the bell to ring on one of those slightly chaotic days, Justin was standing next to someone he wouldn't usually talk to or work with. The young woman was reading a book—I don't remember the title—and Justin struck up a conversation with her about it, asking her what it was about, if she liked it, and why she did. "Can I borrow that book from you when you're done?" he asked. Such an exchange, glimpsed in passing, confirmed what our class community had accomplished: a culture in which students saw themselves as readers, club members who took themselves and each other a bit more seriously than they did the first day they walked into class.

Use Sustained Silent Reading (SSR)

RATIONALE

If it is done right, SSR improves readers' stamina, fluency, and engagement. Teachers need to dedicate specific time to this activity and maintain that commitment, so that students come ready to read, and learn to settle down to the task. SSR is considered one of the most effective means of improving students' reading capacity at any grade level (Pilgreen 2000). How much time teachers devote to it will usually depend on the time available to them and the demands of the course. The outcome of a good SSR program is that students learn to make connections (through writing and talking about their books) and gain exposure to other books through hearing about them from their peers.

WHAT TO DO

• Decide how much time you can commit to SSR and if it will be a daily or weekly activity. Remember that one goal of SSR is the development of stamina, so students should have at least ten minutes to read.

• Keep in mind that students must be allowed to choose their own books for SSR (see Reminder 53), and they may not use the time to read school books, magazines, or newspapers, or do homework.

• Encourage students who did not bring their book to class to choose one from the class library.

• Give students time to reflect on and discuss their SSR books via the following formats.

• Small-group discussion using these questions as guides:

▸ Why did you choose this book?

▸ What about it holds your interest?

▸ How/why would you recommend this book to someone or, alternatively, not recommend it?

▸ What so far is your favorite moment in the book?

- Journal writing using the following prompts from *Reading for Understanding* (Schoenbach et al. 1999), which asks students to focus not on *what* they read but *how* they read it:
    - I got confused when . . .
    - I was distracted by . . .
    - I started to think about . . .
    - I got stuck when . . .
    - The time went quickly because . . .
    - A word/some words I didn't know were . . .
    - I stopped because . . .
    - I lost track of everything except . . .
    - I figured out that . . .
    - I first thought . . . but then I realized . . .
- Whole-class discussion during which students discuss:
    - What book they are reading
    - Why they chose that book
    - Who else would like it
    - How they are reading it
    - If they are going to abandon it and why
    - How they will choose their next book
- Keep track of students' SSR performance using any of the following methods:
    - Wall chart recording students' names, books read, and number of pages
    - SSR log
    - Daily journal
    - Summative evaluation (e.g., an essay or other project that serves to bring closure to and integration of all their reading) when they complete a book or the semester
    - Conferences
- Set up and consistently maintain rules (such as no talking, no doing homework during SSR) to ensure the program's success.

SAMPLE SSR LOGS

I was reading *Redwall* by Brian Jacques. So far I've read 320 pages, but during today's reading I probably read 20. Today I just dived right into the book. I was at an exciting part and I wanted to know what happened. Because of that, I would rate myself as a 4. I would of paid more attention but I was constantly bothered by Mike. I didn't notice much happening because I was too busy in the land of *Redwall*.

—*Felipe Lopes*

What Girls Learn, by Karin Cook

This book is more challenging than my last so when I hear noise or come to a difficult word I get easily distracted, but because this book is about children about my age I am interested to find out about their problems. I am often a very eager reader when I find a good book. Time passed very quickly and I found myself not wanting to stop. Twenty minutes just didn't seem like enough time.

—*Laurel Hackelman*

When I was reading I started thinking about what it would be like to be the character in the book. The character was a high school football star who got hurt and his season was over. I thought to my self and began to think that if it happened to me and I thought that I wouldn't play ever again and know and realize that anything can happen you just have to be careful.

—*Philip Jordan*

FIGURE 1-1   Dan Neylon reads Victor Martinez's *Parrot in the Oven* during SSR.

FIGURE 1-2   Brandon Howe and Chris Dannels during SSR time.

FIGURE 1-3   Joe McCarthy begins the day by reading during SSR.

2 Read Aloud

RATIONALE

Reading aloud, whether it is done by the students or the teacher, is one of the most helpful techniques for improving reading skills and engaging readers of all ages. Hearing the text while looking at it on the page helps many readers process the information more effectively and understand how it should be read. As they listen to the teacher's emphases and pauses, they see how those accord with the punctuation and structure of the sentence. Janet Allen (1995) writes, "I learned that reading aloud was a risk-free way to turn many individuals into one group and share literature with students who believed they hated to read. The questions I asked during and after the reading might have sounded very similar to end-of-story questions I had experienced, but the texts were at least relevant to these students' lives." Reading aloud also develops students' language sense as they hear the ways words are used, pronounced, and interpreted.

WHAT TO DO

- Read aloud

  - When hearing the text will help students enjoy it or process it in a more effective way
  - When introducing new or difficult texts
  - When reading poetry or plays (see Reminder 72)
  - When you don't have time to copy and distribute a text but want to expose your students to it (e.g., an editorial on gun control you want your senior government students to hear)
  - When you want to focus your students' attention
  - At the beginning or end of class (as an opener or wrap-up)

- Choose diverse materials to read aloud, such as

  - Directions
  - Class books (i.e., a novel you read from a little bit each day)
  - Literature (to help students grasp relationships and hear the sound of the language)

- Observations (e.g., from a scientific report used to begin a class or group discussion)
- Kids' books
- Random items you discover in your own reading that you think are fun, powerful, or useful to share
- Note: My high school economics teacher read to us from the stock page each day, showing us in the process how to read such a text. Mr. Baxter, my sophomore English teacher, read to us each Friday, a memorable occasion in an otherwise dull sophomore year.

- Read aloud in various configuratioans, such as

  - Students to a small group
  - Students to the whole class
  - Teacher to the students

- Provide a safe, supportive environment (see Reminder 5) to ensure successful read-alouds.

- Don't force students to read aloud, *invite* them; as they see it is safe, fun, and helpful, continue to encourage them to try it.

- Have booktalks: Read aloud from a book or several books that you think will appeal to students, choosing exciting segments that you can read well, then stopping at the crucial moment when they are hooked and will want to take the book up where you left off.

- Keep in mind Janet Allen's (1995) guidelines for reading aloud to students:

  - Determine if this is the right book to meet the needs of these students at this time.
  - Ask yourself if you can read this book in such a way that students will not be bored by it.
  - Choose books that you yourself enjoy, as this will help you read them better.
  - Choose a book that matches your instructional goals.

- Use reading aloud across subject areas (e.g., reading story problems aloud in a math class helps to emphasize their narrative structure).

- Before, during, and after you read aloud have students:

  - Make predictions about what will happen or how it relates to what you are studying or have studied in the past.
  - Summarize what happened.

▶ Take notes.

▶ Follow along on the page while the text is being read aloud.

• Keep in mind that reading aloud should *not* replace silent independent reading. In the face of students' reading difficulties, many teachers bypass the textbook entirely by reading it aloud; students quickly learn that they do not need to do the assigned reading since the teacher will summarize the main ideas or read it aloud to them in class the next day.

Help Students Write Their Reading Autobiography

RATIONALE

Stories help us understand the world and ourselves. Identifying the traits of effective and ineffective readers makes students aware of what they should do when reading, but it doesn't help them understand their own history as readers (i.e., how they became the kind of reader they are) or develop their current attitude toward reading. Reading is a personal experience. We all enter into the world of stories through our early years—at home or later on through school—but many readers lose sight of the pleasure they once found in reading or being read to. Writing their autobiography allows them to retrace the steps of their reading life and identify those events or people that helped turn them on or off to reading.

WHAT TO DO

• Use the information collected through their reading survey (see Reminder 34) and their discussion of effective and ineffective readers as notes for their autobiography. They might consider using one of the graphic organizers (see Reminder 17) to help them structure their narrative and examine the different influences that shaped their attitude.

• Use the sample autobiography in Reminder 28; this letter originally appeared in my book *I Hear America Reading: Why We Read, What We Read* (1999). Take time to read it closely and discuss with students those elements they might want to include in their own story. Note: this would also provide your students the opportunity to read for a special purpose: not for the purpose of enjoyment of a text (though they might enjoy it) but to learn from it, to study how it works so that they can emulate it.

• Have them share their drafts in groups, using their writing as a tool for discussion and the discussion as a tool for reflecting on how their own story is similar to or different from others'. Encourage them to take notes on their drafts or on separate paper as they discuss their stories.

• Make room for useful conversations. One of the more moving discussions I witnessed was when a group of struggling readers in a

> When I see books that I have read on library shelves, it is like running into an old friend on the street. I often take the book down and browse through it. . . . Like friends, these books have gone into the making of whatever and whoever I am.
>
> KEVIN STARR

freshman reading class began talking about the books they loved as kids. Each seemed to realize that there had been a time when they enjoyed reading, when books were positive forces in their lives.

• Provide alternative assignments that will enable them to think about how people become readers and nonreaders.

    ▶ Have them write the biography of "the best reader" they know using the same ideas and guidelines used to write their autobiographies.

    ▶ Ask them to complete the following sentence, then go on to develop the idea in a paper: "As a reader I would compare myself to a . . . "

• Reflect on their completed work and related discussions throughout the unit. A good starter line if they don't know where to begin might be, "I now realize the following things about myself as a reader."

• Keep in mind that if students have not already developed reading goals (see Reminder 98), now is the perfect opportunity, since having written their reading autobiography, they realize many things about themselves as readers.

• Have them present to the class their finished reading autobiographies or that part of them that they think is most important.

• Consider using or adapting the following writing prompt for this assignment:

By this point in our lives, reading seems like something we just know how to do. While some of us read better or enjoy reading more than others, we all have an important story to tell about ourselves: how we became a reader. You may come from a home where the walls were covered with bookcases and everyone read. You may have had an uncle who took you to the library on Saturdays and read to you on the couch while he drank tea and you ate the chocolates he bought you. You may have had a kindergarten teacher who brought every book to life by reading them aloud. Or you may have had a different type of experience, one in which reading was difficult because you had to learn English first or had some reading difficulties. Tell the story of how you became a reader, including in your story those details that will help the reader understand why you feel the way you do about reading. Read the example provided for you before beginning, and make notes in preparation for writing.

Keep Reading Fresh

RATIONALE

As you read the following passage, which appeared in my previous text, *The English Teacher's Companion: A Complete Guide to Classroom, Curriculum, and the Profession* (1999), think about the importance of approaching texts with a "beginner's mind."

After reading the same books again and again and again, boredom threatens the joy we initially felt when we first taught them. It would be nice if we could all mix things up whenever we felt like it: I get dangerously envious of private school teachers I meet during the summer. They might be reading a book like Charles Frazier's *Cold Mountain*, and will say something like, "I just love it. I think I'll have my kids read it this year." The harsh reality for most of us is that we are stuck with the books we have. For one reason or another I have taught *Lord of the Flies* every year since I was a student teacher. How do I keep from reverting to automatic teaching?

Zen master Shunryu Suzuki (1988) describes the "beginner's mind" as one of "many possibilities"; he goes on to say that "in the expert's mind there are few." According to Suzuki, "The goal of practice is always to keep our beginner's mind. Suppose you recite the Prajna Paramita Sutra only once. It might be a very good recitation. But what would happen to you if you recited it twice, three times, four times, or more? You might easily lose your original attitude toward it. . . . [If] you continue to practice one, two, three years or more, although you may improve some, you are liable to lose the limitless meaning of original mind." Aside from the endless flow of papers, nothing seems to threaten the English teacher's lively practice like repetition. It was largely for this reason—the danger of falling asleep at the wheel of our own reading, and thus our teaching—that Ron Padgett wrote *Creative Reading*. While I don't agree with all his ideas, Padgett's premise is important: we must each reinvent the reading experience for ourselves if we are to continue to find in it the satisfaction we did when we began. Poet Rainer Maria Rilke's admonition that we are always a beginner each time we sit down to the task of writing is true, but it's an ideal and requires a discipline we can't always muster in the course of the daily grind.

If reading becomes a bore, mental death is on the way. Children taught to read by tedious mechanical means rapidly learn to skim over the dull text without bothering to delve into its implications—which in time will make them prey to propaganda and to assertions based on scanty evidence, or none.

JOAN AIKEN

13

WHAT TO DO

Reading literary criticism has not satisfied my need to plumb the depths of the books I teach. For one, such reading only helps if you teach AP classes, since few American high school students are interested in such things as the literary and philosophical influences on J. D. Salinger's writings. I like books such as David Denby's *Great Books* or even Harold Bloom's *The Western Canon* because they invite you to participate in a serious conversation about a book's worth and meaning. This kind of literary writing leads you back into the books you have taught so many times, in part demanding that you challenge them as to why they should be taught all these years. My colleague Elaine Caret exemplifies for me this habit of reflecting on books she has taught again and again. Elaine keeps a journal in which she writes about the different stories or poems she teaches, dating each entry. She can go back and check what she thought the previous year about *Hamlet* after writing this year from her new perspective. A more social variation is to have literary dinners, as my former department chair, Doug Rogers, did. Doug thought we should engage in regular conversations about the books we taught to appreciate why we taught them. Each month we agreed on a different book and met for a delicious dinner at his house.

Whether through conversations over gourmet meals or reflections in a journal, we realize that we cannot step into the same text twice from the very same vantage point. We are always reading a book as if for the first time. As Suzuki writes, "The most difficult thing is always to keep your beginner's mind. There is no need to have a deep understanding of Zen. Even though you read much Zen literature, you must read each sentence with a fresh mind. You should not say, 'I know what Zen is,' or 'I have attained enlightenment.' This is also the real secret of the arts: always be a beginner."

Create the Conditions for Effective Learning

5

RATIONALE

Students cannot succeed in an environment that will not support their learning. *Environment* in this case refers not only to physical surroundings but to the emotional and intellectual climate. If students are to participate, to engage, to learn, they must believe that they can take risks, feel safe, and have those material necessities their work requires. I realize that we do not always have control over our physical environment—we do, however, have control over the emotional and intellectual environment of our classes.

WHAT TO DO

Materials

• Supply all students with their own copy of any text the class reads, unless sharing a copy provides an educationally beneficial experience.

• Ensure that materials are of the best quality possible. When students get books with tattered covers and ripped pages they do not develop positive associations with or respectful attitudes toward these objects. Any photocopied materials should also be as clear as possible (i.e., crisp lines) to ensure that struggling readers do not suffer unnecessary visual interference.

• Have available the necessary tools for good reading—dictionary, thesaurus, paper, pencils, highlighters, Post-its, butcher paper—to support a range of instructional strategies.

• Do everything you can to build a classroom library that includes books and magazines on a range of subjects. Ask your head custodian if there is an old magazine rack or a bookcase in storage. Ask students to recycle magazines from home instead of throwing them away.

Physical Environment

• See to it that the arrangement of the desks in particular and the room in general supports a range of reading approaches (e.g., pairs, groups, SSR).

"Why don't you go and do something?" my mother would say.

"I *am* doing something. I'm reading."

"It isn't healthy just lying there with your nose in a book," she would say, just as she said to my father. Thus harassed, I would find places to read where I couldn't be found—in the attic, in the woods, and at night under the bedclothes with a flashlight.

ROBERT MACNEIL

• Remember that adequate light, appropriate temperature, and reasonably comfortable chairs will ensure that students focus on their reading instead of their discomfort.

• Evaluate your room for causes of distraction, offense, or mixed messages. To the greatest extent possible, the environment should express the value you place on reading. One of the ways this is accomplished in my own class is through posters and postcards of book covers, book fair announcements, authors, and other literary subjects.

Emotional Environment

• Establish and maintain a culture that supports diverse perspectives and reading ability levels.

• Foster an environment in which students feel secure enough to make their individual voices heard, either through reading aloud or sharing their views during group and class discussions.

• Allow students choices in what they read whenever possible (see Reminder 53).

• Support students' learning by providing clear, concise directions (see Reminder 23) about how to read assigned texts. Check to see that they understand. Students should know that they can approach you to ask for extra assistance without being subject to ridicule.

• Make your priorities clear. What do you want your students to perceive is most important in your class—reading books that will challenge them or reading books that will enable them to get an A?

Intellectual Environment

• Give students frequent opportunities to engage in meaningful conversations about what they read.

• Encourage them to participate in discussions about those ideas and issues that are central to their lives and the adult lives they will eventually lead.

• Facilitate their consideration of a variety of texts from multiple perspectives; have them read for multiple reasons and apply their knowledge from and about these texts to other situations.

Procedural Issues

• Be consistent. Students quickly develop expectations about how the class works; upsetting the familiar too often and unnecessarily can undermine their comfort and thus their performance.

• Make sure your instructional practice makes sense. For learning to be effective, information must be meaningful and delivered to the student in a way that achieves the desired outcome effectively.

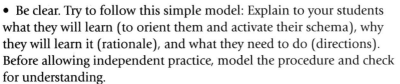

• Be clear. Try to follow this simple model: Explain to your students what they will learn (to orient them and activate their schema), why they will learn it (rationale), and what they need to do (directions). Before allowing independent practice, model the procedure and check for understanding.

6   Be a Model Reader

RATIONALE

Our job as literature teachers should be to model reading and thinking about a text, not to dictate meaning.

CAROL JAGO, FROM
WITH RIGOR FOR ALL:
TEACHING THE CLASSICS
TO CONTEMPORARY
STUDENTS

Harkening back to the apprentice system, we must function as master readers whose job is to show the novice how it is done. We must also show them, through both words and deeds, why it should be done (and when and where it *can* be done).

WHAT TO DO

• Get to know your students so that you can provide them with appropriate recommendations about what to read.

• Talk whenever appropriate about your own reading, not only to show them that you practice what you preach, but to illustrate how your reading applies to a range of situations. Specifically, talk about when, why, where, how, and what you read, so that they are able to see that books are a viable source of information.

• Talk to students about how you choose and read your books, with the goal of demystifying these processes.

• Model for them any assignments that you give. This means thinking aloud as you read so that they can hear how you approach reading any particular text.

• Set up a bulletin board in your room to post articles that support the idea of reading and its importance (e.g., article about a barber whose back room is an African American bookstore and reading room).

• Reinforce the importance of reading, but also of ideas, information, and thinking skills, all of which are best developed and improved through reading.

• Improve your ability to read aloud so that you can make a powerful impression during this activity.

• Talk about the role that you, as a parent, play in your child's literacy, to remind your students that whatever their attitude toward reading, it is something they would want their own children to be able to do well.

- Read and talk about a wide range of texts, including different genres and subjects, so that you can recommend books in all fields to your students and demonstrate how vast the world of reading is.

- Recycle your magazines from home: keep different kids in mind, and when you come across an article that you think one of your students would find interesting, bring it in and present it in a way that piques their interest.

- Remember Thoreau's words: "How many men's lives have been changed by a single book?"

- Remember Lincoln's words: "He is my friend who will give me a book I have not yet read."

- Provide opportunities for your students, whatever grade, to be mentors to those who are younger than they. Students who participate in Reading Buddies programs at elementary and secondary schools develop a sense of pride in their accomplishments and an understanding of the importance of reading.

- Teach them how to be independent readers who can find and choose their own books and read them on their own for personal satisfaction or a specific use.

- Tell students what you do when you have trouble reading a book or get bored with it. This shows them that everyone gets stuck once in a while; it also shows them how to solve particular problems.

- When you see kids reading a book with which you are not familiar, ask them how they like it and if they would recommend it to their peers. This allows you to develop recommendations for other students.

- Read your own book on SSR days or during other reading occasions.

- Talk about the role of literacy and reading in the larger world so students gain an understanding of, for example, the obstacles faced by an illiterate person in the economic and political spheres.

- Model effective reading at all times so that students see the skills of predicting, questioning, inquiring, challenging, clarifying, and so on, properly executed. If appropriate, explain to students why you do what you do when you read so that they appreciate the importance of, for example, asking questions of themselves, the author, and the text as they read.

7 Use Literature Circles

RATIONALE

Literature circles as studied and described by Harvey Daniels (1994) offer powerful benefits to readers of all ages. The circles are structured to move readers through a range of cognitive roles as they discuss books the groups select themselves. This method, adaptable to various subject areas, allows kids to connect with each other and with books. They also learn to take responsibility as members of a group who, together, must construct meaning through debate, discussion, and reflection.

WHAT TO DO

When students are in literature circles, stress that they:

- Make notes and drawings to help organize or convey their ideas
- Ask open-ended questions
- Read favorite passages aloud
- Discuss difficult or crucial passages to better understand or help other group members understand the meaning
- Anchor their discussion in the text, continually returning to it for evidence to support their ideas or settle disagreements
- Make sure everyone participates in and contributes their ideas to the discussion

Keep in mind the four basic roles the students should be encouraged to take on to help them independently discuss topics on their own:

1. *Discussion director*: responsible for creating provocative discussion questions, convening the meeting, and soliciting contributions from the other members (discursive/analytical)
2. *Literary illuminator/passage master*: directs group members to memorable, important sections of the text and reads these passages aloud (oral/dramatic)
3. *Connector*: helps the group make connections between the text world and the real world (associative)
4. *Illustrator*: offers visual responses and explanations of the written

text (a crucial role, as it often elicits insightful contributions from students who are less analytical)

Remember the importance of self-selection in literature circles. This is not a forum for reading works chosen by the teacher or any person not a member of the group.

Assess students' progress as readers in a way that best serves your assessment goals. Teachers can:

- Observe group discussions, focusing on each individual within the group
- Use a performance or evaluation rubric designed for literature circles
- Hold student conferences in which you discuss and monitor students' knowledge
- Have students keep learning logs about their literature circle discussions and reading

Keep in mind the twelve ingredients of literature circles:

1. Children choose their own reading material.
2. Small, temporary groups are formed, based on book choice.
3. Different groups read different books.
4. Groups meet on a regular, predictable schedule.
5. Kids use written or drawn notes to guide both their reading and discussion.
6. Discussion topics come from the students.
7. Group meetings aim to be open, natural discussions.
8. In newly formed groups, students play a rotating assortment of task roles.
9. The teacher serves as a facilitator.
10. Evaluation is by teacher observation and student self-evaluation.
11. A spirit of playfulness and fun pervades the room.
12. New groups form around new reading choices.

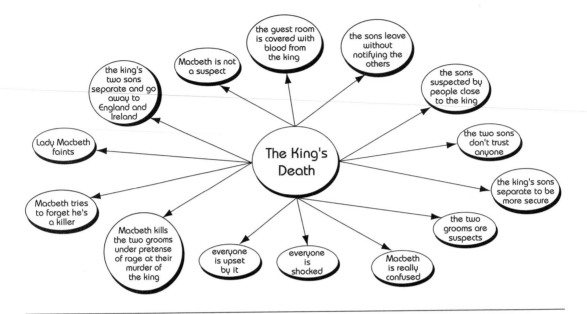

FIGURE 7-1   This brainstorm shows the different connections India, Maria, Erica, and May were able to make during a group discussion about the importance of the king's death in *Macbeth*.

Talk About Reading

. . . .

RATIONALE

We talk more than we will ever write or read. Conversation is one of the primary ways we make meaning: through sharing, asking, discussing, clarifying. As Jerome Bruner wrote somewhere, it is a human need "to share the objects of our attention with others." Using talk for different purposes in different contexts allows students the important opportunity to figure out what they think by, in part, hearing what others think. Talking also helps a wide range of students whose verbal skills need practice and development. (See Reminders 93 and 94 about elaboration and reporting strategies). ESL students, for example, need to hear how English is used and have the chance to practice it for themselves in authentic academic contexts if they are to develop the academic literacy they need to succeed. Talking about reading also brings energy and vitality into the classroom as individual viewpoints are expressed.

WHAT TO DO

- Encourage various configurations of classroom talk. Have students

  ▶ Pair up to briefly discuss an idea that the class is studying in order to make connections and meaning.

  ▶ Huddle into small groups for a discussion or to use talk for a specified purpose.

  ▶ Gather around as a whole class to share what was said in individual groups.

- Use talk to explain, explore, share, comprehend, solve, process, and appreciate.

- Use talk in both formal and informal contexts to help students better understand and allow the teacher to evaluate understanding and performance.

- Sequence learning so that each stage prepares the student for the increased intellectual demands of the next. Stages include

I asked the kids to say what they thought about the story, and one after the other, they did. Then I was ready to move on—but they wouldn't let me. They kept talking. I wasn't refereeing. They stopped raising their hands. They talked to each other. At one point I was going to say something, but I decided no: keep quiet, I told myself. Be glad they are talking to each other, and to Tillie Olsen. That's what it was—a conversation between twenty-six Atlanta kids . . . and Tillie Olsen.

ROBERT COLES FROM *THE CALL OF STORIES*

> Solo reading and written response to formulate initial ideas and questions

> Pairs discussion, to share and compare with a peer before returning to individual reflection with information and insights gained from the dialogue

> Group discussion, to assemble and expand understanding

> Class discussion, during which groups report what they learned and discuss how they arrived at these interpretations

• Define your role as teacher throughout the process. Because such a discussion-oriented approach makes students responsible for their own learning, it is essential that we know what to do and how to do it. During discussions of any kind, the teacher's role is to facilitate, challenge, clarify, support, evaluate, and model.

• Use talk to help students focus their attention by discussing:

> Implications of results and actions

> Consequences

> Possibilities

> Meanings

Follow up these discussions with a conversation about how the reader arrived at a given conclusion or interpretation.

• Provide the safe, supportive, stimulating environment needed for discussions to be successful. Readers engaged in "exploratory talk" exemplify the habits of mind common to effective readers: speculation, hypothesis testing, predicting, clarifying, risk taking (in terms of possible meanings and connections). But to think in public like this requires a conducive environment (see Reminder 5).

• "Talk our way into the text," as Douglas Barnes (1992) suggests. By using literature circles, Socratic seminars, shared inquiry, or any other discussion-based methods mentioned in this book, students will learn the skills they need to make sense of what they read.

• Scaffold discussions so that questions about a specific reading move from simple to complex. Similarly, help students in their discussion of Text B to build on what they learned from studying Text A.

Make Room for Essential Conversations

RATIONALE

We spend a lot of time talking about *how* we read or *what* we read but we need to make room for the essential conversation, the one that answers the question *why* we read. Each discipline has at its heart certain vital questions its practitioners have spent decades, even centuries, trying to answer. When we make room for the essential conversations in our disciplines, when we invite students to enter into those discussions, we create opportunities for deep learning and thoughtful reading. As Arthur Applebee (1996) writes, "Learning is most effective when classrooms emphasize knowledge derived from active participation in meaningful conversations within important fields of study."

WHAT TO DO

Encourage students to enter into the essential conversations with themselves, with classmates, with their teachers, with society, and with the authors/thinkers you are studying. Such conversations can be carried on through writing (journals, e-mail, online threaded discussions, letters, imaginative fiction), discussions, or interviews. Central to the idea of curriculum as a conversation is the notion that a book, regardless of its genre, is a conversation between:

- The reader and the author
- The reader and themselves
- The reader and the characters/events/ideas in that book

Depending on your discipline or the ideas your students are studying, consider how you might fit any of the following conversations into your curriculum:

- What is the nature and role of story?
- What role does or should the imagination play in our lives and work?
- How does character determine the outcome of events?
- What is true?

No wonder the really powerful men in our society, whether politicians or scientists, hold writers and poets in contempt. They do it because they get no evidence from modern literature that anybody is thinking about any significant question.

SAUL BELLOW

25

- What is beautiful?
- What is good?
- What are the meaning and implications of liberty, equality, and justice?
- What is the value of doubt?
- What is the importance of failure and what it teaches?
- Why are we here?
- What is my role, my obligation, my purpose in relation to myself and my community?
- What matters?

Discuss the criteria by which ideas, skills, or subjects are deemed "essential" given that others are necessarily excluded when judgments of this kind are made.

Make room for students to initiate and learn how to use books to support inquiries of serious personal importance. This means teaching them how to frame such inquiries and how to pursue them using a range of texts and other sources as tools for thought and investigation.

Invite a range of perspectives to participate in any such discussion. This might mean having others from outside the class visit to complement the discussion of a text or it might mean bringing a range of other texts to the discussion to allow for more voices on the subject.

Keep in mind that participating in the essential conversation requires that people know how to think out loud and elaborate on their thinking. See Reminders 93 and 94 for helpful ideas.

STUDENT EXAMPLE

Sophomore Ross Webber wrote the following short essay after reading one of his SSR books.

LIFE

Everybody must go through life getting thrown some rough deals and hardships. No matter who you are, life always gives you an obstacle, and you must somehow find a way to overcome that particular obstacle. Then, right when you think that the worst is over, life hits you again.

Hocus Pocus shows an especially brutal side of life in all of its many characters. The main character, Gene Hartke, handles all of his obstacles particularly well, which is surprising because of how difficult most of his life has been. He had fought in the Vietnam War, where he was nicknamed "the Preacher" for all the encouraging speeches he made. He killed so many innocent people without even thinking about it at the time. Later in his life, it shocked him how coldhearted he had once been. He was an adulterer because he liked older women and he didn't see any problem with what he was doing. He lived with his wife and mother-in-law, whom he loved dearly, but who turned insane because of a genetic defect in their family, in a small valley across the lake from a black prison. He taught at a college for challenged students. He was fired for many things including discussing inappropriate topics with the students, making them question their government, and being an adulterer. He had two children who hated him because he did not send their mother and grandmother to a mental hospital. And he had an illegitimate son whom he had never met. And that is just the main character.

Hocus Pocus was written in 1990 and begins in the year 2001. Throughout this book, the author describes the current state of the United States and its government. Many of the things that are said are exaggerations, but on the other hand, many are true. It made me think about what's going on in this country, as well as the rest of the world, and how it affects me. It also made me question many things, such as racial barriers, government, and social classes, which I would not normally think about. It made me realize that while a lot of things are made to look good and innocent, they are still corrupt inside.

Almost every character in *Hocus Pocus* has led a very tough life. For example, a Japanese man working in the same place as Gene Hartke opens up to him and tells Gene about when he was a young boy in Japan. He lived where the atom bomb had been dropped. He was in elementary school playing on the playground with his friends during school. The ball rolled away and into a ditch. He went to go get it, and when he bent over in the ditch to pick up the ball, he felt a hot wind and heard a weird sound. He immediately stood up to see that everyone he knew had died, and the city he had lived in had been completely destroyed. He was the only one around so he had to walk to the next town just to find somebody to help him. He lived the rest of his life wondering why he had survived. He also never forgot the graphic images of the people, young and old alike, lying dead on the ground, their skin detached from their bodies except for a few pieces where the sinew was burnt to the muscle. He never really got over it.

It's almost depressing to read this book. It made me think about how tough their lives had been compared to mine and people around me, and how much I and the people I know complain about the little things that really aren't all that important in the long run anyway. It also made me realize that life is an endless cycle of obstacles that is escapable only by death. And that is just taking the easy way out.

Take a moment to reflect on your reading and teaching. You may find the following discussion points useful, or you can come up with your own:

- Write a summary of the last section. Include in this summary three main ideas—techniques, strategies, tools—that relate to your own classes.

- Which reminders from the preceding section might help you the most?

- Looking ahead to the next section, consider its title and, before you begin reading, create your own list of reminders for this topic. After checking yours with mine, discuss which of these reminders—from your list and mine—will help you and your students the most.

Teach and

Support Students

Amy Hirsch absorbed in one of the many books she read during the semester.

> We are all apprentices
> in a craft where no one
> ever becomes a master.
>
> —ERNEST HEMINGWAY

Given the range of needs and abilities in our classrooms, we must use various strategies and techniques to help our students improve. We are also challenged by the demands of the different types of texts our students must know how to read; thus we must sometimes be quite direct in our teaching, though always trying to develop in our students the independence and mastery that they will need as adult readers.

I support my students' reading in different ways depending on what we are reading or learning to read. When the state tests come around, for example, I download sample questions from the Internet and copy them to an overhead so we can walk through them together. I give them other sample questions that they can annotate in order to better understand the texts by manipulating them. When we read difficult literary texts such as *Macbeth*, I might incorporate video segments to help them see what is happening or how the director and actors are interpreting the words.

My goal is always to make available to them and teach them to use an array of tools and techniques, then allow them to choose those that are most helpful to them. No matter how much good work I do, however, if they cannot eventually read these texts on their own, I have not been successful. One additional means of supporting certain students—special education and ESL students, specifically—is to put an extra copy of any handouts in the ESL and special education teachers' boxes so that we can work together to help those students succeed.

Teaching and supporting students involves a range of complicated and important tasks. Sophomore Jenna Goldberg reminds us that, despite their quick resistance, students know what they need to learn.

> Reading through [the state standards summary of what students are expected to know], I realized I know a lot but just not very well. One thing I think teachers should do more is keep reviewing things over and over because whenever I don't go over things a lot I seem to forget a lot of things. Another thing I feel teachers should do more is have more vocab and make it a bigger deal because I've noticed that whenever I know more vocab I seem to write and speak better. Some things I like that teachers do is when they have kids get creative like with artsy things. I also like when teachers make time for us during class to read more—so far this year I think my teachers have done a good job with it. When I read a lot I think it makes a difference when I work.

We support students in many different ways, but never more effectively than when we give them room to practice with texts that mean something to them. Moreover, we must remember that we should always model for them what we hope they will do as readers. In *Reading for Understanding* (Schoenbach et al. 1999) teachers are described as master readers and students as apprentices; this relationship makes sense to me and honors the role we have to play in supporting our students' progress toward improved performance and mastery.

Make
Connections

RATIONALE

Making connections—between ideas, authors, subjects—is what good readers do; in fact, that *aha!* moment is one of the most satisfying experiences of reading. We need to make connections to what we have taught and will eventually teach so that students recognize these links and experience any particular discipline as a coherent field of study. But readers need cause to make other sorts of connections also: between themselves and the outside world, between this subject and others, between the past and the present, the personal and the public. We can and should help them develop the strategies needed to think across domains and see all knowledge as integrated.

WHAT TO DO

Remember that reading is primarily a process through which we make connections and construct meaning. We can help students make more connections and construct more sophisticated understandings by

- Asking them how this text or idea relates to those they studied in the past
- Asking them to find connections to what they are studying in other subject areas, using examples from those domains to support the connection
- Inviting them to look for different types of patterns within the text
- Allowing them to make both intellectual and emotional connections to what they read so that they can take into account both private and public responses
- Encouraging them to challenge a particular text's meaning by speculating about connections that might seem unfounded but reveal deeper insights

Ask readers to make various types of connections: structural, thematic, cultural, personal, rhetorical, political, chronological, curricular.

Encourage students to make connections by asking the following types of questions:

When you read a novel, even if it's one you don't like much—or you have a hard time getting into it, and staying into it—you can't help trying to figure out which characters resemble you.

17-YEAR-OLD STUDENT TO ROBERT COLES'S *CALL OF STORIES*

31

- How does that relate to the theme of _____ we studied last semester?
- Can anyone explain how Huck Finn's and Jim's attitudes relate to the Bill of Rights, which you are studying in your history class this week?
- What would this poem sound like if you played it as music? What instruments would you use and why?
- Can you explain how the story "The Tortoise and the Hare" relates to Einstein's theory of relativity?
- If you used grammatical terms to describe this math equation, what would be the verbs and the nouns? Is it possible for there to be adjectives?
- Edwin Tufte wrote two books, one in which he looks at images as nouns and another in which he describes images as verbs. Looking at this image, what are the nouns and verbs that come to mind?

Keep in mind that making connections means making learning personal, live, real. When we allow students to choose what they read and what ideas they investigate, we increase the likelihood that they will make meaningful connections that result in powerful learning and improved skills.

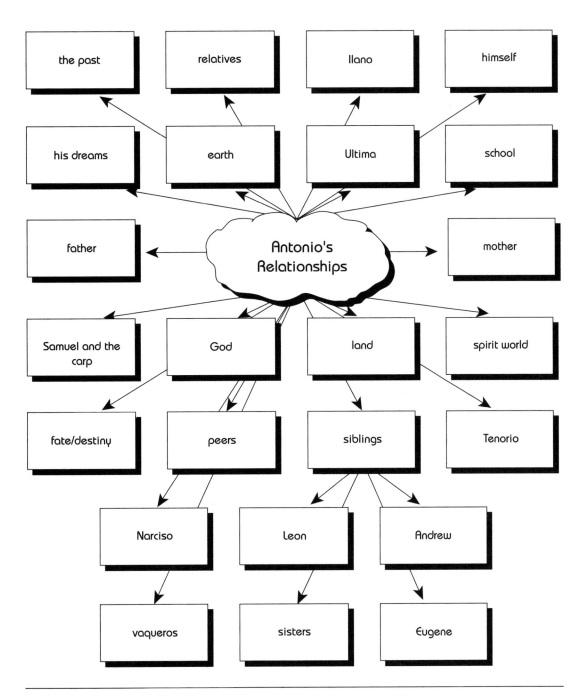

FIGURE 10-1   During a class discussion we made these connections regarding Antonio's relationships in Rudolfo Anaya's *Bless Me, Ultima.*

11 Make Available the Necessary Reading Tools

RATIONALE

I like writing with a peacock's quill because its feathers are all eyes.

THOMAS FULLER

Given that our students will be reading for a variety of purposes, we need to keep on hand the tools to support such work. Tools are essential for other reasons. Many students come to us with special needs; our classrooms must be equipped to help them. Obviously some of the books or materials listed below are not necessary for all classes or subject areas. Teachers will have to determine which are most appropriate to their own work. Consider using the open space on this page to make your own list, or add to this one those specific materials your students might require.

WHAT TO DO

Based on your students and your practice, gather together the resources and materials that will make your classroom an effective and powerful learning environment. Your list of necessary tools might include the following:

- Dictionaries
  - ▶ College level
  - ▶ English-language-learner version
  - ▶ Unabridged version
  - ▶ Scientific
  - ▶ Literary terms
  - ▶ Phrase and fable
  - ▶ Word origins
  - ▶ Biblical
  - ▶ Mythology
- Thesauri
  - ▶ *The Synonym Finder*
  - ▶ Antonym/synonym reference book

- Encyclopedias
  - *Merriam-Webster Encyclopedia of Literature*
- Literary anthologies (e.g., to research allusions)
- Bible
- Atlas
- Almanac
- Extra copies of class texts that everyone is reading
- Cliffs Notes or similar text guides
- Annotation Tools
  - Post-it notes
  - Highlighters
  - Transparencies
  - Overhead pens
  - Overhead projector
  - Graphic organizers
  - Butcher paper
  - Individual copies of texts
  - Internet connection

12 Choose Texts Wisely

RATIONALE

Every choice counts when it comes to reading. If we select a passage that is too difficult, we will not only lose our students' interest but waste the time spent trying to read it. We should always ask ourselves the following questions when deciding whether a text is useful and appropriate for our students. On occasion we choose a text we just love, say an article from the *Atlantic Monthly*, for a high school freshman history class, only to find that it would be a challenging read for some college graduates. Better to have asked the following questions, to determine students' needs and clarify our educational purposes.

WHAT TO DO

Ask the following questions when evaluating reading selections for your students.

GENERAL QUESTIONS

• What will they need to know and be able to do in order to read this piece?

• How does it relate to what they read before and will read in the near future?

• Is this passage of genuine interest to the students?

• Is the layout of this book (font size, margins, length) suitable for your students' needs?

• Does this text support your goals as a teacher and your students' goals?

• Does this text help your students prepare for any mandatory tests the state or district requires?

• Will this text and the ideas within it inspire good conversation and engaged learning?

• Is it clear to the students why you are having them read this?

• Does it pass the "dinner table test" (i.e., if the students went home and said they were reading an article about this subject, would their parents get upset?)?

• Does it challenge all your students while being accessible enough to *all*?

• Are you using this as a primary text or one that will supplement the primary text?

• If supplemental, what is the relationship between the two (i.e., why did you choose it?)?

• Is this similar in form and function to the other texts they have read—or does it help you bring some textual diversity into your curriculum to expand their reading repertoire?

QUESTIONS ABOUT EXPOSITORY TEXTS

• Does it have a title?

• Does the text include subheadings to orient the reader by signaling new chapters or sections within a chapter?

• Does the passage include an introductory paragraph that helps the reader orient themselves to the rest of the text?

• Does the text include a conclusion or summary paragraphs?

• Are the paragraphs in this text organized, focused, and developed using the following elements?

  ▶ Topic sentence that provides a controlling idea
  ▶ Examples that illustrate the main ideas throughout the text
  ▶ Transitional words that keep the reader oriented

• Does the author use typography (bold, italics, font style, font size) to help the reader (e.g., using bold to indicate that a word is defined in the glossary)?

• Does the author use graphic devices (e.g., illustrations, maps, tables, or charts) to support the reader?

• Does the text provide other forms of support (e.g., listing objectives, focus questions, key concepts, or words to know at the beginning of the chapter) for the reader?

• Does the article include useful, challenging comprehension questions that can be used for writing or discussion?

• Is this text more challenging (e.g., in length, sophistication, or assignment) than those that came before it?

13 Provide Options for Student Response

RATIONALE

Because students read for a variety of purposes, they need a range of options when they respond to their reading. Such choices allow for increased engagement and improved comprehension through, presumably, the use of those options they find most effective. Finally, allowing for different options across genres (e.g., writing, speaking, drawing) invites students to think about their reading in different ways, an essential trait of effective readers.

WHAT TO DO

Offer students the following options for responding to what they read:

WRITTEN FORMS

- Keep a journal

- Create their own story

- Write a collection of poems

- Keep a diary (as a character, the author, the reader) while they read

- Write letters to the characters, the author, or someone else

- Recast the text as a brochure, story, newspaper article, editorial, or advertisement (see Reminder 99)

- Use written conversations (Reminder 81)

- Explain or interpret a visual response to the text

- Imitate the author's style

- Write into the story (by putting themselves in the story as a character or narrator)

- Write an essay (literary, analysis, narrative, interpretive, reflective)

- Make a list (details, aspects, examples, ideas, associations)

• Write a conversation (in the form of a script) that takes place between a character in this text and another during which they examine the ideas the class is studying. (Examples: a conversation between Einstein and your teacher, between Gatsby and Fitzgerald, between FDR and JFK)

• Write a manual for the procedure or process they read about (e.g., in a science class)

SPOKEN FORMS

• Perform the text (see Reminder 72)

• Teach the text

• Discuss the text in small groups or as a full class (see Reminder 18)

• Read aloud (traditional format, choral reading) (see Reminder 2)

• Retell the text (see Reminder 71)

• Role-play the author, a character, or other (e.g., expert) in an interview or other type of interpretive discussion during which the class asks questions

• Conduct a panel discussion

• Engage in a student-teacher conference

VISUAL FORMS

• Draw the action (see Reminder 73)

• Draw a scene

• Create a Web site

• Plot the action

• Create a multimedia presentation

• Create a computer game based on the text

• Use graphic organizers—target, mandala, storyboard, conversational roundtable (see Reminder 17)

STUDENT EXAMPLES

When she was a freshman, Anna McCord wrote the following poem in response to Amy Tan's *The Kitchen God's Wife*.

THE SILVER CHOPSTICKS

Representing so much
At first
Hope, happiness, love
But never living up to their promises

The silver string
Connecting the chopsticks
Like a husband to his wife
No easy way to break the tie
No way for escape
Bound together forever.
—Anna McCord

Brandon Baciocco, a senior in Jimi Baloian's English class, wrote the following creative response to Ken Kesey's *One Flew over the Cuckoo's Nest*. The creative-fiction option helped him to read the story better— i.e., as both a reader *and* a writer looking at the story as a model—and also gave him occasion to sharpen his writing skills on a story he was motivated to write well.

Chapter 1: The Awakening
Date: January 15, 2025
Place: NOT IDENTIFIABLE

As his eyes slowly came into focus, all Sampson could see was a blinding light, even more blinding than the sun. He had the common response that he always had to light and that was to reach down his side to get his glasses out of his pocket. But when he tried to move his hand, he found it bound to a table. He tried to struggle free, but all his limbs were bound square and sturdy onto a table. He looked around the room; he was trying to find another source of life. But the room was empty. The table suddenly began to move him to an upright position.

As he finally saw the other end of the room, all he could see was a wall that was covered by a large mirror. Then like thunder, a voice spoke over a loud speaker. "Sampson Derrik Kessel. You have been chosen to serve your government." A smile curled over Sampson's lips as he spoke back in a defiant tone. "And what if I don't want to?" The voice hesitated before speaking again. "You don't have a choice. We are not asking you, we're telling you." Sampson bared his teeth and growled a little. "Now now Sampson, no need to be upset. You may find that the advantages of being an agent for the people will be far more rewarding then any common life." Sampson

realized now that he was not being chosen to work for the government.

"For the people?" Sampson fired back. "Don't you mean for a Syndicate operation? Isn't that why I am here? You must be one of the big companies. Come off it now, who are you?" The voice behind the glass again hesitated. "You are an intelligent man, Kessel. Much more than I predicted. We are a program for bettering the human race. We are known simply as The Combine."

Sampson felt shock flood his body. He knew what the Combine was. It was an order that wanted to bring chaos to the world and then rebuild it in their visage. The same Combine that took his father from him. The voice continued. "We live by seven words, Sampson. Chaos, Order, Massacre, Blood, Intelligence, Network, and Evolution. It is through these words, or our codes if you will, that we have prospered into what we are today. And soon, you will learn them too."

Sampson, feeling the burn of tears from his face, cried out in horror. "Weren't you happy with my father as an agent? Why me? What service could I possibly perform?" The voice, without missing a beat, said calmly, "Your father like you disapproved of our methods and morals. He would not accept the seven codes. We hope you will be different. We don't want what happened to him to happen to you." "You bastards!" Sampson screamed. A small opening in the window slid open. A small dart flew across the room and hit Sampson square in the neck. As the drug started to take its toll on Sampson he could only feel tears on his face. He knew that he would be subjected to their training and if he didn't go their way, he would be killed.

Jasmine First coming to America

Jasmine's telescope comes into focus Visions of America flood her view Its arms are wide open Accepting her into its world of people as sweet as Angels and opportunities waiting to be hers When the fog clears and she begins her first step onto the path her fate has taken her Her screams aren't loud enough to be heard by the world forgetting to let her in Was this choice fate or free-will? She asks herself as the day spent with the astrologer under the bayan tree burns on her tail. This world & new life she has entered has yet to tell her who she will become and where it will take her. Echos of Prakash, Jasmine & Jhoyti can be heard ringing in the distance until she runs so far they are burried forever away in the past. The person so alone, vunrable and Lost is about to be introduced to people that will change and be her life forever.

FIGURE 13-1 Hannah Tucker combined words and images, facts and metaphors to convey her insights into and understanding of Bharati Mukherjee's novel *Jasmine*.

Use the Dense
Question Strategy

· ·

14

RATIONALE

This strategy walks students through a structured sequence of questioning that culminates in the kind of sophisticated, or "dense," question we hope to see them ask. This strategy, which I learned from Leila Christenbury, has many uses, one of which is to teach students how to ask different types of questions. I often have students use this process to develop their own essay topics.

The wisdom of the novel comes from having a question for everything. When Don Quixote went out into the world, that world turned into a mystery before his eyes.

MILAN KUNDERA

WHAT TO DO

Have students develop and respond to each type of question (e.g., text, world, dense) as they work through the text, then develop one dense question in summation.

EXAMPLE

See the sample dense-question-strategy sequence shown in Figure 14-1 (on page 44).

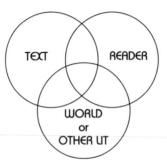

Type of Question	Description	Example
TEXT	Info found in text	*Who is the narrator of the story?*
READER	Reader's experience, values, ideas	*Have you ever felt fed up with everything and just wanted to take off, get away on your own?*
WORLD or OTHER LITERATURE	Knowledge of history, other cultures, other literature	*What other character—in a book or a movie—would you compare the main character to?*
SHADED: TEXT/READER	Combines knowledge of text with reader's own experiences, values, ideas	*What characteristics do you share with the main character?*
TEXT/WORLD	Combines knowledge of text with knowledge of history and cultures	*In what ways is Holden similar to teenagers today? In what ways are today's teenagers different?*
TEXT/OTHER LITERATURE	Combines knowledge of text with knowledge of other pieces of literature	*How does Holden's relationship with his sister compare with Esperanza's in* The House on Mango Street?
READER/WORLD	Combines knowledge of reader's own experiences with knowledge of other cultures, people	*In what ways are teenagers in other countries similar to American teens? In what ways are they different?*
READER/OTHER LITERATURE	Combines knowledge of reader's own experiences with other pieces of literature.	*In what ways are you similar to and/or different from Holden and Esperanza?*
DENSE QUESTION	Combines knowledge of all three areas into one Dense question	*Why does Holden feel alienated and how is that related to what many of today's teens feel? Include in your answer a discussion of the extent to which you do or don't share these same feelings and why.*
TEXT/READER/WORLD or TEXT/READER/OTHER LITERATURE		

FIGURE 14-1   This sample sequence of the dense question strategy shows a series of questions a student created while reading *The Catcher in the Rye.*

Prepare Students to Read
(Prereading)

15

RATIONALE

Work that teachers do to prepare students to read certainly improves student performance; however, students must also develop reading habits on their own so that they are prepared to read difficult texts independently. Prereading accomplishes the following: familiarizes students with ideas and content; activates their prior knowledge; establishes a purpose; clarifies how they should read a particular text; allows them to evaluate their needs and the demands of the text; helps them create a mental outline so that information can be effectively organized as it is read; increases interest; identifies potential problems (e.g., vocabulary or concepts).

WHAT TO DO

• Independently or as a group, try any or all of the following activities before reading:

  ▶ Have students predict what the text will be about or what will happen, and support their speculations (e.g., "The word in the title suggests . . . ").

  ▶ Discuss and brainstorm questions about possible meanings and implications of the title or the text's subject.

  ▶ Determine how the text should be read (e.g., say: "We are going to read this to get some ideas about the concept of democracy, so just skim it to glean some of the primary examples or implications of democracy").

  ▶ Evaluate the text's organizational structure to determine:

   • How it works
   • How it should be read
   • Its genre/type

  ▶ Use various techniques to activate students' prior knowledge. (see Reminder 61 and 80)

The first line reads, "As Gregor Samsa awoke that morning from uneasy dreams, he found himself transformed in his bed into a gigantic insect. . . . " When I read that line I thought to myself that I didn't know anyone was allowed to write things like that. If I had known, I would have started writing a long time ago.

GABRIEL GARCÍA MÁRQUEZ

> ▶ Remind them what effective readers of such texts do. (Reminder 36)

> ▶ Focus on the opening: the opening sentences and paragraphs often contain the kernel of the entire text.

> ▶ Review the directions if there are any so that they know what is expected of them.

• Don't spend too long on prereading activities: you don't want to undermine students' interest in the text. Spend just enough time to orient, intrigue, and prepare.

• Model how to read it by narrating your own reading process as you begin reading the text. Make a point of explaining how you make sense of textual features and difficult vocabulary.

• Ask the following questions:

> ▶ What questions do we need to ask to read this successfully?

> ▶ What question(s) might this book help us answer?

> ▶ What do we know from our previous reading and discussion about _____ that might help us read this text better?

• Provide any necessary background information and develop those skills needed to read the text.

• If you are asking them to do something specific with the text—e.g., annotate it—provide an example so that they can see what you expect and what it looks like.

• Have students follow these steps when prereading a text

1. Read and consider the title.
2. Find the author's name and any other information about the writer.
3. Identify the source (i.e., the original publication and date) of the article.
4. Read the introduction or opening paragraphs carefully, checking these against the title.
5. Skim through the article and read all boldface subheadings, pullout quotes, or sidebar information.
6. Skim through the article and read the first sentence of each paragraph; if this sentence is clearly not the topic sentence, locate and read the topic sentence.
7. Examine any other typographical features such as italicized words.

8. Examine any graphic content (e.g., maps, illustrations, images).

9. Read the last paragraph carefully.

10. Study any questions or additional information provided at the end of the article.

11. Read the entire article, keeping in mind what you have gained from your prereading and checking your new understanding against the initial understanding, revising as needed.

Use Video to Support, *Not* Replace, Reading

RATIONALE

The availability of film versions of literary texts, some of which are quite good, challenges teachers to use them at the right time and in a way that supports students' learning. Their use should never replace reading the texts, however. This goes for all subject areas: if a teacher includes only material from lectures and videos on tests, students quickly conclude that there is no compelling reason to read assigned books. In this way students can end up reading significantly less across all subject areas.

WHAT TO DO

• Anchor the viewing of video in the written text whenever possible. Example: After viewing Martin Luther King's speech "I Have a Dream," return to the written text and identify the guiding images King uses. After reading his "Dream" speech, read his "Letter from a Birmingham Jail" and compare the style and message of each.

• Use video clips to help students make the abstract more concrete. These clips should be cued up to help students quickly focus on that part of the video text that will help them prepare to read or better understand what they just read.

• Ask yourself when you consider using a video if its use in that instance preempts a reading of the text (i.e., if you are using video to replace reading).

• Use video to do what print cannot. Example: When reading a Shakespeare play, show clips of the same scene from different productions so that students can see and study various interpretations of the text.

• Use video before you begin reading if the material is unfamiliar or abstract. Depending on the material they will read, students can activate their schema efficiently by watching a well-chosen selection of video.

• Use video while reading to allow for a wider range of types of text and to increase engagement. Always anchor such viewing in the text, if possible. After viewing *Hamlet* starring Mel Gibson, for example, ask students how Gibson's interpretation of Hamlet in a particular scene compares with what the text actually says. (For example, "Gibson is rather morose in this scene; are there words in the text that support such an interpretation?")

• Use video after they read to supplement their reading with additional information or the same information in a different medium. You can also use video after reading a text to provide an alternative version against which to compare the printed text.

• Treat video as a text to which students should bring the same range of textual skills to bear. Many graphic organizers and reminders naturally adapt themselves to "reading" a video text or comparing a video and printed text.

SAMPLE ASSIGNMENT

Here is a set of sample questions I assigned my freshmen, who watched the film version of *Lord of the Flies* after reading the book. The questions confront them with the difference between the book and movie and provide useful information to me about the extent to which they are reading and how well they are doing it.

MOVIE ASSIGNMENT: *LORD OF THE FLIES*

1. Pick one character to pay close attention to and follow them throughout the film. How does the portrayal of the character in the film compare with your understanding of that character in the book?

2. Find five points throughout the movie where the director changed the book's story line. What was the change? What is the effect of that change on the story?

3. The "Siskel and Ebert" review: In a paragraph, critique the film for its overall quality as an adaptation of the book. Be sure to provide examples from both the film and the book to support your ideas.

17 Use Graphic Organizers

RATIONALE

Graphic organizers are essential tools for both teachers and readers. They come in many forms and have proven valuable for readers at all levels because they:

- Support all learners, but especially those with special needs

- Provide structure and guidance as readers move toward greater independence

- Offer a visual means of explaining and organizing information and ideas

- Ask students to evaluate and actively manipulate information, which helps them to see the connections and relationships between ideas

- Teach students to think categorically

- Provide useful tools to prepare for and facilitate writing, thinking, and discussing

- Help students remember and make greater cognitive associations between information and ideas

- Force students to evaluate information in order to determine what is important

- Prepare students for the world of work, where such tools are used with increasing frequency

- Improve readers' understanding of the text

- Help to develop students' knowledge of textual structures and their general textual intelligence

WHAT TO DO

- Try out the graphic organizer(s) you want to use before assigning them to students. Sometimes it turns out that they do not work as we imagined, or we find better ways to adapt them to the unit. Either way, using them ourselves provides a model to show our students; it helps us think better about the text; and it tests the appropriateness of the tool with respect to any particular assignment.

• Before reading, have students use organizers such as the KWL form (see Reminder 61 and Appendix 11) to prepare them for the reading ahead. This and other such forms, included in the Appendix, help readers activate their schema for particular types of text by getting them thinking about not only the organizational structure of the information but the actual content of the text as well.

• Note that while some graphic organizers—e.g., KWL—are prescriptive and very structured, some are more open-ended and adaptable (see Figures 17-1 and 17-2), allowing students to think outside the box. I think of these organizers as somehow archetypal— i.e., they tie in with the ways we are naturally inclined to think. The target diagram (shown in Figure 17-1), for example, makes immediate sense to most people, yet can be used in many different ways. The conversational roundtable (shown in Figure 17-2) also allows for many alternative uses.

• Avoid the reflexive use of graphic organizers. If their use becomes predictable, you lose the element of surprise that makes them a source of energy to students.

• Use graphic organizers to help students:

> Classify ideas, words, and characters prior to writing about or discussing a text

> Organize a sequence in a process they are reading about

> Take parallel notes—e.g., comparing what they read with the experiment or lecture that follows

> Identify what is important in a text

> Examine and understand the organizational pattern of the information or story

• Use graphic organizers to develop students' skills and strategies, and as you use them, discuss why you chose the ones you did. Gradually allow students to choose the method that works best for them so that they can become more independent. Be sure to ask students why they made the choices they did so that they can be made aware of their thought processes when making decisions about how to read and respond to a particular type of text.

STUDENT EXAMPLES

The organizers shown in Figures 17-1 and 17-2 helped sophomores Jeff Harber and Sandy Borelli understand Shakespeare's sonnets and write with greater focus, as shown in the following passage Jeff wrote:

> Shakespeare reminds us that beauty cannot last forever. He illustrates this belief of his through many, if not all, of the sonnets that he wrote. Shakespeare believes that everything has an end as he points out when he writes, "When I do count the clock that tells the time, And see brave day sunk into hideous night." (12:1) This is his way of subliminally saying that nothing can last forever, including beauty. Shakespeare also uses his strange style of writing to tell us

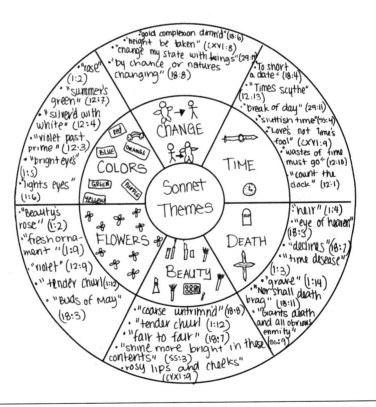

FIGURE 17-1   Sandy Borelli used the target organizer to help her make sense of a series of Shakespeare's sonnets.

that everything must grow old and there is no defense to this fact, "And nothing 'gainst time's scythe can make defense." (12:13) Lastly, William Shakespeare illustrates his beliefs quite clearly when he states that everything, even the most lovely, must wither in time, "Then of thy beauty do I question make, That thou among the wastes of time must go." (12:9)

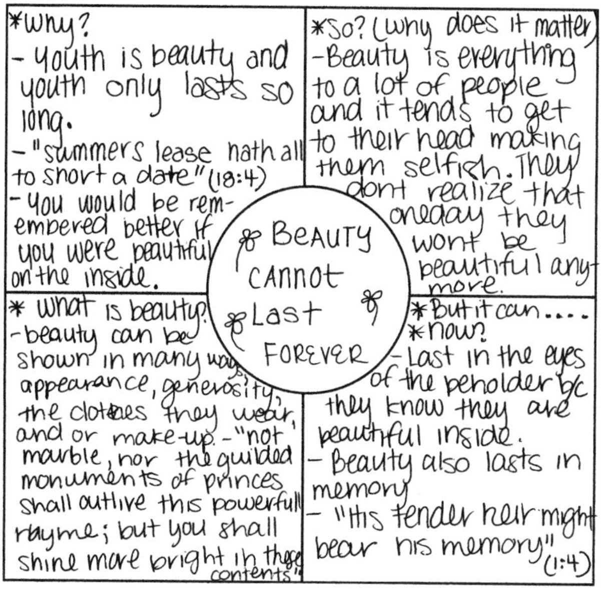

FIGURE 17-2   Sandy then used the conversational roundtable to help her prepare to write about the sonnets. It was this kind of preparation that helped Jeff Harber to respond so effectively to the sonnets.

18 Develop Guidelines for Group Discussion

RATIONALE

Good class discussions are no accident: people require nurturing and training to learn how to discuss ideas and texts. Discussions, whether they be in small groups or with the full class, offer students social occasions for learning and demonstrating their own learning to others. Because we tend to make meaning through our relationships and conversations with other people, group discussions are essential to any effective reading program.

WHAT TO DO

• Ask yourself if a group configuration is appropriate for any particular activity. Some activities are more suited to independent work. Solo activity can often be followed up with group or class discussions, giving individuals the chance to compare ideas and integrate their learning with that of others.

• Ask yourself whether pairs, small groups, or large groups are best suited to your particular instructional aims.

• Depending on the nature of the assignment, consider whether you should have students take on any or all of the following roles:

  ▶ Facilitator
  ▶ Timekeeper
  ▶ Taskmaster
  ▶ Director
  ▶ Resource specialist (looks up words and references in dictionary, textbook, or other reference books)
  ▶ Secretary
  ▶ Reporter

• Make sure that, however you structure the assignment, everyone has the opportunity to participate.

• Consider the following questions when you assign students to groups:

- ▶ Should you group all the ESL students together to provide each other with secondary language support? Or should you divide them up so they have to work independently?
- ▶ If you have a very small group (e.g., 2–4 students) from one ethnic group who may feel uncomfortable if separated, should you let them work together or make them work with others?
- ▶ Should groups be assigned for a long period (e.g., the semester) or should group configurations change frequently?

• Try to ensure that all contributions to the discussion, from teacher or student, move the discussion forward in a productive way.

• Prevent any person or persons from dominating the discussion.

• Have small groups discuss what points they will emphasize when they report to the class.

• Circulate throughout the room, reminding students to:

- ▶ Have patience
- ▶ Listen!
- ▶ Anchor their discussion in the text they are reading
- ▶ Show respect for different views
- ▶ Support their thinking with examples from the text

• If time permits, ask groups and individuals to evaluate their performance, determining the quality of their work based on such questions as:

- ▶ What did we do well?
- ▶ What could we do better next time?
- ▶ What method or strategy did we use, and how effective was it?
- ▶ What was our intended outcome?
- ▶ To what extent did we achieve this outcome?
- ▶ To what extent did everyone participate?

• Try always to provide them with the tools and examples—by first modeling successful discussion for them with a student or small group—they need to do this activity right and well.

STUDENT EXAMPLE

The three transitional ESL students shown in Figure 18-1 wrote the following in response to the prompt, "What questions do you need to ask to help you read *Macbeth* more successfully?"

What are the witches doing? The three witches greet Macbeth as "thane of Glamis," "thane of Cawdor," and "king Hereafter." They promise Banquo that he will create many kings and then they disappear.

What happens? As soon as they are gone, Ross and Angus arrive with news that the king has named Macbeth thane of Cawdor. Then Macbeth considers killing Duncan so he can become king "hereafter," which is what the witches called him.

What changes (in their minds, the action, their status, relationship)? Macbeth changes his mind and acts because of the witches. Now he is thinking of killing the king, so he can have all the power.

How or why did things change? By talking to the witches. They changed his mind, action, and relationship with Banquo, etc. He changed his relationship with Banquo because Macbeth knew that if he kills the king, Banquo's son is going to be the next king.

What will happen in the future? One prediction was that Banquo never is going to be a king, but someone related to him will be.

FIGURE 18-1 Annie, Susanna, and Monica read *Macbeth* together to help them better understand it.

Use Questions to Support Reading

19

RATIONALE

"What ultimately counts is *the extent to which instruction requires students to think, not just report someone else's thinking*" (Nystrand 1997). If asked engaging questions—as opposed to find-the-fact questions—students engage more fully. Better yet, if they are allowed to formulate their own questions, they read more carefully, since they are reading to answer their own questions. Questions, in short, invite engagement when they provoke thought and discussion about those aspects of the reading that are important to students. Alternatively, if the teacher takes into consideration what is important to the students, he or she is likely to pose questions that students find engaging.

Why do people always expect authors to answer questions? I am an author because I want to ask questions. If I had answers I'd be a politician.

EUGENE IONESCO

WHAT TO DO

Questions are used for "building understanding not checking . . . understanding" (Beck et al. 1997) My first question, once we have established the foundational information—who, where, why, when, what, how—is usually, "What are the questions we need to ask about this subject (or text)?" This changes my role from poser to facilitator as I solicit questions and help students decide which ones we should consider. Throughout this process, students are not only practicing developing good questions (which, I always try to remind them, is what good readers do while they read), they are helping to establish criteria for good questions. If there is time, we might stop to evaluate what makes those we chose particularly good questions, so they can internalize these standards.

Remember that the type of questions you ask depends on what you are reading or where you are in the document. You ask different questions early on, but all should support good discussion. Here are some examples:

- What do you think the author is trying to accomplish here?
- What does the subject seem to want more than anything else in the world?

- Why is this the desired outcome?
- Can anyone find examples in the text to support that explanation?
- What do you think is the question this article (or story) is trying to answer?
- So far, how does the author seem to feel about the main character of this story?
- How does this information connect with what we read last quarter?

Keep in mind that the time to ask questions is when students are fully engaged in the text. Waiting until they finish reading detracts from the fundamentally social nature of learning. By using questions to facilitate and direct their learning we allow readers to see books as conversations, as interactions with other people, including authors and their ideas.

Consider that the kind of questions you ask will depend on whether the discussion is taking place as a class or as a group, and whether the groups are expected to report back to the class. Two options arise: Give each group a different set of questions to use or have them develop their own. If they all respond to and then later discuss the same questions, they benefit from seeing how others responded to the same query.

Use the following list as a starting place in developing your own questions:

- What was your first reaction to the text?
- What do you think now?
- What is the text about?
- What was one thing that stood out?
- Did you like it?
- How does it mean?
- What does it mean?
- Why did the author write it?
- Does it bring to mind any similar ideas or experiences you have had?
- What was one question you had while you read it?
- If you could ask the author one thing, what would it be?
- What did you learn from reading this?
- What would you compare it to?
- Do you agree with the author's main point?
- What seems most important to the author when you read?

- Why do you think the teacher chose this for you to read?
- What would this look like as a painting or sound like as music?

Try giving groups a list of such questions to choose from and ask them, when they report back to the class, which questions they chose and why.

If time allows, remind them to use the different reporting strategies (see Reminder 94) you have been practicing in class, since students, especially those lacking formal academic skills or academic language, often do not know how to frame their responses. If you are working with struggling readers, a good intermediary step is to have them discuss the questions and write down what they think or what the group said; such a script makes it easier for them to report to the class and gives them additional writing practice, while simultaneously helping all students to participate.

20 Teach Vocabulary Strategies

RATIONALE

Readers need a range of strategies for making sense of the trouble-some words they encounter while reading. Readers encounter words they do not know but must understand if they are to read a certain passage. They also find familiar words used in new ways that make no immediate sense to them; this might be especially true in literature—for example, in poetry—where authors take some license with the words they use. Another possible source of confusion, especially for English-language learners, could be cultural references or the use of idioms that are not familiar to them. Students need strategies they can use, not words they can memorize. In this respect, teaching vo-cabulary involves teaching students how language works at both the literal and figurative and connotative and denotative levels. Equipped with these skills, students can become the independent readers we want them to be.

WHAT TO DO

• Recall the twelve strategies identified by Janet Allen (1995); students should know how and when to use these when reading:

1. Look at the word in relation to the sentence.
2. Look the word up in the dictionary and see if any meanings fit the sentence.
3. Ask the teacher (or someone else who might know).
4. Sound it out.
5. Read the sentence again.
6. Look at the beginning of the sentence again.
7. Look for other key words in the sentence that might tell you the meaning.
8. Think about what makes sense.
9. Ask a friend to read the sentence.
10. Read around the word and then go back again.

11. Look at the picture if there is one.

12. Skip the word and read on.

• Heed Allen's warning against spending too much time preparing students to read a text; too many vocabulary words and too much review of prior knowledge will intimidate the readers and undermine their interest in the reading selection.

• Use the linear array worksheet (see Appendix 12 and the example shown in Fig. 20-1) to help students develop a better sense of the continuum of meaning (a range of words with, for example, *freedom* on one end of the continuum and *slavery* on the other end, with words like *servitude* in between).

• Use semantic mapping (see Appendix 18) to help students generate a range of associations from a word or its root (e.g., *auto*).

• Substitute the word with others to help students gain a sense of why it is the right word and see how changing it can alter the meaning (e.g., replace *freedom* with *independence*). Write up the possible substitutes on the board and discuss their different meanings. Such discussions develop students' language sense—i.e., which words to use when, why, and how.

• Teach students to cluster words into smaller phrases to help them orient themselves in longer sentences (see Reminder 74). Example: In the beginning / when I first moved to San Francisco / I found it disorienting, / because I was used to living in a smaller town / where everyone know everyone else.

• Teach them to use the book's available supports for language (e.g., table of contents, glossary, index, sidebars, pullout quotes, graphic illustrations).

• Have them compare the unfamiliar word to words they know to see if the familiar words help them.

• Have them read the troublesome passage out loud so they can process it by a different instrument (their ears instead of their eyes).

• Have them summarize the passage in their own words, checking to see if this makes sense in the larger context of the text.

• Have them look at synonyms and antonyms to better understand the scope of the word's meaning (by contrast).

• Discuss with students how the author is using the word (connotative or figurative meaning) compared to its denotative or literal meaning.

• Teach them to assess both the word and the source of their trouble with it: Is it because it is new or used in an unfamiliar way?

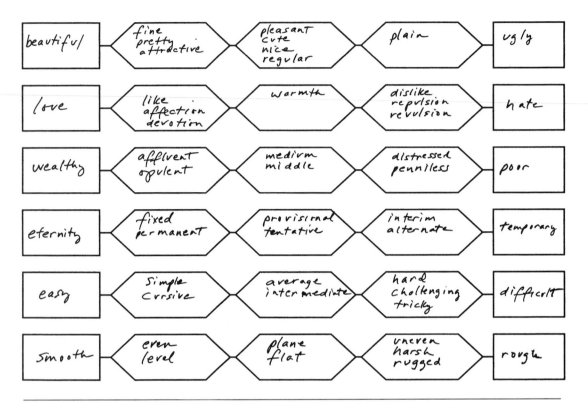

FIGURE 20-1   Rebecca Farac's use of the linear array graphic organizer to expand and refine her vocabulary.

- Help them to see the range of uses: e.g., can the word be understood in various contexts as a noun, a verb, or even an adjective (e.g., *school, play, class*)?

- Have students brainstorm words appropriate to a specific category (e.g., the category for a science class could be "speed") prior to reading about it to activate their knowledge and orient themselves to the subject.

VOCABULARY WORK: THEMES

NATURE	DEATH	BEAUTY
• bud	• heir	• fairest creatures
• rose	• memory	• sweet self
• ripe	• famine	• gaudy spring
• baudy spring	• grave	• golden complexion
• creatures	• eternal	• bright eyes
• lofty trees	• die	• sable curls
• breed	• changing course	• lovely
• violet	• heaven	• sullen earth
• summer	• heaven's gate	• marriage
• rough winds	• war	• love
• lark	• judgment	• lover's eyes
• star	• sword	
• bark	• doom	

FIGURE 20-2   Students reading Shakespeare's sonnets develop their vocabulary and their language awareness by analyzing and categorizing words according to themes they identify within the poems.

Teach Students
How to Ask for Help

RATIONALE

Often students know they need help but do not know how to ask. This might happen for several reasons: language limitations, personal pride, or undeveloped social skills. They might know they need help but not what kind of help they need. Regardless, learners must know how to determine when they need help and how to ask for it.

WHAT TO DO

• Provide, when possible, clues that will indicate to students that they are in trouble or at least going down the wrong road. These are the educational equivalents of "If you see the gas station with the rusted tractor out front you know you've gone too far." An example might be, "If you find yourself saying 'this is a story about a boy and his dog,' you're not grasping the idea and need to ask for help."

• Model for students in different circumstances how they might ask for help. I will say, when discussing a certain text, "One way I often get confused is with complicated syntax. So when I come across such trouble, I will ask someone else how *they* read that passage."

• Brainstorm ways that students might ask for help with their reading. You might begin with an example—"Could you help me understand this poem?"—and examine whether it is a well-phrased question. You could then move on to brainstorm alternative ways of asking this question, taking time to discuss how they improve upon the original.

• If a student asks a question that is particularly clear and useful as an example to others, stop and discuss it, explaining why it is such a good question.

• As you progress through the year, developing questions as you go, put the best ones, or prompts for them (e.g., "What is the author _____ing . . . ?) up on a side board or make a poster so that they can be referred to during discussions.

- Use the bookmarks provided in Appendixes 30 and 31 to give students the samples and tools needed to ask good questions about their reading.

- Model and teach them to use the following strategic questions:

  - I don't understand . . .
  - Could you please explain . . .
  - How did you arrive at that explanation/answer?
  - Could you read that passage again?
  - Would you mind reading that aloud so we can hear how it should sound?
  - Could you please say more about that?
  - How does this relate to what we have been studying?
  - What did you say this meant?
  - What examples can you give me to help me better understand?
  - Could you please provide us with an example of that?
  - This is what I think you are saying. . . . Is that accurate?
  - I'm sorry, could I interrupt to ask a question about something in the text?
  - Could you suggest a different way for me to read this text?
  - Do you have a specific strategy to recommend when I read this text?
  - Could you please go over the directions again?
  - Why are we reading this?
  - What do you want us to find or do while we read this text?
  - I came up with a very different interpretation of that text: (Explain). Am I wrong?
  - What if you/we/the author/the character . . . ?
  - Would you please read a little slower? I'm having trouble following along.
  - I don't understand you. Is there a different way to explain this?
  - Why do you think that?

22

Challenge and Support Students While They Are Reading

RATIONALE

When your students are reading, different needs emerge: some students need additional support to be successful while others need extra challenges to engage them and keep them enagaged. The teacher's role grows more complicated: you must monitor their progress and needs, determining whether they are ready for more sophisticated tasks. Using multiple means of evaluating understanding and assessing performance, you must determine whether the level of instruction is appropriate or needs to be revised. The emphasis should be on moving away from guided instruction to more independent reading.

WHAT TO DO

- Regularly remind yourself and your students:

  ▶ Why they are reading this text

  ▶ How they should be reading it

  ▶ What reading the text successfully looks like (e.g., by modeling, using exemplars)

- Keep the reading experience alive and fresh by:

  ▶ Using different approaches throughout the reading

  ▶ Using different discussion configurations (e.g., pairs, small groups, whole class, and teacher-student discussion)

  ▶ Integrating, where appropriate, supplemental texts (e.g., articles, essays, poems, images, or Web sites) in different genres that represent different or complementary perspectives on the same subject

  ▶ Pausing to look at another text written by the same author, to observe the contrast

  ▶ Including a variety of activities—e.g., perform the text, draw it, recast it, etc.—that allow students to experience it from different angles, deepening their understanding (see Figures 22-1 and 22-2)

- Evaluate your role as you go: moderator, facilitator, tutor, lecturer, master reader.
- Teach them to read recursively by checking what they think or know now against what they read earlier.
- Make connections to earlier portions of the book or other texts they have read.
- Use multiple measures to determine their understanding and performance:

INFORMAL

- ▶ Class discussions
- ▶ Teacher-student quick conferences
- ▶ Paraphrases or other short writing assignments that require synthesis
- ▶ Group discussions you monitor
- ▶ Journals (e.g., learning logs, double-entry journals)
- ▶ Graphic organizers designed to organize and represent their understanding

FORMAL

- ▶ Quizzes
- ▶ Tests
- ▶ Essays
- ▶ Presentations

- Throughout the reading, make connections between:
  - ▶ The current text and those they have read or will read
  - ▶ Current and previous studies of this or related ideas
  - ▶ This and other subjects (e.g., music, history, industrial arts, science)
  - ▶ This text and themselves
  - ▶ This text and the world
- Help them to visualize, hear, and understand the evolving structure of the text.
- Stop often to reflect on what they are reading and why: such metacognitive habits are essential to becoming better readers. Brainstorm or share strategies you and the students are using to read the text.
- Revisit as needed what effective readers of such texts do.
- If students get stuck, teach them to use a variety of "fix-up strategies" (Keene and Zimmerman 1997):

  ▶ Reread

  ▶ Skip ahead

  ▶ Read aloud

  ▶ Consider the larger context

  ▶ Look at other available information (typography, graphics, sidebars, etc.)

  ▶ Explain it to someone else (or to themselves, in their journal)

• Make room for students' questions and essential discussions as they read to increase or sustain intellectual and emotional engagement.

STUDENT EXAMPLES

FIGURE 22-1   Darren Mayer illustrates Macbeth's "split mind" through words and images, showing how such approaches can help students better understand what they read.

Amy Hirsch's explanation of her open mind drawing shows her insight into the story:

> On the left side of the picture, there is a crown which represents that Macbeth wants to be the king. The first place ribbon represents that he wants to be number one. The knife shows that he wants to kill king Duncan to become king. He says that the king is great, but that is obviously not what he is thinking. The lips represent that he is a kiss up. On the right side there are two hands shaking that symbolizes that Macbeth acts like he is friends with Duncan. "Come over" is what he tells the king so that he can kill him. The man killing the other man is Macbeth killing king Duncan.

Steve Gomez's explication of his open mind, shown in Figure 22-2, helps him to better understand the subject as well as to make powerful connections between the class text and his own life:

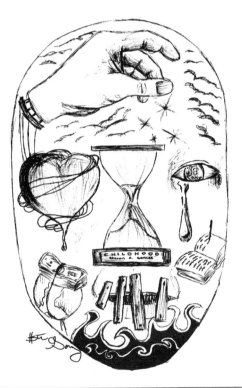

FIGURE 22-2   Steve Gomez, taking advantage of the option to represent his own mind (to help him better understand Macbeth's) used his artistic talent to express himself. Such opportunities give students a chance to respond to texts in ways that are personally meaningful to them.

Clouds represent my thoughts and mind always lingering in the clouds. My hands are only controlled by my heart which sprinkles little miracles on to paper with very little thought. My crying eye throws wishes into a pond of stars so high above. The hour glass shows a childhood so long coming so close to an end. The book shows a new love for writing. The globe shows the fact of life that truly makes me mad: "Money rules the world." My mouth is a prison to so many words, my pen says them for me. The first shows I can act in the heat of the moment.

Provide Good Directions

23

RATIONALE

In order to read successfully, students must understand the assignment. Directions—written, spoken, explained, or created—are helpful only to the extent that they consider the student's needs. A single word in a sentence—*define* instead of *describe*—can make a crucial difference in a student's performance on a task.

> Every text is a lazy machine asking the reader to do some of its work.
>
> UMBERTO ECO

WHAT TO DO

• When creating and delivering instructions orally, keep in mind that the ideal sequence is as follows:

1. Read the directions aloud while students follow along on a handout.
2. Have them underline any important words (such as *define*, which indicate specifically what they are supposed to do) so that they can revisit the directions and refocus throughout the reading.
3. Model for them what the assigned task looks like, narrating your decisions and actions as you go.
4. Provide a student example if appropriate and possible, so that they see what a student should be able to achieve.
5. Have them try it on their own, stopping to check their initial effort against the criteria for success that you have already established.

• Teach them to use any of the following strategies when reading directions:

▶ Annotate the directions with useful information or questions they want to ask.

▶ Turn the directions into a checklist of what they should do.

▶ Look first for the verb (e.g., *categorize*); then ask what this should be applied to (e.g., the elements of a cell); and finally the extent to which it should be applied.

▶ Establish the sequence in which the activities should be done or in which they occur.

> ▶ Paraphrase the directions in their own words to better understand them.

- Think in threes: students should hear the directions, read them, and try the activity before getting under way.

- Be sure to establish the following in your directions:

  ▶ Purpose (why they are reading this)

  ▶ Method (how they should read this)

  ▶ Specifics (how much they should read and by when)

  ▶ What the assignment is asking them to do that they have not done before

- Keep in mind that good directions are:

  ▶ Written in short, coherent sentences

  ▶ Organized sequentially (using numbers or bullets to emphasize each step)

  ▶ Complete with illustrative examples

  ▶ Grammatically, syntactically, and semantically correct and clear: (Instead of writing "The definition of *looming* is . . . " write "Define *looming*." Not only is this more efficient, it's more clear by virtue of the verb and sentence structure)

  ▶ Designed with the reader in mind, not the task or the teacher

- Make clear any constraints or warnings (e.g., "Do not write on the form") by using typography and layout for emphasis.

- Remind them—and in the early stages of the learning process, interrupt their reading to remind them—to return to the directions throughout the task so that they can check what they are doing against what they are supposed to be doing.

- Show students how to read directions on their own. While it is essential to go over directions with them in the early stages, teachers must move kids toward being independent readers. Having students read and then annotate and/or paraphrase directions provides a useful opportunity for the teacher to ask what they underlined, why they thought something was important, or what they thought the directions asked them to do.

SAMPLE DIRECTIONS FOR EXAMPLE ASSIGNMENT SHOWN IN REMINDER 22

DIRECTIONS: WHAT'S ON YOUR/MACBETH'S MIND?

- Decide your topic: a character from the play, yourself, a historical figure, or a representative persona (e.g., teenagers, men, women, leaders).

- Think in threes: e.g., what the character (1) thinks, (2) does, and (3) says.

- Fill the different spaces with symbols, words, images, or whatever else helps to represent the character's mind as you understand it.

- Add features—clothing, hats, hands, a body, etc.—to your image if they help you convey your ideas (or just to spice up your illustration).

- Write an explanation of your drawing either on the back of it or on a separate sheet of paper. If at all possible, make connections between your work and the text.

24

Create and Use Study Guides

RATIONALE

Study guides, also known as reading guides, are tools that help students understand what they read. They accomplish this through questions that serve to focus the reader's attention on those aspects of the text most appropriate to the unit of study. These guides are different from the traditional "study questions" that typically appear at the end of a reading selection. Wood, Lapp, and Flood (1992) characterize study guides as "tutors in print form," by which they mean that the guides are designed specifically to aid readers *as they read*, not after. There are many types of useful guides, each providing structure to students as they learn to read in new ways or encounter difficult texts on their way toward independence. Guides are especially helpful to learners with special needs.

WHAT TO DO

• Decide whether a study guide is necessary in the first place by asking yourself the following:

> What concepts do I want students to understand/know after reading this text?

> Which terms must they know to understand those concepts?

> What level of independence is appropriate for reading this text?

> Are there organizational and conceptual structures that suggest a study guide would be a useful tool to achieve the desired learning result?

> Would a study guide prepare them well for those activities that follow the reading?

• Determine how best to use the study guide by asking the following questions:

> Which strategies and skills are students focusing on now, and how can this guide enhance those?

> What use do you want to put this information or these skills to after they finish reading?

- Review the various types of study guides (adapted from Wood, Flood, and Lapp 1992):

   Anticipation guide: designed to stimulate discussion and prepare students to read by activating their prior knowledge and integrating that with what they read.

   Point-of-view guide: expands students' perspective through elaboration and prior knowledge.

   Textbook activity guide: helps students monitor their comprehension through predicting, retelling, and outlining.

   Interactive reading guide: used to facilitate discussion, retelling, brainstorming.

   Levels-of-comprehension guide: asks students to distinguish between literal and figurative, to infer, evaluate, and interpret levels of meaning.

   Guided learning plan: uses open-ended questions and students' prior knowledge to evaluate the text.

   Process-of-reading guide: sequence of activities or questions designed to develop or improve students' ability to draw conclusions, predict outcomes, and identify main ideas and sequences.

   Pattern guide: develops and enhances students' knowledge about organizational patterns of information (see Reminder 90) through use of graphic organizers or questions.

   Concept guide: enhances students' ability to identify the main ideas and supporting details through questions and graphic organizers.

   Analogical study guide: uses analogies and metaphors to help students understand and remember; such guides also expand their thinking through such associations.

   Content guide: asks students to find specific information and helps them to establish purpose for their reading.

- Have students create their own study guides (e.g., teacher's edition, Cliffs Notes) for a text.

- Create your own study guides (instead of using those provided by publishers) so you can align them with your curricular needs and goals as well as your students' needs and abilities.

- Use the guides to help students develop the six facets of understanding (Wiggins and McTighe 1998): explanation, interpretation, application, perspective, empathy, and self-knowledge.

- Use the study guide as a means, not an end in itself. Little if any emphasis should be placed on grading; completion and ability to use the guide is what matters most. Wood, Flood, and Lapp emphasize this point, calling the guides "adjunct aids" designed to assist student reading. Grading turns an otherwise useful tool into little more than an open-book test.

SAMPLE STUDY GUIDE QUESTIONS

The Scarlet Letter Journal Guiding Questions

Overview Please keep a separate *"Scarlet Letter* Journal" during the course of our study of this novel. This separate journal can be in your "regular journal" so long as entries on the novel are kept together; you may also use separate sheets of paper. These questions are intended to help you read more deeply in the text, focusing on aspects of character, the tone of the story, the changes in the plot. You should answer these questions thoughtfully and thoroughly (e.g., about four to five sentences per answer in most cases) in your journal unless otherwise directed by me and/or the weekly assignment sheet. Here are a couple questions to guide you and help you respond with greater insight.

- What happened?

- Why is it important?

- Why do you think this?

- How do you know that?

- What is the relationship between this event/person and some other event or character in this (or another) story?

CHAPTER ONE

1. What do you think are the three primary or most important images in the first chapter? (Please explain your answers.)

2. Why does the narrator offer us a rose at the end of the chapter? What might this mean? What has it to do with Ann Hutchinson? (Please explain your answers.)

3. Why would Shirley Jackson in "The Lottery" name the woman who gets stoned "Mrs. Hutchinson"? (Please explain your answer.)

4. After reading Chapter 1, go through and mark (on the photocopied page provided to you) all the adjectives you can find. When you finish, look them over and then, in your journal, explain what you think they have in common with each other. (Another way of thinking about these adjectives: what effect do they have on the tone or mood of the story's opening?) *Don't forget to explain your ideas.*

Support Students with Special Needs

25

RATIONALE

Students enter our classes with a range of challenges, some easier to address than others. The following suggestions are intended to help those students with special needs, though the truth is, they will help all students in one way or another. My background is in special education, and every strategy and tool in these pages should help challenged learners, a point I have tried to make throughout this book by using examples from special needs students, even though I may not identify them as such.

What one knows is, in youth, of little moment; they know enough who know how to learn.

HENRY ADAMS

WHAT TO DO

• Be multimodal and multimedia: Whenever possible, let students hear the subject of study, talk about it, see it, and touch it.

• Sequence your activities and assignments logically.

• Provide a weekly assignment sheet to help students check off work they have done or need to do.

• Check frequently for understanding. Do this in a variety of ways (e.g., paying attention to students' expressions, circling the room to look at their work, asking them at the period's end if they understood the lesson).

• Discuss learning strategies you think will help them with specific areas or assignments.

• Allow adequate time for completion of tasks or reaction to questions you ask.

• Provide additional time to those students who need it.

• Whenever possible, break up new information into small units, present it slowly and sequentially, and review frequently.

• Be patient.

• Provide immediate feedback whenever possible to help students measure their progress.

- Ask individual students what helps them the most and what is most difficult for them.

- Provide time to practice or rehearse: whether it is an upcoming writing test or a speech they must give, be sure to give them time to prepare.

- Use small groups to support English-language learners. Such groups, if made up of fluent speakers and considerate students, provide the developing speaker with an opportunity to listen more carefully and speak more often without the usual anxiety of raising their hand and speaking when the whole class is listening. One other tip: do not let students huddle together into single-language groups too often, but do let them help each other by using their primary language to explain things to each other.

- Provide handouts whenever possible. These make it easy for students to follow along; also they help remind students of what is required of them when they are doing classwork at home.

- Use the board. The board provides visual text that the struggling and diligent alike can write down and clarify later.

- Do not depend on (but feel free to use) verbal directions.

- Do not talk too fast.

- Provide clear, concise directions.

- Find out if there are audiotape versions of the book you are reading at the local library and suggest that they try these; most states provide books on tape for adopted texts at little or no expense through their department of education.

- Recommend that they watch the film version of a book you are teaching, though point out that there might be significant differences in the film version (e.g., *The Scarlet Letter*).

- Make CD-ROMs (e.g., dictionaries, reference works, encyclopedias) available if you have students who would benefit from such tools.

- Allow them to use Cliffs Notes. Though controversial, these study aids provide much needed support for the student whose language ability makes it hard enough to understand literary texts, especially those with dialect, idioms, and slang used by writers like Mark Twain or J. D. Salinger.

- Make yourself available outside of class. Many ESL students are reluctant to demand attention until they gain some confidence with their new language; you must go to them and remind them that you are willing to meet with them if they need extra help.

Support English-Language Learners

. . . .

26

RATIONALE

My classes include a generous number of ESL students, all of whom are supported by a strong ESL department. I mention this because perhaps the most important lesson I have learned when it comes to helping my ESL students is the importance of collaborating with their ESL teacher. The following suggestions, as well as many of those in Reminder 25, come from such collaboration.

Life is a foreign language; all men mispronounce it.

CHRISTOPHER MORLEY

WHAT TO DO

• Assign the ESL student a language partner who is specifically responsible for helping that student understand assignments and words they do not know.

• Make available a dictionary in their native language and dictionaries that are specifically designed for English-language learners (see the *Longman Dictionary for American English: A Dictionary for Learners of English*).

• Use gestures to emphasize and illustrate your points whenever possible.

• Create a questionnaire that asks students specific questions that will help you develop a profile of them as a student and a learner (Briggs 1991).

• Allow students, as part of your outside reading program, to read at least one book in their native language.

• Allow them to write first drafts in their primary language as a means of getting their ideas together, then work on the translation and writing in English later.

27 Support Students with Learning Difficulties

RATIONALE

I began my career working with kids who had various, and sometimes extreme, learning difficulties. I don't pretend any expertise in this area, only a commitment to their success. The following strategies and ideas have served me and, more importantly, my students, well. Many other techniques are available in Reminder 25, but those listed here are specifically aimed at helping students with learning difficulties.

WHAT TO DO

• Alter the format of written handouts to reduce the amount of material in the student's visual field, or use graphic displays and diagrams to convey information.

• Let students have a partner who understands their needs and is supportive and willing to work with them. I have had girls who were very understanding and supportive of those boys in the class with learning disabilities and provided extra help to them both in and outside of class.

• Enlist the help of a scribe to share note-taking responsibilities; if one is not provided through the student's IEP, look for a student in class who would be willing to help in this area.

• Use graphic or other organizers to help with reading. Even if you are not requiring that such tools be used on a particular reading, try to make available some helpful means of organizing information (e.g., before the reading, review how to make an outline).

• Understand the constraints that individual students' challenges impose on them and do your best to address their needs by clarifying intended outcomes (e.g., students with ADD typically are very tired by day's end, after trying to overcome distraction and confusion all day).

• Provide clear and logical transitions between ideas and units of instruction.

- Provide concrete examples to illustrate the ideas you are discussing, relating them to the student's background, experience, and personal interests (which are usually available in their IEP or student file).

- Seat students with learning difficulties up front and away from those people or conditions that would distract or otherwise undermine their performance.

- Assess their learning style and discuss with students how they can best learn different types of information.

- Allow students to demonstrate their knowledge through alternative means (e.g., using a tape recorder in place of written notes, a scribe during tests, or a computer).

- Establish and maintain high but reasonable expectations.

Take a moment to reflect on your reading and teaching in this space. You may find the following discussion points useful, or you can come up with your own:

• Write a summary of the last section. Include in this summary three main ideas—techniques, strategies, tools—that relate to your own classes.

• Which reminders from the preceding section might help you the most?

• Looking ahead to the next section, consider its title and, before you begin reading, create your own list of reminders for this topic. After checking yours with mine, discuss which of these reminders—from your list and mine—will help you and your students the most.

Evaluate Your

Own Teaching

A black woman had just presented a paper entitled, if I remember correctly, "First, Teach Them to Read." [Martin Luther] King leaned over to me and said, "first, teach them to believe in themselves."

—JOHN GARDNER, FROM *EXCELLENCE*

Helen Garcia reads one of the many books she devoured during the semester.

To self-evaluate is to ask yourself how you can be better, to remind yourself that you can always improve. My favorite example of such critical evaluation concerns Wilt Chamberlain. Apparently Wilt gave himself a score of 1–5 at the end of each game, a 5 being the best score possible. The reporters learned about his ritual of evaluating his performance and would always ask him, "What did you give yourself today, Wilt?" He rarely gave himself a score higher than a 2; when asked to explain, he said that he was always aware of all the ways he could have played better.

Such thinking is not "the glass is half empty" thinking, but rather is reflective, a means of improving one's performance by refining it. The same habit of reflection, the willingness to make mistakes—so long as you learn from them—is common to strong readers who know not to give up.

I take my own criticism differently and can use it to better ends than the criticism we often hear from students or the public. Here is a sample from my own notebook, to which I periodically retreat to think about my teaching.

> I had one of those days when time runs out, you try it a bit differently in each period in hopes of getting it just right and even make progress but don't win the prize. I began to reflect (for .5 seconds) at one point on the fact that I am making a transition at this point in the semester from focusing on skills to opening up the conversation, and that's tricky because it means helping students take the next steps more on their own, and not all of them are ready for that I think. So I will have to keep at it in the coming days to get a better grab on it. Such days remind me as usual of Pat's [my master teacher] frequent remark about the difference between what you should or want to do and what you actually can do.

Mostly I measure my own teaching and what I am accomplishing by looking at kids like Phil Jordan. It's kids like Phil, a good kid but not always a motivated student, who give you the real measure of your own success. I know I'm doing something right when I read comments about independent reading like this one of Phil's:

> I read a book called *A Season on the Brink* by John Feinstein. Now, I'm usually the kind of person who doesn't like to read much, but as soon as my friend recommended and gave me this book, I knew it was right up my alley. When I began to read this book I found myself reading every night. I noticed that the time would go by so quickly when I was reading that my mom had to come to my room and tell me to go to bed. I guess it was just because I was really enjoying the book.

Phil reminds me that I can and should measure my teaching by various criteria, in his case by asking myself not only what I am trying to accomplish but what I have helped students learn to expect from and know about themselves.

Finally, though it's nice to sit down and record my thoughts in my journal, have a written conversation with myself, a student, or some author I'm studying, my time is limited. I have learned to ask these questions about myself and my teaching as I drive home, while I wait beside the copy machine, as I plan for the next day's lesson. Evaluating your teaching, in the end, means keeping the conversation going, the one between you and your profession, your colleagues, and, of course, your students, who are always willing to help you evaluate your teaching for the simple reason that they want the best teacher they can get, the one you are always trying to be.

28

Remember *Why We Read*

RATIONALE

We read to know we
are not alone.

C. S. LEWIS

We work so hard to help our students read that we sometimes lose sight of that essential question: Why do we read? It is not an obvious question to a teenager living in a world filled with distractions and surrounded by an almost infinite number of forms of entertainment. Questioning why we read also challenges us to reflect on what we are trying to accomplish as teachers. The following letter, written by a student, reminds us why we read—and why we want our students to read, too.

WHAT TO DO

Read the following excerpt from my book *I Hear America Reading: Why We Read • What We Read* (1999), and think about how powerful the experience of reading can be for all children.

Dear Mr. Burke:

"How has reading changed my life?" My memory runs back to when I was seven years old. "Ding Dong!" My dad finally came home.

It was my birthday party. I was waiting for him the whole day. A week ago, he had told me that he would give me a big surprise on my birthday party. "What will it be? It must be that red skirt I saw in the shopping center!" I've looked forward this moment for a week that I was almost impatient.

I immediately ran over to him. He was very excited. There was a careful wrapped box in his hand. "Oh, my dear red skirt. I finally have you." My heart was pumping. Without my dad's consent, I took over the box.

"Oh, no!" My heart was sinking when I opened the box. It was not the pretty skirt I'd longed for so long. It was a BOOK! I was like falling down from the top of the world. "No, I never want the stupid book. Where is my dress?" I cried out. Tears were filled in my eyes. I've waited for a week for the useless book. I felt I've been cheated. How can he give me the cheap, nonsense book for my birthday gift? He didn't like me at all. I would never read it.

At night, I can't fall asleep. Looking at the big book, my anger was running inside me. It had ruined my party. Why did dad lie to me and said it was a surprise to me? Suddenly I grew curiously: "What is the book about? Is it so evil that I hate it and want to tear it apart?" I opened the book—*Chinese and Foreign Stories*—and read my first real story in my life.

There was a little virtuous duck. It's so ugly that nobody liked it. It didn't have any friends. Every animal around the lake laughed at her wherever she went: "Look at this little duck. Get away from her." Comparing to her, her sister was as pretty as a princess. Wherever she was, there were always friends around her. They would say: "Come here, dear. Come in my house." One day, they were playing around the lake. Suddenly, a little chick fell into the lake. He shouted "Beauty, save me." The pretty duck shook her head selfishly: "Why should I save you. I can't get anything." The ugly duck just passed by. It saw what happened and jumped in the water bravely without a word. It saved the chick. From then on, everyone liked to play with warm-hearted ugly duck. The story ends with a motto, which I remembered most—"It's the inside that counts the most."

I was ashamed when I finished reading it. I felt I was like one of the animals that only look at the outside of the things, but ignore what they really are. I liked the red skirt because it was pretty. But pretty outfit can't cover my inside. Only the knowledge can fill my mind. And reading is one way to get the knowledge.

I moved on to the next story. . . . I was deeply attracted. I can't put the book down anymore. I kept reading. I read during the break of the class. I read as soon I got home. Soon, I had a habit—I can't go to sleep unless I read some pages. Like what my mom said, "I fell in love with reading."

I fell deeply in love with the beautiful earth when I read "Our Home—Earth." I decided to preserve the earth like the guards who fight against bad people destroying the earth. I cried for Cinderella when she was tortured by her wry sisters. And I can't stop laughing at funny action of the little bear when it danced.

I read, and I learned. My mind was not empty with only pretty dress anymore. I was filled by books and knowledge. I began to understand what is true beauty, and to realize our burden as the residents on earth. I never felt I was alone and boring. I have books—my dearest friend with me.

As I grew up, my knowledge grew. I had regretted what I did wrong when I was young. But I never regretted to pick up the book on my birthday night. It's that moment I began to open the door lying between me and wonderful world, people and knowledge. It's reading that helps me find my true self and our value of living. I am still reading. When I get home after a day's tire work, my first hope is to lie down on the sofa, and read a book a while. It's the only time I can forget all the unhappiness. At that time, my book and I are the only two existing on earth. Every time when my dad asks me what I want most for my birthday present, I say it out without thinking: "I want books. I want to read."

Sincerely,

Grace Zheng
High school ESL student

Consider These Ten Principles of Good Instruction

RATIONALE

Richard Allington, who has spent much of his life thinking about reading, offers the following synopsis of the most important principles to keep in mind. These principles form their own useful list of "reminders" for us to consult when planning or teaching.

What I like in a good author is not what he says, but what he whispers.

LOGAN PEARSALL SMITH

WHAT TO DO

Read "Ten Principles for Looking at Reading/Language Arts Lessons in Your Classroom," by Richard L. Allington, University of Florida, and think about the extent to which you are applying these principles in your own classroom.

Ten Principles for Looking at Reading/Language Arts Lessons in Your Classroom

Much has been learned in the past decade about classroom instruction that effectively develops the reading and writing of all children. The ten principles below provide a brief summary.

1. **Nothing is better than reading and writing to develop children's reading and writing.**
   Do kids read for at least one hour each day? Do kids write for at least one-half hour each day?

2. **Most reading should be easy reading (high accuracy/good comprehension). An 80/20 ratio (of easy to harder) seems about right.**
   Do all children have texts of appropriate complexity? Do they choose some of their books?

3. **Children do not develop comprehension strategies by answering questions after reading.**

Are active comprehension strategies explicitly modeled on a daily basis? In content subjects as well as reading sessions? Do children write daily to demonstrate understanding?

4. **Children do not develop composing strategies from red ink corrections (nor from just writing).**
Are composing strategies explicitly modeled in front of children on a regular basis?

5. **Children do not develop decoding strategies from drills or dittoes (nor from just reading).**
Are useful decoding strategies explicitly modeled for children on a regular basis? Is decoding instruction linked to spelling/composing? Are decoding lessons focused on word structure?

6. **Children benefit from an integrated, content-oriented reading/language arts curriculum.**
Are the interrelationships between the language arts obvious in the curriculum children experience each day, each week, each year? For instance, is the decoding strand linked to the spelling/composing strand? The composition strand to the comprehension strand? Do each day's instructional activities exhibit linkages? Do children learn from reading?

7. **Some children need access to larger amounts of more intensive instructional support and enhanced opportunities to read and write with instructional support.**
Do lower-achieving students (e.g., Title 1, learning disabled) participate in instructional support efforts that substantially increase the amount of reading and language arts time they have and is personalized instruction provided? Do they actually read and write more daily?

8. **Thoughtful literacy is the new general goal for reading and language arts instruction. Basic literacy/minimum competence will no longer suffice.**
A wealth of school tasks emphasizing summarizing, organizing, synthesizing, comparing, analyzing, creating, and presenting texts are evidence of thoughtful instruction K–12.

9. **Developing independent readers and writers is critical to developing thoughtful, lifelong learners. Easy access to books is critical support for fostering independent reading activity.**
Do classrooms have large and enticing supplies of books and magazines nicely displayed and available to read at school and home? Is the school library open weekends and summers?

10. **Access to consistently high-quality classroom instruction is more important than which parents children have or which special programs they attend.**
    Good classroom instruction is absolutely central to student achievement. Do not expect either parents or special programs to solve children's literacy learning problems.

30 Teach by Design

The prepared man is the lucky man.

SUN-TZU, *THE ART OF WAR*

RATIONALE

Planning lessons is the phrase we most commonly use to describe what we do, but *designing lessons* is more accurate, given all that we have to achieve within a period, a unit, a semester. Teaching by design recognizes the structural nature of curriculum development: good lessons and effective learning require that certain elements be placed and used in specific ways. If we can learn to ask and eventually internalize the following questions, we can create consistently effective assignments and activities that culminate in improved reading and learning for our students. The subsequent set of points addresses those concerns that arise before, during, and after our students read; the purpose of the first list is to help you decide *what* to teach and how to design assignments for optimal student learning.

WHAT TO DO

Ask yourself the following questions:

- What do I want my students to be able to do? (See Reminder 32)
- Why do I want them to be able to do that?
- What activities and learning will lead to this outcome?
- What examples can I provide to help students see what strong and weak performances look like on this assignment?
- What do they need to know or be able to do to accomplish that?
- What evidence of their performance/achievement is acceptable?
- To what use can I then put that assessment data?
- In what capacity can I best support their learning in this instance?
- What conditions are necessary to ensure effective learning in this instance?
- What obstacles should I anticipate?
- How can those obstacles be most effectively and efficiently overcome?

- How does this objective align with my curricular priorities? Establish your curricular priorities by asking these questions:

  ▶ What should my students be familiar with?

  ▶ What is important for them to know and do?

  ▶ What are the "enduring" ideas or "understandings" that should anchor this unit or lesson? (Wiggins and McTighe 1998)

Reflect on the following points:

- Which texts will best support the curricular conversation the class is engaged in at this time? (See Reminder 9)

- How can this activity or unit support and further develop students' previous learning to ensure growth and continuity?

- Which standards will support my choice of method and content?

- How will this activity or method help my students meet the state standards? (See Reminder 9)

- What special needs might some students have prior to and during this activity—and how can I best meet those needs to ensure that they are successful? (See Reminders 25, 26, and 27)

- How should I organize and write the directions to ensure ultimate clarity and student success? (See Reminder 23)

- How can you structure this assignment so that students use their emerging skills, strategies, and knowledge with greater independence than in the past?

- What connections can you—and through this lesson, your students—make to what you have already studied and will study in the future? (See Reminder 10)

- How can I achieve understanding instead of "coverage"? (depth versus breadth)

- What resources or materials are necessary to support this activity?

Keep in mind these essential considerations when assigning reading:

- How much time is needed to read the text as expected (e.g., skimming vs. reading for understanding)

- Length of the text

- Difficulty of the text

- Preparation necessary to read the text successfully

- Appropriateness of the content

- Strategies that will help students read the text most effectively

31 Stop and Reflect Periodically

I always know the ending. That's where I start.

We get so busy, it is hard to remember to stop, look, and listen: Are we doing all that we should or could to help our students and ourselves? Are we reaching all students or just the ones who always seem to "get it"? Use the following questions (and the table of contents of this book) to remind yourself of what you can and should try to do, especially if things are not going as you wish.

WHAT TO DO

Whenever you can or feel the need to, ask yourself any of the following questions to evaluate your own teaching. It's up to you to determine the value and implications of the answer to any of the questions.

- How many pages per week are students actually reading in my class?
- Am I having them read too much, too little, or just enough?
- How many types of text (see Reminder 75) do students read in my class?
- What specific techniques or instructions do I offer them when they read these different types of text?
- How much time do I expect students to read each night?
- How long do my assignments take students to do?
- Am I allowing them time for SSR in my class?
- Do I clearly establish the rationale (why) and the purpose (how) for reading whenever I assign it?
- What is the area in which my students most consistently struggle when it comes to reading?
- What am I doing to address that?
- Am I doing anything—overusing film, lecture, handouts—to help them avoid reading?
- What sort of assessments do I most consistently use to evaluate their reading?

- What type of information do these measurements yield?
- How do I use that information to improve my teaching and their learning?
- Do I allow room for students to ask their own questions about the subjects and texts we read?
- Are my expectations—of amount, frequency, level of work—reasonable and appropriate given the skills of and demands on my students?
- What specific support am I offering—i.e., what adjustments or accommodations—to students with special needs?
- Which students consistently do not read, or get the lowest grades in that area?
- What common traits do they share?
- Have I talked with them to find out why they do not do the reading or avoid it?
- Do I know the reading levels of all my students?
- Do I scaffold and sequence my instruction in a logical and developmental way so as to move them from what they know how to do toward what they must learn how to do?
- Am I spending an appropriate amount of time preparing them to read the texts in my class?
- Am I modeling (or using students as models to show) how assignments should be done, strategies used, or texts read?
- Am I developing students' awareness of the strategies they use so that they can improve their ability to self-monitor what they do while they read?
- Am I reading aloud enough—and doing it effectively?
- Am I providing exemplars to show them what they should do and how it should be done?
- Am I checking what I teach against the standards of my district or state so my students will learn and be able to do what they are expected to know and be able to do?
- Do I structure my class and what we read based on essential questions and ideas?
- Who talks the most in my class?
- Do I use graphic organizers and other tools to help students read better?
- What evidence can I provide that I use graphic organizers well and that they make a difference in students' learning?

32 Consult the Standards

RATIONALE

Standards, whether they are state or local, our own or our department's, offer useful guidelines, particularly for new teachers who lack a complete understanding of all that they must teach in any one class. While some teachers resist and even resent the standards developed by states and districts, they remain in place and are thus something our students and we as teachers must use in a productive way. Standards remind us that our work is not about what we can say that we *taught* but what our students can *do*.

WHAT TO DO

• Share, discuss, and post the standards in your classroom so that students know what they (and you) are expected to accomplish in your subject area.

• Refer to them without allowing them to be intrusive, incorporating the language of the standards into your lessons so as to reinforce and remind students of the importance of these skills. Example: "One thing we know good readers do is use questions to help themselves better understand what they read. What are some questions we might ask while reading this text that could help us read it better?"

• Provide—through a Web site, overhead transparency, or photocopy—exemplars to help students see what any given standard looks like. This might also include you modeling the behavior they are expected to master.

• Identify and explain the criteria by which students' performance on any standard will be measured and evaluated. Provide, if possible, examples of the different levels of performance so that they can develop a clear understanding of what success looks like.

• Use the standards (see Figure 32-1 and Appendix 32) to guide your thinking, or locate those governing your own discipline at www.mcwrel.org.

GENERAL STANDARDS FOR READING IN ALL SUBJECT AREAS

IDENTIFY

- ❏ conventions that govern the particular text and how those help shape meaning
- ❏ the main idea in a text
- ❏ the main argument in an expository text
- ❏ literary devices used in a text and how they function to convey meaning and affect the reader
- ❏ organizational patterns used to convey information
- ❏ rhetorical devices and how they are used in different texts
- ❏ figurative language (metaphor, simile, analogy) and how it functions within the text
- ❏ the genre to which the text belongs
- ❏ archetypes and symbols used in the text and determine how they contribute to its meaning and affect the reader
- ❏ subtle differences between words and ideas and how those affect the reader and contribute to meaning

EVALUATE

- ❏ stylistic elements and how they contribute to the writer's voice and convey meaning
- ❏ an author's ideas for bias and the extent to which this bias affects the integrity of the text
- ❏ the author's choice and use of a particular medium to determine its effectiveness
- ❏ a document in order to determine how it should be read
- ❏ an author's approach to a particular idea and the effectiveness of their perspective, argument, or idea
- ❏ the accuracy and clarity of any information
- ❏ the philosophical assumptions that underlie the author's ideas or the text itself
- ❏ the effectiveness of the point of view from which the text is written
- ❏ a particular idea across a range of texts to understand it more fully
- ❏ the author's choices in terms of how they contribute to meaning and affect the reader
- ❏ the author's style or this text in light of others by the same author or within the same genre
- ❏ the validity of an argument according to the context in which it is used

INTERPRET

- ❏ current information in light of what they have read so far in order to revise their understanding
- ❏ the point of view from which the text is written
- ❏ the current text in light of other works by that author or from the same era or culture
- ❏ a range of types of information—numerical, statistical, graphic, expository—to arrive at a complete understanding of the text in context
- ❏ observable patterns within the text in order to arrive at a complete understanding of the text in this context

USE

- ❏ a range of strategies to comprehend different texts, choosing the most appropriate one for that particular text
- ❏ representational strategies to make abstract material concrete
- ❏ a range of strategies to determine the meaning of a particular word in its context
- ❏ information from the text they read in order to make a decision
- ❏ information provided by the text to solve a problem

FIGURE 32-1   These standards were culled from a wide range of standards documents in all subject areas in order to find a common set of habits, skills, and knowledge needed to read successfully in all disciplines.

EXPLAIN

- ❏ how the structural components of the text influence meaning and affect the reader
- ❏ the motivations of fictional characters, drawing examples from the text to support the reading
- ❏ how an author's use of sensory detail contributes to the form and function of the text
- ❏ the conclusions they draw using information from the text to support their thinking
- ❏ the relationship between different elements or parts of a text and how those contribute to meaning and affect the reader
- ❏ the process by which they arrived at their understanding of a particular text (or solved a problem posed by the text)

DETERMINE

- ❏ the veracity of information within any text
- ❏ whether the information is fact, opinion, or rumor
- ❏ the author's intent and the devices used to achieve the desired outcome
- ❏ whether this is a document they need to read at all and if so, which parts of it should be read
- ❏ the extent to which the culture, era, or other factors affect the text's meaning and reader's response
- ❏ the type of text and how it is supposed to be read (according to its textual conventions and genre)

KNOW

- ❏ the core terms appropriate to the textual domain (i.e., vocabulary specific to a novel, a legal text, a scientific text)
- ❏ origins and roots of certain essential words
- ❏ the fundamental conventions that govern a text in this particular genre, discipline, or domain
- ❏ how a text functions to create a specific response in the reader
- ❏ the different types of text or genre within a discipline
- ❏ essential background information necessary to read this document successfully
- ❏ the defining characteristics of a variety of informational texts
- ❏ the principles of grammar, syntax, and semantics as they relate to a particular text

COMPREHEND

- ❏ words using the most appropriate strategy (context, roots, connotative or denotative meanings)

INTEGRATE

- ❏ information from a variety of sources and types of texts to arrive at a more complete understanding of a subject

ORGANIZE

- ❏ information as you read to suit the demands of the reading task

DEVELOP

- ❏ an appreciation for the beauty and power of language as it is used to convey meaning in different types of texts
- ❏ their own questions while reading and use their experience and knowledge as readers to find those answers within the text.

FIGURE 32-1   Continued

- Use the example standards checklist shown in Figure 32-1 (and the variation of this in the Appendix) to help you create your own adaptation using state or local standards.

- Know the different types of standards and how they apply to your subject area:

  - *Performance standards:* articulate the degree or quality of proficiency students must demonstrate to achieve mastery on any standard.

  - *Content standards:* identify and describe what students should know and be able to do in any subject area.

  - *Assessment standards:* identify and describe the qualities of or means by which standards can be effectively assessed.

  - *Delivery standards:* identify and describe the materials, tools, or other means necessary to help students achieve each standard.

- Align the standards with your local and state standards and framework to achieve consistency in your interpretation and implementation.

- Consult the standards when planning and use them to:

  - Identify a topic or essential question
  - Select standards appropriate to the assignment
  - Use local curriculum objectives
  - Design learning and teaching activities
  - Decide which products and performances are appropriate to this assignment
  - Define the assessment criteria
  - Write performance descriptors
  - Create scoring guides that are linked to the standards
  - Collect and display exemplars (Harris and Carr 1996)
  - Provide multiple means of demonstrating and assessing mastery of each standard in order to accommodate a range of learners

Revisit the Six Features of Effective English Instruction

RATIONALE

The following six features come from a study conducted over several years by Judith Langer at the Center on English Learning and Achievement. This study, "Six Features of Effective Instruction" (2000), focused on middle and high school English classes, though in truth these same six features would apply equally well to other subject areas. Throughout the study, Langer and her team emphasize that these six features are not independent of each other but are instead interrelated and supportive of one another. Langer provides examples of activities to illustrate how each feature might be addressed in the classroom. The following information is adapted from Langer's report.

WHAT TO DO

Reflect on the text below, keeping in mind how it relates or could relate to your own practice.

Feature One: Students learn skills and knowledge in multiple lesson types.

ACTIVITIES THAT WORK
- Providing overt, targeted instruction and review as models for peer and self-evaluation;
- Teaching skills, mechanics, or vocabulary that can be used during *integrated* activities such as literature discussions;
- Using all three kinds of instruction to scaffold ways to think and discuss (e.g., summarizing, justifying answers, and making connections).

Feature Two: Teachers integrate test preparations into instruction. Using district and state standards and goals, teachers and administrators collaborate on the following.

ACTIVITIES THAT WORK

- Analyzing the demands of a test;
- Identifying connections to the standards and goals;
- Designing and aligning curriculum to meet the demands of the test;
- Developing instructional strategies that enable students to build the necessary skills;
- Ensuring that skills are learned across the year and across grades;
- Making overt connections between and among instructional strategies, tests, and current learning;
- Developing and implementing model lessons that integrate test preparation into the curriculum.

Feature Three: Teachers make connections across instruction, curriculum, grades, and life.

ACTIVITIES THAT WORK

- Making overt connections between and across the curriculum, students' lives, literature, and literacy;
- Planning lessons that connect with each other, with test demands, and with students' growing knowledge and skills;
- Developing goals and strategies that meet students' needs and are intrinsically connected to the larger curriculum;
- Weaving even unexpected intrusions into integrated experiences for students;
- Selecting professional development activities that are related to the school's standards and curriculum framework.

Feature Four: Students learn strategies for doing the work.

ACTIVITIES THAT WORK

- Providing rubrics that students review, use, and even develop;
- Designing models and guides that lead students to understand how to approach each task;
- Supplying prompts that support thinking.

Feature Five: Students are expected to be generative thinkers.

ACTIVITIES THAT WORK

- Exploring texts from many points of view (e.g., social, historical, ethical, political, personal);

- Extending literary understanding beyond initial interpretations;
- Researching and discussing issues generated by literary texts and by student concerns;
- Extending research questions beyond their original focus;
- Developing ideas in writing that go beyond the superficial;
- Writing from different points of view;
- Designing follow-up lessons that cause students to move beyond their initial thinking.

Feature Six: Classrooms foster cognitive collaboration.

ACTIVITIES THAT WORK

- Students work in small and large groups to
  - Share their ideas and responses to literary texts, questions, etc.;
  - Question and challenge each others' ideas and responses;
  - Create new responses.
- Teachers provide support during discussions and group work by
  - Moving from group to group;
  - Modeling questions and comments that will cause deeper discussion and analysis;
  - Encouraging questions and challenges that cause students to think more deeply.

Take a moment to reflect on your reading and teaching. You may find the following discussion points useful, or you can come up with your own:

• Write a summary of the last section. Include in this summary three main ideas—techniques, strategies, tools—that relate to your own classes.

• Which reminders from the preceding section might help you the most?

• Looking ahead to the next section, consider its title and, before you begin reading, create your own list of reminders for this topic. After checking yours with mine, discuss which of these reminders—from your list and mine—will help you and your students the most.

Evaluate

Your Students

The decent docent
doesn't doze;
He teaches standing on
his toes.
His student dassn't
doze and does,
And that's what
teaching is and was.

—DAVID MCCORD

Holly and Jenna read collaboratively to help them understand an article from
Time magazine and a poem by Nikki Giovanni about rapper 2Pac Shakur.

We are so committed to helping our students become readers that we can forget about the larger context of their lives. As the Martin Luther King epigraph from the previous section reminds us, it is important to teach kids to read, but it is as important to help them believe in themselves. Thus we must consider their lives, their emotional and existential needs, when we evaluate their progress and performance as readers. Maritza's candid journal response allows me to evaluate what she did (or did not do) as a reader; it also explains why she thinks or does what she does, information I can use to anticipate her needs in the future.

> Today I didn't read a lot. I was actually thinking about writing that I did and that it was great and all but I don't see the point in BSing you or myself. I didn't read because I forgot my book at home and the book I picked out today [for SSR] even though it looks interesting isn't half as good as real life. What did I do for 20 minutes, you might ask? Well, I read, but not a book. I read what my friend wrote to me in our little notebook. I read about how she feels, her problems, concerns, troubles, etc. which to me is better than any book I can read. Then I answered her and wrote about my own feelings, problems, troubles, etc.

How do I get such information? I ask for it: in their journals, on index cards, in quick conferences at their desk, in the last minute before class ends. Such information, as I said before, allows me to keep track of where they are as readers—and as people. I can give Guadalupe all the handouts and suggestions I want to help her as a reader, but it's not likely to accomplish much when her mind is elsewhere, as this journal entry shows:

> I didn't read well today because I couldn't concentrate and be in an environment where it is peaceful. When I was reading my book I kept thinking about how my mom is getting an operation [in Mexico] and I can't be with her to support her and all I could do is hope and pray that she will be okay.

As this book continually seeks to remind us, however, our work is to help our students develop their reading abilities, to instill in them a love for and commitment to reading. We can evaluate their progress toward these goals through informal means (conversations, observations, reflective writings) and more formal approaches (portfolios, exams, rubrics). Entries like the following one from Alice, a student who had moved here from Korea the previous year, provide the most valuable information when it comes to evaluating our students' progress as readers:

I was going to read a book written in my own language this time, but I changed my mind and read a book called *How to Make an American Quilt*. I only finished this book throughout 12 weeks but I definitely improved in some areas of reading. Now I can read faster, without falling into some other thoughts; moreover, my vocabulary slightly improved, too. I can tell that I improved whenever I read. I get to write more in my journal than before nowadays—not because I got more to say, but now I can express what I was thinking clearly.

As you can see, Alice's reflection allows me to evaluate her progress as a writer, a thinker, and, of course, a reader. When sophomore Kenny Bowden writes the following response I know that he is growing as a reader and *how* he is growing (e.g., in capacity, engagement, patience): "I especially enjoyed the last couple of pages because the author incorporated a lot of Spanish into the book. I think it serves as a good tool in helping me visualize the situations posed in the book." Such observations as Kenny's remind us that to evaluate our students is to evaluate ourselves and our classes; if we listen, we, too, will learn, and improve.

34 Use Reading Surveys

RATIONALE

Reading surveys allow us to get to know our students and help them get to know themselves as readers. These surveys, which can serve many different purposes, help any teacher clarify students' attitudes and capabilities as readers. The surveys can also provide a powerful opportunity for discussion in the class at the beginning or end of the year.

WHAT TO DO

• Use the survey provided in Appendix 33 or one you create yourself to facilitate a discussion about reading across the curriculum, in and out of school, and in different contexts (e.g., the workplace; for personal research).

• Have students read the survey prior to using the profile of effective and ineffective readers. This will help them better understand what they themselves do when they read. It will allow them to get more out of the discussion and to identify where they stand on the continuum of readers.

• Use the information here as prewriting information for an essay in which they evaluate their ability as a reader. This more analytical essay might come after they have written the reading autobiography.

• Use a survey at the beginning of the year—to get to know students and help them evaluate their current status—and at the end of the term or school year to help them reflect on any progress they have made and the source of that improvement.

• Have students use the survey to interview others, from different age groups and backgrounds, to create a more complete picture of readers.

• Use the data from the survey to practice summarizing and synthesizing data into a written form, drawing examples to support your reading from the text at hand (in this case their survey).

• Put the survey in students' portfolios so that they can revisit it during teacher-student reading conferences or at semester's end. It provides a useful if informal measure of their progress as readers and attitude toward reading.

• Use the data gathered from the survey to create their reading goals.

• Note the following summary, based on survey information gathered from my sophomore classes during the semester I wrote this book. My 150 sophomore students said that they

FREQUENTLY READ

> ▶ Magazines
> ▶ Web sites
> ▶ E-mail
> ▶ Textbooks
> ▶ Poems/lyrics

OFTEN READ

> ▶ Novels
> ▶ Reference books
> ▶ Autobiographies and biographies
> ▶ Manuals
> ▶ Comics

35 Develop Portfolio Guidelines

RATIONALE

Given that reading is a skill we expect to improve the more we do it, it helps to have a process to document that growth. While there are various formal and informal methods for assessing reading performance, portfolios provide the reader (and teacher) with a tangible record of what the student has read over the course of the year. They also allow readers to revisit their goals and, by adding evidence of progress, to monitor their progress toward those goals. Finally, portfolios provide teachers with a powerful means of evaluating their own work, since they invite teachers to reflect on what their students read, how they read it, and how much they improved their reading attitude and ability during their tenure in the class.

WHAT TO DO

- Decide who chooses the content of the portfolio and the criteria by which it will be evaluated.

- Establish and communicate to students the portfolio's purpose.

- Show them what a good portfolio looks like by sharing, if possible, exemplars from previous students. (If you are just beginning to gather exemplars, ask students if you can photocopy theirs as an example for other students, now or in the future. It is also ideal to gather examples of strong, good, and weak portfolios, so that students can see the difference between these.)

- Ask yourself and/or your class the following questions about portfolios as they relate to your specific class and subject area:

  - What would be acceptable evidence/data to include?
  - What are the criteria by which the portfolio will be evaluated?
  - What categories and criteria should be included on a rubric used to evaluate these portfolios?
  - What examples, anchored to the rubric's categories, would help them to better understand what a successful portfolio looks like?
  - How much choice should students have as to what they include?

- Consider including any or all of the following in the portfolio:

  - Record of what students have read
  - Annotated bibliographies of books read (see student example that follows)

- Representative examples from their learning log
- Before-and-after reading surveys (see the reading surveys in Appendix 33)
- Reflective essay on their progress as readers during the year
- Scores from a variety of reading tests, including class, district, and state tests
- Creative responses in different forms or media, including artistic and multimedia productions inspired by or in response to their reading (other possibilities include reviews, précis, written conversations, think-alouds, or comments about a dramatic performance of a text)
- Reading goals, as revised over the course of the year
- Example of a close reading of a challenging text (this might be represented by a carefully annotated text and a subsequent critical analysis of that text)
- Cover letter introducing the contents to a reader, in which students explain what the contents show about them as readers
- Reading autobiography

STUDENT EXAMPLE

The following personal evaluation accompanied Ricardo Lopez's freshman portfolio in Diane McClain's freshman English class.

Annotated Bibliography

Alvarez, Julia. *How the Garcia Girls Lost Their Accent.* © 1991. 290 pages. Fiction.

Ashe, Arthur. *Days of Grace.* © 1992. 352 pages. Autobiography.

Hinton S. B. *The Outsiders.* © 1997. 180 pages. Fiction.

Kingsolver, Barbara. *Pigs in Heaven.* © 1994. 343 pages. Fiction.

Lenz, Frederick. *Snowboarding to Nirvana.* © 1997. 225 pages. Fiction.

McCourt, Frank. *Angela's Ashes.* © 1997. 309 pages. Autobiography.

Quindlen, Anna. *One True Thing.* © 1995. 400 pages. Fiction.

Seinfeld, Jerry. *Seinlanguage.* © 1993. 180 pages. Comedy.

Verne, Jules. *From the Earth to the Moon.* © 1896. 400 pages. Fiction.

Never did I ever stop to think about the type of reading skills that I had. I always thought that if I could read pronouncing all the words correctly and reading in a smooth rhythm is all I need. But never did I imagine that there were many types of readers, each with different skills and qualities. It's kind of weird that I never realized this, because it is obvious. Now that I look back to September, I wasn't the best reader in the world but I wasn't the worst, but I could have done better. Reading wasn't really a thing that I enjoyed. I consider reading to be a task. I hadn't discovered the thousands of books that I like to read. In the reading scale [see Reminder 37], I think I was somewhere around the less inexperienced reader slot. I was developing fluency and I enjoyed reading books that had a lot of reasoning and mystery. Reading as a leisure activity was something that never crossed my mind.

The blend of books that intrigued me and the time spent reading in class made it almost impossible for me to put down a book. I could not put the book down and do any activity. I was always wondering what was going to happen in the next chapter. My bibliography reflects the image of a reader that enjoys books with a sense of humor and books about activities that I do in real life. However, books like *The Outsiders* and *Angela's Ashes* are books that try to make the soul understand the tragedies of life such as poverty, the death of a loved one and plain human suffering that is not wished upon any living thing. I have read nine books in six months. I can't recall reading more than four books a year and now I've finished nine in six months. I have read more than 2,000 pages and I have learned from the lives of hundreds of people, characters in books.

I believe that in the reading scale I am now in the experienced reader category, a self-motivated, confident, and experienced reader who may be pursuing particular interests through reading. I have changed in thousands of ways. My word bank has immensely expanded and whenever there is a word that I don't know the meaning to, I don't just ignore it but I write it down and figure out what it means. My reading in other classes and at home has improved greatly. I can enjoy reading and it has become a pastime. The only way that I can improve my reading skills is to read books. There is no other way to improve by staying at the same level. I have to read books that are harder than the books I usually read.

Compare Effective and Ineffective Readers

RATIONALE

We often learn best by comparing one performance with another, by examining, in this case, the habits of effective and ineffective readers. By recognizing the habits and needs of both types, teachers and students can become more cognizant of what they must or already do to read effectively. Regularly referring to these different habits and problems also creates a common vocabulary that allows teachers and students to discuss what they are doing or need to do if they are to become more effective readers. Finally, discussing what readers do demystifies the process of reading, which is sometimes perceived as an activity people either can or cannot do, a harmful and illogical fallacy.

A good reader is one who has imagination, memory, a dictionary, and some artistic sense.

VLADIMIR NABOKOV

WHAT TO DO

• Post the effective/ineffective readers comparison on the classroom wall, where everyone can see it. This will provide many opportunities to remind students of what they should do while reading.

• Post the Northwest Regional Educational Laboratory's "The Traits of an Effective Reader Reading a Literary Text Scoring Guide" rubric (see Appendix 39) on the classroom wall or give a copy to students. This will allow you to review what effective readers do while reading literary works. (Note that a similar guide for reading expository or "informational texts" is also available in Appendix 38.)

• Model the behaviors of an effective reader or point out to the classroom those students who exemplify different traits.

• Provide examples of written work from current or past students to help readers better understand what certain aspects of reading look like.

• Use the scoring guide rubrics and/or the comparison of effective and ineffective readers in the following contexts, to help readers focus their attention on how they should read any particular text:

> Before reading, review the characteristics of successful readers, modeling or providing exemplars of work produced on similar assignments to help students see what successful reading looks like.

> During reading, interrupt students and use the scoring guides and descriptions as tools to help them reflect on their performance. Evaluators commonly use these "anchoring sessions" to help remind readers of what to look for and what a successful performance looks like.

> After finishing, have students use the scoring guide or descriptions to evaluate their own performance, identifying those specific behaviors they employed or skills they used to read at that level. They could use the scoring guide in subsequent discussions with their group, the class, or the teacher, as a tool to help them talk about how they read (see Reminder 94).

> Throughout the day or year teachers can revisit these scoring guides and descriptions to help them remember what they are helping students learn to master and what they themselves must teach. It is also a good idea to consult the standards periodically (see Reminder 32).

• Have students use the different scoring guides and their own notes from discussions as the basis for a reflective or analytical essay about reading. Susan Allen, author of several books on reading, asks students to identify "the best reader" they know and explain why they are such a good reader. The scoring guides and comparison (see Figure 36-1 and Reminder 37) would help students write such a paper.

• After evaluating their current ability according to the rubrics, and completing the reading survey (see Reminder 34 and Appendix 33), students can use this information to help them write their reading autobiography (see Reminder 3).

• Provide students time to discuss *how* they read a particular text; such exploratory talks allow students to learn how others their age solve problems while reading and to better digest their reading.

STUDENT EXAMPLES

The following examples come from students who were, as part of a class assignment, asked to identify the characteristics of good readers. By involving them in the identification of these traits, the hope is that they will begin to increase their awareness of these habits.

EFFECTIVE READERS	INEFFECTIVE READERS
BEFORE THEY READ	
Determine what they already know and need to learn.	Begin reading without asking themselves what they know or need to learn.
Read the directions for the reading and related work carefully, making sure they know how they are supposed to read the selection and what they are supposed to know or do after they read it. If they do not fully understand the directions, they consult those who do.	Ignore or barely look at the directions, getting from them no sense of what might help them read well or do the subsequent assignments that are based on the reading.
Assemble any tools or materials they might need and determine how best to use them (for example, being sure they have a highlighter and deciding how they should annotate a selection).	Do not have or retrieve the tools or materials that would help them be active readers.
Set themselves up to read in an environment conducive to reading and thinking.	Try to read in an environment filled with distractions.
Establish appropriate and reasonable goals for the assignment, taking into consideration the demands of the text, their personal reading goals, and the time needed to read this particular text.	Do not evaluate the demands or difficulties of their reading assignments. Begin reading without defined purpose or any personal goal to direct their efforts.
Identify the type of text in order to activate their textual intelligence about how such texts are made and how they work to create meaning.	Treat most texts as equivalent, making no distinction between how they work and should be read.
Even before reading, begin making predictions, based on any available clues or features, as to the content and its meaning.	Make no effort to predict what the text might be about, due to indifference or lack of habit of doing so.
WHILE THEY READ	
Continually check what they read against the predictions they made, revising their understanding as needed based on new information.	Do not process what they read, but just take it in without asking questions, wondering, or responding mentally to what they read.

FIGURE 36-1   Characteristics of effective and ineffective readers.

Engage all their faculties, bringing their full attention to the text at hand.	Allow their mind to wander off to other subjects unrelated to what they are reading.
Monitor their understanding.	Do not monitor their understanding.
Make connections between what they know and have read, between this and other classes.	Do not make any connections but see the reading as isolated from anything else.
Troubleshoot their reading, determining the cause of any confusion or other problems, and solving these problems effectively and efficiently.	Are not aware that reading is a problem-solving process through which the reader can use various techniques to improve understanding or overall reading performance.
Pace themselves, recognizing the importance of stamina in reading longer, more difficult texts.	Plunge ahead until they get tired or frustrated, then give up, failing to return to the reading as promised.
Read the text at both the literal and figurative levels according to the demands of the text.	Read mostly at the surface or literal level, missing the deeper levels of meaning available to them through the text.
Know which questions to ask and strategies to use while reading. Are active, recursive readers.	Do not ask questions or read strategically; if they do ask questions, they may be the wrong ones or simply useless. Are passive, linear readers.
Expand and use content knowledge and vocabulary needed to read the text.	Do not pay attention to new words or concepts that will help them.
AFTER THEY READ	
Evaluate the extent to which they understood what they read according to their own and the prescribed criteria. If necessary, they return to the text or consult others who can help them better understand what they read.	Do not determine the extent of their understanding.
Revisit their personal reading goals and reflect on the extent and reasons for any progress toward these goals.	Do not have goals in the first place and thus cannot evaluate their progress toward such goals.
Summarize, clarify, and question the text and how it relates to past, present, and future reading and learning.	Make no effort to complete the transaction: when they finish the last word they are done.

FIGURE 36-1   Continued

May be copied for classrooom use. Reading Reminders by Jim Burke (Boynton/Cook, a subsidiary of Reed Elsevier Inc., © 2000).

	Pee-Wee	Amature	Professional
Speed	Slow	Average	fast
Distraction	easily	Somewhat	Never
interpretation	takes everything Literaly	understands it, but doesn't find meaning	understands the Book, and the authors interpretation
interest	interested in things having to do with their own.	can either hate it or like it.	very interested because they analyzed and choose books well
inteligence	can't understand meaning of words	understands most words	can find a word meaning by the words around it
frequency	rarely reads for pleasure	reads when needed	reads whenever they get the chance

✱ I AM A PEE-WEE READER ✱ I NEED HELP!

FIGURE 36-2   This student created a very honest and insightful description and set of criteria for what readers do.

Dear Mr. Burke:

I think reading is very big subject since we do it so much. We do it without even realizing. I think most people read a lot everyday even if they won't admit to it. I personally don't really like to read books, because I prefer reading magazines and manuals so that I get something useful of it.

A good reader likes reading everything from novels to people emotions. A bad reader hates reading books, but they read people and signs and other literature that interests them. I think the only real difference between all readers is their will to read. Everyone could be a good reader if they found something they liked to read.

I am a good reader because I can concentrate well on reading and keep good pace. The thing that separates me from being great is that I can never really find something I like to read. I am confident in my abilities and am able to tackle almost any book. I have some trouble keeping up with all the class reading and keeping undistracted. This is the way I see myself as a reader.

Sincerely,

Mike Costaglia

Upon entering school in September, students in my freshman Honors class submit letters in which they reflect on the books they read that summer. This assignment not only gives them an opportunity to build bridges between the different books, but it allows me to evaluate their performance and figure out what my course needs to offer them. The following example, from freshman Amy McElhany, offers a good example of what I hope to see: comprehension, insight, connections—between the different books but also between the students and the world in which they live. I include here only the first page of Amy's letter; it provides a concise example of what I wish all students could do by the time they enter high school.

Dear Mr. Burke,

My name is Amy McElhany. I was a student at and am now a graduate of Burlingame Intermediate School. This fall I will be attending your English class at Burlingame High School as a freshman. This is my first assignment as a high school student. This may not be a momentous occasion for you, but it is for me. This summer I read the two assigned books *To Kill a Mockingbird* and *Bless Me, Ultima*, and one additional book, *Pigs in Heaven*. These books had many similarities and many differences.

To Kill a Mockingbird, by Harper Lee, is a story set in the southern town of Maycomb, Georgia in the 1950s and is told by Scout, the daughter of a lawyer. She has a brother named Jem.

The story portrays people judging each other before they ever get to know each other. One example was Mr. Dolphus Raymond. He hung around with black people and drank out of a brown paper bag. Most people just assumed he was a drunk and kept a whiskey bottle in the bag, so he would not upset the ladies. Because of these traits he was considered evil. Most people gave him one glance and knew for certain that he was a drunk, but that was not the truth at all. The truth was that he associated with black people because he enjoyed their company, and he drank Coka-Cola out of the brown paper bag to keep his image. Another example was Arthur (Boo) Radley. The town came to the conclusion that since he never came out of his house, he was bad. One lady said he peeked in her bedroom late at night. The children at the local school thought that the nuts that fell off the trees in his yard were poisonous. But Scout and Jem found out that he was a good person who watched out for them. When Jem broke his arm, Boo carried him home. Scout found out the reason Boo never came outside. He just didn't want to.

The story is also about the prejudices people have towards each other. The best example of this is the trial of Tom, a black man who is accused of raping Mayella Ewell, a white woman. There was no physical evidence to prove Tom committed the crime. In fact, some of the evidence shows Mayella was hit on the right side of her face, probably by a left-handed punch, and Tom was crippled in his left arm. The only thing pointing to Tom's guilt was the testimony of Mayella Ewell and her father Robert E. Lee Ewell. The prosecutor and the town assumed the all-white jury would convict Tom. They were right.

Have Them Use
the Reading Scale

RATIONALE

It is fine for us to give students grades or notes, make comments in passing, or praise their observations during a class discussion of a text, but we must also ensure that they are able to monitor, correct, and evaluate their own performance. The following continuum, or reading scale, originally developed as part of *The California Learning Record* for the California Department of Education, provides a useful means of having students conduct such a self-evaluation. See the accompanying example of a student's reflection on his progress based on his self-evaluation. I have adapted the original scale into a checklist.

WHAT TO DO

Have students use the following checklist/continuum to determine their current standing as a reader and their progress since the last evaluation. The self-evaluation provides the perfect opportunity for formal or informal reflection, as the featured example shows. (The example is from freshman fall semester in Diane McClain's class. She made and maintained a strong commitment to SSR for the semester. The bibliography and reflective writing bear witness to the benefits of the program.)

Inexperienced Reader (1)

❏ Limited experience as a reader.

❏ Generally chooses to read easy, brief texts.

❏ Has difficulty with any unfamiliar material.

❏ Needs a great deal of support with the assigned reading.

❏ Rarely chooses to read for pleasure.

Less Experienced Reader (2)

❏ Is developing fluency as a reader and reading certain kinds of material with confidence.

❏ Usually chooses short books with simple narrative shapes.

❏ Reading for pleasure often includes comics and special interest magazines.

❏ Needs help with the reading demands of the class, especially complex literary, reference, and informational texts.

Moderately Experienced Reader (3)

❏ Feels at home with books.

❏ Is developing stamina as a reader.

❏ Is able to read for longer periods and cope with more demanding texts, including novels and poetry.

❏ Willing to reflect on reading and often uses reading in his/her own learning.

❏ Selects books independently and can read juvenile fiction and nonfiction.

❏ Can use information books and materials for straightforward reference purposes.

❏ Still needs help with unfamiliar material.

Experienced Reader (4)

❏ Is a self-motivated, confident, experienced reader who may pursue particular interests through reading.

❏ Capable of tackling some demanding texts.

❏ Can cope well with the reading required in all classes.

❏ Reads thoughtfully and appreciates shades of meaning.

❏ Capable of locating and drawing on a variety of sources in order to research a topic independently.

Exceptionally Experienced Reader (5)

❏ Is an enthusiastic and reflective reader who has strong, established tastes in fiction and/or nonfiction.

❏ Enjoys pursuing reading interests independently.

❏ Can handle a wide range and variety of texts, including some adult material.

❏ Recognizes that different kinds of texts evoke different reading stances.

❏ Is able to evaluate evidence drawn from a variety of information sources.

❏ Is developing a critical awareness as a reader.

STUDENT EXAMPLE

After compiling their list, students reflect on how reading those books affected them.

Bibliography

Bradbury, Ray. *Fahrenheit 451*. © 1953. 119 pages. Science Fiction.

Bradbury, Ray. *The Martian Chronicles*. © 1946. 181 pages. Sci Fic.

Bradbury, Ray. *Dandelion Wine*. © 1975. 239 pages Science Fiction.

Cooney B., Canine. *Driver's ED*. © 1994. 199 pages. Fiction.

Krakauer, Jon. *Into The Wild*. © 1996. 207 pages. Fiction.

McCourt, Frank. *Angela's Ashes*. © 1996. 364 pages. Autobiography

Paulsen, Gary. *Night John*. © 1993. 92 pages. novel

READING SCALE SEMESTER

In September, I wouldn't have ever called myself a "reader." I just hated to read. It didn't matter what kind of book I had, whether it was adventure, horror, mystery, romance, war, drama, fantasy, or memoir, I hated it. I knew I should start to read more so maybe I could improve at it. I thought this way because whenever I was called upon to read in my other classes, I would say "pass" just because I knew I would mess up on reading out loud. Teachers always say to get better at reading you have to read, which is pretty logical advice. Whether I like that advice or not, in September, in the 9th grade, I had no choice but to take that advice. The kind of reader I think I was in September would be a 1 Inexperienced Reader. I had difficulty with any unfamiliar material, and I still hated to read. But if I wanted to get an "A," I had to become better at reading, so even though I hated it, I read.

As I take a look at my bibliography, I see that in a period of five months, I read seven books, 1,401 pages, with an average of 200 pages per book. To some people that is probably nothing, but to me, that is more than I have read so far in my life, in one class. To tell you the truth, I am proud of myself for reading seven books in five months. The kinds of books that I have read are adventure, novels, autobiography, and science fiction. The books that seemed the most challenging were the science fiction books, which is kind of weird because I read three of them. I think the reasons I read three science fiction books is because I liked the challenge and the author.

They were all written by Ray Bradbury. The reason I like science fiction books is because they make me think about things like, "Is this what the future is going to be like, as it is in the book, *Fahrenheit 451*?" Basically, I like science fiction books because they make me think about topics that are really deep, like space, time, and the future.

Today, as of this moment, I believe that I am at a Three— Moderately Experienced Reader. Some of the ways that I think I have changed are, well, I like to read as long as I think it is a good book. Also, I think I have improved my speed of reading, as I can read a lot faster than back in September. I think now I know all of this happened because I have been reading. One way that I have not changed is that I still do not like certain kinds of books. For instance, horror and drama are two kinds that I cannot stand! My reasoning for this is, well, I just don't like them. I also see changes in how I read in my other classes and at my home. In most of my classes, I found that I read a lot faster than I used to. In my history class, it used to take me about an hour to read a chapter and now it takes me about 30 minutes. Not only at school but at home, I read for pleasure. Sometimes when I have nothing to do, I just read the newspaper. Just by reading the newspaper, I now know a lot more about the things happening in the world.

I think I can bring myself to the next reading level, on the reading scale, by following some advice someone gave to me. "To get better at something, you must do it again, again and again and when you think you're better, keep on doing it." So for me to get to the next level, I will just have to read, read, read, and read.

Troubleshoot Reading Difficulties

RATIONALE

There are three rules for writing the novel. Unfortunately no one knows what they are.

W. SOMERSET MAUGHAM

Teachers and students all need to develop "fix-up" strategies, means of identifying, evaluating, and repairing their problems with a given text. Reflective readers (and teachers) begin to notice certain patterns of error, recognize specific types of text as difficult for themselves; the difference is that they learn to troubleshoot their own or their students' difficulties. Use the following table to help you find the strategies that will help your students the most.

WHAT TO DO

• Use the following table, which refers you to places throughout this book, to help you troubleshoot your teaching or your students' difficulty with reading.

• As you get to know the book better, add your own list of difficulties and cross-references to this page so it can serve as a useful guide to the answers you seek.

• Keep in mind that most graphic organizers are designed to help students solve or avoid many of the problems they encounter in reading. Organizers such as the "think-in-threes" schema offer useful tools to help students make sense of difficult texts; examples of these organizers, which I have included throughout the book, will show you how they might be used and offer students exemplars to help them understand.

IF THE READER IS	SEE REMINDERS
• Confused	2, 14, 16, 17, 23, 24, 25, 52, 54–74, 83, 86, 95, 97
• Unfamiliar	12, 14, 15, 17, 19, 20, 24, 52, 86, 87, 95
• Frustrated	8, 10, 12, 13, 20, 21, 23, 24, 29, 78, 80, 81, 91, 93, 94, 96
• Bored/not engaged	4, 5, 7, 9, 28, 39, 50, 53, 75, 79, 99
• Not reading	1, 2, 6, 8, 12, 34, 81, 82, 96

IF YOU ARE	
• Discouraged	4, 9, 10, 28–33, 97
• Bored	4, 10, 13, 22, 99, 100
• Confused	14, 17, 28, 31, 32, 33, 35–39, 100

Check for Understanding and Growth

RATIONALE

Whether it's a matter of revisiting personal reading goals or our purpose in reading a given text in the first place, both teacher and student must ask what they achieved when they finish a reading. The only way to improve is to evaluate how you did against what you wanted or were expected to accomplish. Such information is only useful, however, to the degree that it improves future performances and helps the teacher refine lessons. Finally, understanding can best be assessed using multiple measures, all of which contribute to a more complete picture of the students and their performance. While periodic evaluations and assessments help to determine students' needs and performance, postreading summative assessments serve to bring the unit to a close and allow the class to move on to the next unit of study.

My mother, Southern to the bone, once told me, "All Southern literature can be summed up in these words: 'On the night the hogs ate Willie, Mama died when she heard what Daddy did to Sister.'"

PAT CONROY

WHAT TO DO

• Use the dense question strategy (see Reminder 14) to help students develop their own final exam or essay topic on this reading.

• Consider which of the following is most appropriate or provide students the opportunity to choose from and create their own culminating assignment:

> ▶ Quiz/exam
> ▶ Performance task or project
> ▶ Essay
> ▶ Academic prompt (e.g., for a paper)

• Keep in mind that any final assessment, regardless of the type of task, should be useful and make sense to the student (i.e., help them improve their performance), the teacher, and parents.

• When designing culminating activities or final assessments, consider using these words in the prompt:

> *Explain*

> *Interpret*

> *Apply*

> *Demonstrate*

> *Synthesize*

• Ask yourself how this assessment will allow them (and you) to compare their performance on this unit/text with their performance on previous tasks or texts in order to measure their growth.

• When assessing understanding or performance, consider what is adequate in terms of data, time, and task.

• Decide and communicate honestly to your students the purpose of the assessment, which might be any of the following:

> To verify that they read a text

> To measure their understanding

> To determine mastery of a type of reading or a specific skill

> To determine what they need to learn or do next

> To reflect on and thus deepen their understanding before moving on

> To integrate all the different knowledge they've gained in the course of a unit

• Ask yourself what examples of a successful performance (via exemplar or rubric) you can provide students in the process of assessment. Make these available early on, so they know what success looks like.

• Decide the proper balance between the following sources of questions and answers after students finish reading:

> The text

> Their heads

> Their hearts

> The world

> Other texts

> Their experience

• Create assessments that will likely reveal critical misunderstandings/misreadings.

• Allow students to explain or demonstrate their understanding using one of the following means: visual, written, spoken, or performed explanations—or a combination of these.

STUDENT EXAMPLE

The Big Idea organizer allows you (and the student) to assess quickly whether or not the student understood the main ideas in the text.

What's the Big Idea?

The big deal of Dimagios life and death was that he conquered feats of strength and cunning, honorable and loyal, and triumph in conflict. He was admirable and well respectable and was one of the best baseball players of time.

Narrow it Down: What's the Most Important Point?

The most important point is that Joe DiMaggio wasn't like most celebrities. He didn't talk to any news people and wasn't concerned with all of the Hollywood gossip. This is one of the reasons he was so admirable.

How do you know that's the most important idea? Write three examples or comments that support your assertion that this is the most important idea. If they are quotes include the page number so you can refer to it later when writing about or discussing this idea.

1. People didn't try to invade his personal space

2. People didn't want to get to know him, but they admired and respected him.

3. All people knew about him was that he was a great baseball player

---

FIGURE 39-1   Amy Hirsch used the What's the Big Idea? graphic organizer to help her make inferences about an article on Joe DiMaggio.

Take a moment to reflect on your reading and teaching in this space. You may find the following discussion points useful, or you can come up with your own:

• Write a summary of the last section. Include in this summary three main ideas—techniques, strategies, tools—that relate to your own classes.

• Which reminders from the preceding section might help you the most?

• Looking ahead to the next section, consider its title and, before you begin reading, create your own list of reminders for this topic. After checking yours with mine, discuss which of these reminders—from your list and mine—will help you and your students the most.

Read a Variety of Texts
for Different Purposes

It's much easier to write a solemn book than a funny book. It's harder to make people laugh than it is to make them cry. People are always on the verge of tears.

—FRAN LEBOWITZ

Ashley Moore, lost in thought while reading after lunch.

A quick skim of most contemporary magazines and newspapers (not to mention Web sites) reminds us how many types of texts there are. And students need to know how to read them all, each one requiring a different set of skills, capacities, or attitudes. Thus we must make room for these different types of texts in our curriculum, no matter what subject we teach, and, ideally, we should use them for different purposes.

In one sequence, for example, my sophomores, preparing to read Erich Maria Remarque's *All Quiet on the Western Front*, were given a packet that included a poem, statistics, graphs, a short essay, letters from soldiers in World War I, and a time line of the years 1914–1918 that I found on a Web site. I had them read these different types of text in order to complete a KWL organizer (see Reminder 61 and Appendix 11) and their own time line so that they could acquire the necessary background knowledge that would help them understand and appreciate Remarque's novel. I didn't have them read the poem as literature but as a report, as a form of information. The poem, Wilfred Owen's "Dulce et Decorum Est," was originally conceived as a letter to his mother. Because in its original form it was offered as a means of informing his mother about the war, to read it that way is not to cheat the poet nor deny the poem its artistry.

Independent reading, which I have stressed throughout this book, provides students with an excellent means of integrating a wide range of texts into their reading experience. Chris Karmiris, a sophomore in my class, took a more historical slant on his passion for basketball by reading John Christgau's book *The Origin of the Jumpshot*. One of the things he found most interesting was the difference between the past and present: "As I read this book, I compare the different styles of basketball on how it was played fifty years ago and how it is played today," wrote Chris.

Another sophomore, Kay Wong, who enjoyed reading all sorts of different and often humorous books, wrote the following after borrowing my book *I Hear America Reading*:

Today after I read Mr. Burke's book, I took a moment and realized what books meant to me. Even though I hate reading school books, I love reading. I love reading books on all sorts of topics from biographies of my favorite stars, to astrology, culture/religion, economics and many more. Books are kind of like the Internet. There are books and web pages on just about everything but it depends on if you can find them or not. A lot of people in the book that wrote letters to Mr. Burke and it's just amazing how both guys and girls like reading so much, too. Books are probably one of the most important things in life. That's probably where you gain most of your knowledge (and TV). My mom's friend's husband was not cared for by his parents as a child. They always yelled at him and beat him and all he could do in his childhood was hide in his closet and read. Now he is a very smart man with a lot of knowledge. The knowledge you get from books is more than anything, from books you learn about the real world, what could happen and what has happened. Every great man reads no matter what it is he reads.

I can't say it much better than Kay did. The reminders that follow address the different types of texts our students must read and we should use; each one also provides ideas to help you and your students learn how to read and use them for different purposes in all subject areas.

Read
Textbooks

40

RATIONALE

People seldom read a book which is given to them.

SAMUEL JOHNSON

Textbooks represent a significant portion of students' academic reading. With increasing sophistication of layout and integration of Internet links, not to mention the range of text types included in these books, students need guided instruction in how to read them and strategies to help them read them independently. The questions that follow offer a starting point. Teachers and students should develop questions specific to their textbook or reading assignment.

WHAT TO DO

Use these questions as a way to begin a discussion:

- What events, ideas, people, or perspectives might the publisher have left out to avoid controversy?
- What is/was the political and social climate in which this textbook was created and how, if at all, might that climate have shaped the content, form, and function of this book?
- What is the perspective of the author/publisher of this text and how does that shape my perceived meaning?
- What is the relationship between what students read in the textbook and hear or learn in class through simulations, discussions, lectures?
- What is the important idea or information in this particular text or assigned reading?
- How do you determine whether an idea is important?
- By what criteria are people, events, places, and so on chosen by the authors or publishers? (e.g., for the sake of coverage? Importance? Test preparation? High interest?)
- What do students need to know and be able to do to read this book, chapter, or specific excerpt successfully?
- Do they know how this text works (e.g., what a word in bold typeface implies)?

- What role (reference, sacred text, supplement to other texts) does the textbook play in the classroom?
- What would _____(e.g., the Japanese)_____ say about the textbook's description of _____(e.g., Hiroshima)_____?
- What does the textbook *not* include—information, perspectives, events, people, places—that it should? (And why do you think these elements were left out?)
- How thorough is the book in its coverage of the subject? (For example, one textbook I looked at offered three paragraphs as its "biography" of General Douglas MacArthur).
- Is the book's vision coherent and consistent throughout the book?
- What is the teacher's role or relationship with this textbook as reflected by the book itself and the support materials addressed to the teacher? (Is it a "teacher-proof" text, or one that expects or at least allows the teacher to use the book to support constructivist, inquiry-based instruction?)
- What is the reading level of the textbook and the students using it? What are the implications for the teacher if the students' reading abilities do not match the demands of the text?
- Is this conclusion or observation still true? (e.g., a history textbook might offer a description of Secretary of Defense Robert McNamara based on his actions and ideas in 1967, many of which he himself has responded to or even debunked in his subsequent memoir about the Vietnam War).
- Are they (e.g., the author of the textbook or given passage from within that textbook) a credible voice in light of what we know now? (For example, the history teacher with whom I collaborate uses an obsolete but excellent textbook called *Tradition and Change*, which consists of case studies and primary source documents. When he has students read about South Africa, he immediately addresses the need for more current information by bringing in *Time* magazine articles and having the students interview South Africans via various resources available through the Web.)
- What other materials or resources might I use to supplement this textbook on this particular issue or subject?
- What is the question that this textbook, teacher, or class is trying to answer and how is the book being used to help answer it?

When power leads
man toward
arrogance, poetry
reminds him of his
limitations. When
power narrows the
areas of man's
concerns, poetry
reminds him of the
richness and diversity
of his experience.
When power corrupts,
poetry cleanses, for
art establishes the
basic human truths
which must serve as
the touchstone of our
judgement.

JOHN F. KENNEDY

RATIONALE

While poems are obviously appropriate for English classes, they have their place in other classes, also. In history, for example, students might read "The Star-Spangled Banner" as the poem it first was, considering its meaning and how it was that this particular poem lent itself so well to becoming our national anthem after its initial debut in a newspaper. Poetry invites attention to the smaller details of the world, enriching students' understanding of "the big picture."

WHAT TO DO

Note the following approach to reading poems, each step of which provides choices depending on what you want to accomplish with the poems you're teaching.

First, look at the poem's title for some clue as to what it might tell you.

Read the poem straight through, without stopping to analyze it. Such a reading is crucial if we are to read the poem for what it is: a performance, an event, an experience at once personal and musical, private and public.

Start with what you know. I give my students any poem so long as there is even one phrase that can help them to climb into the poem. It might be the last line or some other phrase embedded within the poem. It doesn't matter so long as there is some toehold within the poem for them to begin the climb toward their own understanding.

Look for patterns. These patterns might be grammatical, sensory (e.g., a combination of sounds, colors, scents), or object related, evolving and changing from the beginning to the end of the poem. Other patterns reveal themselves in the architecture of the poem. The reader's charge is to understand the relationship between the different pieces of the pattern.

Identify the narrator. Too often we assume that poems are narrated by the poet, unless a persona is clearly established, as in John Berryman's

Dream Songs. We mistake Charley Chaplin for the Tramp and Woody Allen for the fool.

Use writing to think. Periodically, stop and write in your journal to help you digest your thoughts. This reflective writing helps you make greater sense of the disparate insights that won't come together, while taking you deeper into the poems (and other texts) you have read so many times.

Read the poem again. If you haven't read it aloud yet, be sure to do that now.

Find the crucial moments. Often a poem, like a story, has moments when the action shifts, the direction changes, the meaning alters.

Consider form and function. At certain points, some features become more apparent, and seem more important than they at first did. This is the point at which a knowledge of certain poetic elements is helpful. This is the moment when the teacher should be prepared to introduce or review such terms. In this context, the terms will help to explain the poem and, secondarily, illustrate the meaning of the terms themselves. Form and function shape meaning in most poems: this is why you cannot avoid this discussion. Two other elements that often contribute to the meaning of a poem are repetition and compression. *Compression* refers to the way words and images get juxtaposed against or woven into each other, often through the economical use of language (e.g., see how Shakespeare combines images of hands, pilgrims, lips, and prayer in the scene from *Romeo and Juliet* in which the lovers first meet). *Repetition* implies both rhythm and emphasis, each of which needs to be discussed for a full understanding of any poem. Sometimes extra space between words is used, as in some of the poems of Muriel Rukeyser, for example, or John Berryman's *Dream Songs*, to convey meaning. The space between stanzas suggests presence—of time passing, scenes changing, and so on—more than absence.

Look at the language of the poem. Language is everything in a poem. Words are the poet's medium, their paint, and what they do with them merits serious scrutiny if you are going to understand the poem. Punctuation and typography both demand consideration when reading a poem. Typographical considerations are rather straightforward: you might ask, for example, "Why are they capitalizing or italicizing that word or phrase?" Punctuation, on the other hand, often remains a nagging source of confusion in a poem: why doesn't that poet just put a period where there obviously should be one?

Go deeper or call it quits? By this time you have achieved a functional—if not solid—understanding of the poem.

Return to the title before going on. Just as we tell students not to finish an essay without revisiting the initial writing prompt, so the reader should go back to the title of the poem at this point to see what additional information it might offer.

Remind yourself why you are having students read this poem in the first place. Sometimes we get so involved in the reading of a poem that we forget *why* we are reading it.

STUDENT REMARK

READING POETRY

Poems are a lot more difficult and longer to read. I usually have to read it a couple of times to understand. I was stuck when my attention span wore off for a moment. I figured out that a poem (the story of a poem) really reminded me of a person I used to know. I got really interested in that poem so I wrote it down so I could remember it and understand it better.

—*Shawna Nelson*

Read Web Pages

RATIONALE

Of the many new texts students must learn how to read, none demands more immediate attention than the Internet, since our students are spending more and more time online. They need, as we do ourselves, to see Web pages as texts that demand critical reading skills, especially when it comes to determining the quality of the information and the credibility of the people they may encounter online.

WHAT TO DO

Teach students to ask the following questions when reading a Web site text. Point out that the same questions can be used to evaluate other sources and media.

Student Site Evaluation Form

THINKING ABOUT THE SITE

1. Has it won any awards?

2. If the site has won awards, is there a link where you can go to learn if the award is important?

3. If the site has won an award, was it an important one to win? (You might have to check the links given to decide.)

4. Who is responsible for the content of this site?

5. When was the site last updated?

6. When was the information on the site written?

7. Does the information seem current or out of date?

8. Is this site easy to navigate?

THINKING ABOUT THE AUTHOR OF THE SITE

9. Who is the author of what you are reading at this site?

10. What information can you find about the author of this site?

11. Does that information show you that the author has the authority or knowledge to write about the topic at this site?

It is a mistake to think that books have come to stay. The human race did without them for thousands of years and may decide to do without them again.

E. M. FORSTER

135

12. Does the site have links to other sites that give you information about the author?

THINKING ABOUT THE AUDIENCE FOR THE SITE

13. Does the author seem to have a specific audience for this site in mind?

14. Does the site have advertisements?

15. If the site has advertisements, do they give you insight into who the audience is supposed to be?

16. Does the site offer an "About Us" or introduction that helps you understand who the audience is supposed to be?

THINKING ABOUT INFORMATION FOUND AT SITES

17. Has the information been published someplace other than just on the Web?

18. Is the information clear and easy to understand?

19. If the information is about a controversial topic, is more than one side of the topic presented or does the site offer links to sites that would offer the opposing view?

20. Does this site have links to other sites that give you additional information on the topic?

21. Can you tell when the information at this site is a fact versus an opinion?

22. Does the information have a clearly identified author?

23. Are there charts and graphs that summarize or explain points?

24. Is all the quoted information clearly identified and properly cited?

My Evaluation

OVERALL, THIS SITE

❏ Would help me a lot with my assignment.

❏ Links me to other sites that are helpful.

❏ Looks helpful but the information is too technical or hard to understand.

❏ Is more an advertisement than information I can use.

❏ Seems to be just be one person's opinion and contains insufficient information about who the person is and why I should believe that opinion.

Read Narrative Texts

RATIONALE

Because stories are used for many important purposes in our world, we need to know how narrative texts work and how to read them. Advertisers and politicians use stories to persuade us and to influence our thoughts and behavior. Writers of novels and memoirs use stories to entertain and to examine ideas and events. Narrative texts, which include both nonfiction (e.g., memoirs) and fiction (e.g., novels), also help us to understand how other texts work. Finally, narrative fiction often provides students their only encounter with the imagination during the course of the school day; in this one respect, teaching such texts is vital.

What they [the amateurs] are really saying is "I have a story and I want it told." This compulsion is what enables the journalist to get his information. It's a writer's job to flesh out the stories he hears.

TOM WOLFE

WHAT TO DO

Consider the following overview of how narrative texts can be approached.

Purpose is central to the study of narrative texts—the writer's, the reader's, the teacher's, and the characters'—because it directs how the text should be read and taught. Arthur Applebee (1996) suggests that we use texts to create a conversation (see Reminder 9) between ourselves and others, including the authors of the texts we read; in a study of family, for example, the class could read narrative texts that focus on this subject, such as those by Harper Lee and Rudolfo Anaya.

Madison Smart Bell (1997) suggests that teachers and readers focus on design; he believes that "form or structure [or what he comes to call "narrative design"] is of first *and* final importance to any work of fiction." In his study of narrative structure, Bell details the roll of plot, character, tone, point of view, dialogue, "time management," and "imagery and description" in stories.

Donald Graves's (1999) focus is on character. Graves argues that character drives stories because stories are about what people want most and are willing to do to get it. Graves's method is compelling and has been very useful in my own classroom. It creates openings for discussion and allows students to make connections (see Reminder 10) between themselves and the characters they encounter on the page. When you begin by looking at what a character wants most, your sympathies are engaged. Developing an identification with characters can be a powerful experience for students. (See Reminder 89.)

Other approaches are useful, even important. Narrative texts, for example, demand a sequence and can be described as a pattern, though the pattern may not always be obvious. Using graphic organizers or other strategies to help students see these sequences, patterns, or relationships will help them read more effectively. For example, students reading *The Odyssey* benefit from analyzing the story's sequence. Homer begins in the present and then suddenly shifts into the past, to a different place, to a different subject (from Telemachus, the son, to Odysseus, the father) four chapters into the epic. Sketching out the sequence makes this structure more visible to students and even helps them understand why an author would want to use such a device.

SAMPLE ACTIVITY: PLOT THE PLOT

Overview   The plot is what happens in a story. Writers make decisions about not only what to include (or leave out) but how to arrange what they do include. Some plots, such as Homer's famous epic *The Iliad*, begin in the middle of the story (i.e., halfway through the war that is the setting for the story), while others begin at the beginning. Still other plots are difficult to grasp, as they may be made up of many different episodes which, like pieces of a quilt, you must stitch together as you read the story. The purpose of this assignment is to study the story you have finished reading so as to better understand how it was made and why the author made it that way. In short, this assignment asks you to identify the crucial moments throughout the story and, after identifying them, explain why they are important and how they lead to the final outcome. The following questions might help you as you discuss this text with the members of your group:

1. Did this event affect the characters and/or the direction of the story in significant ways?

2. What effect did it have on the characters or the story?

3. Did the character make a crucial decision at this juncture?

4. Why did they make such a decision?

5. What are some other decisions they could have made?

6. How would those have changed the outcome of the play or the characters themselves?

7. Did they make the decision knowing what effect it would have on the others in the story—or on the story itself?

8. What does their decision tell us about their character?

> **plot** *noun*. The plan or main story of a literary work; a graphic representation, as a chart.—*verb*. To make a plot, map, or plan of; to mark or note on or as if on a map or chart; to invent or devise the plot of (a literary work).

Directions   Follow these steps as you work in your assigned group:

1. Appoint a note taker and have them write down everyone's name and take notes on what is said.

2. Get out your time lines from the play. (Students kept a regularly updated time line as they read the play.)

3. After comparing the events on your time lines, identify the most important eight to ten moments in the story, indicating them on your time line with a star.

4. Identify what you feel is the single most important event on your time line.

5. Discuss why it is *the* most important and write down a summary of your group's ideas about it.

6. After plotting out the eight to ten events (using the attached sheet), discuss them, looking for a pattern or logic to the action within the story. For example, if you see a sequence of moments within the story, each one of which required the character to make a decision, you might conclude that each time, they made the wrong decision. You should then discuss *why* you feel they made the wrong decision and find evidence from the text to support your assertion.

STUDENT EXAMPLES

In Figure 43-1, students are asked to identify and evaluate crucial moments in the play. They must then graph these moments to show how those events affect the story.

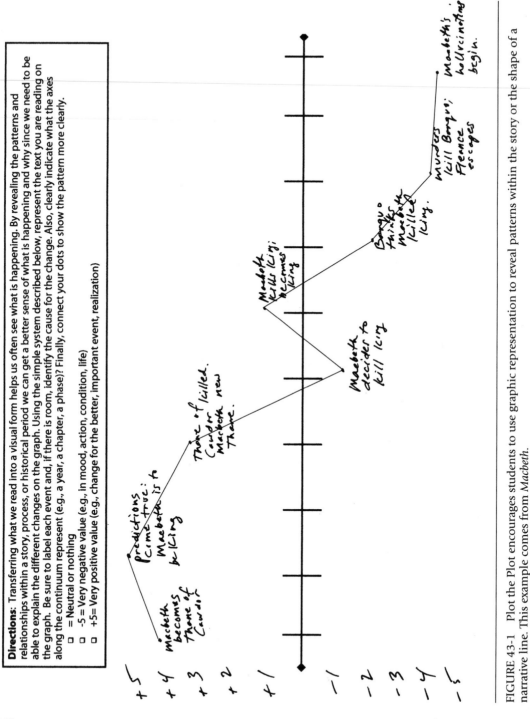

Directions: Transferring what we read into a visual form helps us often see what is happening. By revealing the patterns and relationships within a story, process, or historical period we can get a better sense of what is happening and why since we need to be able to explain the different changes on the graph. Using the simple system described below, represent the text you are reading on the graph. Be sure to label each event and, if there is room, identify the cause for the change. Also, clearly indicate what the axes along the continuum represent (e.g., a year, a chapter, a phase)? Finally, connect your dots to show the pattern more clearly.

- ❑ = Neutral or nothing
- ❑ -5 = Very negative value (e.g., in mood, action, condition, life)
- ❑ +5 = Very positive value (e.g., change for the better, important event, realization)

FIGURE 43-1 Plot the Plot encourages students to use graphic representation to reveal patterns within the story or the shape of a narrative line. This example comes from *Macbeth*.

140

Main Characters	Macbeth Donalbain
	Lady Macbeth
	Malcolm
	Macduff
	Banquo

↓

Setting (time, place, atmosphere)
Scotland and England around 1600s
Dark, suspenseful atmosphere

↓

Primary Conflict	Macbeth wants to become
	King. But he likes the King. To become
	king he must kill the king and
	his sons. He is very ambitious

↓

List the main events in the story
- Witches tell Macbeth that he will be king.
- Macbeth murders the king.
- Sons of the king escape and become suspects
- Macbeth kills Banquo (has him killed)
- Macbeth has Macduff's family murdered
- Lady Macbeth dies
- Macduff kills Macbeth   · Malcolm becomes king

Climax	Macbeth kills
	the king? kills
	Macduff's family?
	Lady Macbeth dies?

Resolution	Macbeth is
	killed and Malcolm
	becomes the king.

FIGURE 43-2   Students used this story structure graphic organizer to improve their understanding of what happened in *Macbeth*.

STUDENTS' EXPLANATION

We put Macbeth becoming the thane of Cawdor as a +4 because he is becoming more important and getting a higher rank. We put Macbeth's decision to kill the king at -1 because it was forced upon him by his wife. We put Macbeth killing the king and becoming king at +1 because it is kind of good for him. He didn't really want to betray the king but he is happy he has power now.

44 Read Expository Texts

RATIONALE

Reading books is good, reading good books is better.

LAWRENCE CLARK POWELL

As adults, expository texts make up the bulk of what we read. In school this is no different. Thus students need to know how such texts work, how they should prepare to read them, and what to do once they begin reading such texts. Expository texts include essays, speeches, lab procedures, journals, government documents, newspaper and magazine articles, and directions, among other things. While each type of text shares certain characteristics with the others, they each make their own demands on the reader through the unique use of structure, devices, features, and conventions. We need to teach students how to read each type as they encounter it if they are to read them successfully. To fully appreciate all that a reader of such texts does, read the Northwest Regional Educational Laboratory's rubric (see Appendixes 38 and 39) for informational texts in the appendix.

WHAT TO DO

Help students understand the characteristics of an expository text. A narrative text includes such elements as a theme, plot, conflict(s), resolution, characters, and a setting. Expository texts, on the other hand, explain something by definition, sequence, categorization, comparison-contrast, enumeration, process, problem-solution, description, or cause-effect. Where the narrative text uses story to inform and persuade, the expository text uses facts and details, opinions and examples to do the same. John Steinbeck used narrative to describe what it was like for people during the dust bowl, but an economist would use exposition to explain the causes and consequences of the same event, drawing examples from various sources to illustrate his points, perhaps even including a graph or some photographs.

Students should be able to:

- Identify the elements of a paragraph and read them
- Recognize the transitional words that signal important information or a shift in focus

- Establish the genre—e.g., cause-effect, definition, persuasive
- Organize the information within an expository text into an outline for subsequent analysis
- Annotate such texts for a specified purpose
- Summarize paragraphs or sections of the text as they read
- Preread these texts according to the current purpose
- Use available information such as subheadings to orient and focus their reading
- Identify the main ideas throughout the text
- Develop their own questions and apply them to the text
- Create their own study guides
- Take effective notes for subsequent discussions or writing assignments

Have students follow these steps when reading an essay or article:

- Read and consider the title
- Find the author's name and any other information about the writer
- Identify the source (i.e., the original publication and date) of the article
- Read the introduction or opening paragraphs carefully, checking these against the title
- Skim through the article and read all boldface subheadings, pullout quotes, or sidebar information
- Skim through the article and read the first sentence of each paragraph (if this sentence is clearly not the topic sentence, locate and read the topic sentence)
- Examine any other typographical features such as italicized words
- Examine any graphic content (e.g., maps, illustrations, images)
- Read the last paragraph carefully
- Study any questions or additional information provided at the end of the article, before, during, and after reading
- Read the entire article, keeping in mind what you have gained from your prereading and checking your new understanding against the initial understanding, revising as needed

STUDENT EXAMPLE

Students understand better what they themselves have learned to do or make. Students who have learned to write practical expository documents, such as the proposal by freshman Erin Johnson that follows, are better equipped to read and use such texts.

SPECIAL OLYMPICS

As we become more and more aware of the problems around us, steps should be taken to prevent these problems from having tragic consequences. In the culture in which we now live, status is based almost completely on what we look like, how we act, or how "perfect" we are. For most people, coping skills are developed enough that these standards don't matter quite as much. But when you're physically or mentally different it can be especially hard to grasp the unrealness of these standards. For people who have mental or physical disabilities, the problem may not be grasping the situation of perfectness, but the fact that they feel left out and think that outside their special classes, there is no place for them to go and just hang out.

In this report I hope that I will be able to demonstrate the significance of the Special Olympics through the minds and hearts of the participants, volunteers, and parents of these special people. A few questions I intend to answer are:

• Why do kids participate in the Special Olympics?

• What needs are participants attempting to meet through participation in the Special Olympics?

• How are the athletes recruited?

• If athletics have inherent value for students, shouldn't schools provide equal opportunities for all students?

I know that my investigation will turn up many different answers, but I know that all answers will show the significance of the Special Olympics.

In addition to reading newspaper articles and magazines, I plan to do the following:

• Interview participants, volunteers, and parents.

• Contact the local Special Olympic committee and see if I can interview a representative.

• Create a documentary based on interviews, clips from Special Olympics advertisement tapes, and other clips related to the subject.

• Search the Internet for information and use the public library system.

I am aware of how time consuming this project is going to be so I am taking steps to prepare myself for it. I have decided that I am going to break it down into days, setting goals that I need to have completed each day. I am also aware that if I do decide to make the documentary, I will have to give up, or leave early from, after-school events so that I will have a better chance of getting the video done. Because some of the people I will be interviewing live in Washington, I will have to spend time organizing my schedule so that I can talk to them over the Internet or by phone.

If my project is a success I should be able to answer this question: What is the significance of the Special Olympics to its participants?

Read
Images

RATIONALE

The age demanded an image.

EZRA POUND

In our multimedia world, we must expand our notion of what a text is and how it should be read. As more audiovisual texts are used to convey the information that print once did, we must bring to these texts critical literacies that will help us construct meaning from their elements. The following questions are designed to help readers make sense of images they encounter in various contexts.

WHAT TO DO

Use these questions to build discussions of how to look at or "read" images:

- Where should you begin as you try to read this? Why there?
- Is this image authentic (i.e., it has not been touched up or otherwise doctored using other materials or software programs)?
- If this image was altered, who did it and why?
- What questions do I need to ask to read this image successfully?
- Why are we looking at this?
- What are we looking for?
- How should we look at this?
- What choices did the artist make and how did those choices affect the image's meaning?
- Is this image in its original state (i.e., no manipulation or "doctoring")?
- What are the different components in this image?
- How are they related to each other?
- What is the main idea or argument the image expresses?
- In what context or under what conditions was this image originally created and/or displayed?
- Who created it?

- Was it commissioned? (If so, by whom and for what purpose?)
- What was the creator trying to do here? (i.e., narrate, explain, describe, persuade—or some combination of these?)
- Can you find any tension or examples of conflict within the image? If so, what are they? What is their source? How are they represented?
- Do you like this image? (Why or why not?)
- How would you describe the artist's technique?
- What conventions govern this image? How do they contribute to or detract from its ability to convey its message?
- What does the image consist of?
- Why are its parts arranged this way?
- What is the main idea behind this image?
- What does this image show objectively?
- What does it mean subjectively?
- Is this presented as an interpretation? Factual record? Impression?
- What is the larger context of which this image is a part?
- What is it made from?
- Why did the creator choose the materials, medium, and perspective they did?
- What is the place to which your attention is most immediately drawn?
- What is the smallest detail that says the most?
- How would it change the meaning or viewer's experience if different materials, medium, or perspectives were used?
- What motivates the creator here?
- What verbs could be used to describe what the components—colors, lines, light, space, objects, characters—are doing in the image?
- What adjectives could be used to best describe the precise details of the objects in the image?
- What nouns most accurately describe the content—colors, lines, light, space, objects, characters—of the image?
- What adverbs most accurately describe the components—colors, lines, light, space, objects, characters—of the image?
- What do we need to know to read the image successfully?
- How did the original artist expect this image to be read (e.g., as an interpretation, a prediction, a documentary)?

147

- Is the creator working within or against a particular genre or school of expression?
- What are the criteria you are—or should be—using to evaluate this image?
- What are the image's motifs, themes, plot, and characters?
- How would you describe the style of this image and why did the artist make the choices they did?
- What is the best or the prescribed angle from which I should view this image?
- How has the artist used the following elements to communicate with the viewer: light, line, space, time, color?
- Does this image achieve—or is it offered as—a symbolic or iconic representation (e.g., Dorothea Lange's "Migrant Mother")?
- Is there an observable pattern used here? If so, what is it and how is it used?
- Does the creator use any devices such as repetition, symbols, visual puns? If so, what are they, and how do they work in the image?

Read
Tests

RATIONALE

Tests are a text like any other, complete with their own demands and features. While we should not give them any special pride of place among the many types we teach, we do need to show our students how to read such tests. We can do this by showing them how langauge works and how tests are designed and must be read.

The test of any man lies in action.

PINDAR

WHAT TO DO

Have students follow these steps when reading and taking tests:

Skim and scan: Depending on how much time you have for the test, flip through to get a sense of the terrain: number and type of questions, what's easy, what's hard. This will orient you and allow you to prioritize your time and attention.

Do the easy ones first. Like in pick-up-sticks, you get just as much credit for the easy ones as the hard ones. After skimming through the test, knock out the ones you know so you have the time you need to read the others more closely. This will also activate your background knowledge, thus making it more likely you will be able to figure out the harder questions.

Read all the possible answers first before answering. Test makers depend on inattentive readers to make mistakes that conscientious readers will not. Even if you see the answer you know is right, read through them all to make sure there is no surprise hiding under answer E (e.g., "All of the above").

Eliminate the wrong answers. If you don't see the obvious answer, work backward by ruling out those that cannot be right.

Paraphrase the question in your own words to help you better understand what it is asking.

Watch out for traps. Some tests use the word *not* to trip you up; stop and ask yourself what it's really asking. Avoid answering questions that include information from the passage, especially on standardized tests. Instead, look for questions that answer the question.

Try to answer the question before looking at the answers on a multiple-choice test. Paired with the previous strategy, this method gets you primed to know the answer when you see it; if you have already determined the answer in your head, you know what to look for when you check the possible answers.

Read recursively. Good readers frequently and habitually circle back around to check what they are reading and thinking against what they have already read to see that they agree. This habit keeps them attentive to what they are supposed to be doing. On an essay test, for example, after reading and underlining the key words in the directions, pause periodically to reread the directions. This will help you measure the extent to which you are answering the question; it might also provide useful information to spark new ideas for your essay.

Read the answer sheet. Know how it works. A group of students in my honors English class neglected to do this and they scored a –2.6 on the reading test. We calculated this to mean that they were reading at the level of a puppy in its second month! They had missed a crucial direction on the answer sheet that made all their answers out of sequence after number twenty.

Answer in the order that works best for you. Work through the test in the order that makes most sense to you and will help you read it best. One important point, however: remember to use some sort of system to indicate which questions you still have to answer, and be sure to erase any "reminder" marks before turning in the test.

Have students ask themselves the following:

- Why is that the best answer?
- Why did I not choose that answer?
- How did I arrive at this answer?
- Is this answer based on my experience and opinion or information found in the text on which I'm being tested?
- Where else can I look for this information (e.g., another section of the test?)
- What does that word mean in this context?
- What does the rubric or other scoring guide suggest I need to understand or look for in this question?
- What are they actually trying to test?
- Is it better to guess or leave it blank?

Read Primary Source Documents

47

RATIONALE

Primary source documents include maps, documents, reports, photographs, letters, diaries, posters, and recordings created by those who participated in or witnessed the events of the past. Their use in all classrooms, all subjects, allows students to touch the living past, to occupy the role of historian within that subject area. Perhaps most importantly, the use of primary sources allows students to see that textbooks and other contemporary writings about the past—or even present—events is merely an interpretation that is shaped by the era, biases, and values of those who write them. There are two places students and teachers can easily find primary source documents: the National Archives (www.nara.gov) and the Library of Congress (www.loc.gov), both of which offer daily and ongoing exhibits and materials to support classroom instruction. Of particular interest is the National Archives' *Teaching with Documents: Using Primary Sources from the National Archives* (two volumes). Primary source documents are excellent examples of texts we read to learn; students must also learn to read them. Thus using them also allows you to integrate writing and speaking in the reading curriculum as students, working as historians, create their own interpretations based on their readings. This invites a valuable discussion about the decisions they make as readers—and writers.

The world will little note nor long remember what we say here today, but it can never forget what they did here.

ABRAHAM LINCOLN

WHAT TO DO

Consider all the following elements when choosing primary source documents:

- Language
- Design and structure
- Materials
- Form and function
- Size
- Voice, tone, style

Use the following questions to initiate class discussion:

- In what context was this document created?
- Why did the individual choose this form or medium?
- What do the visual components of the text convey in terms of its meaning or status?
- Who authored/created it?
- For what purpose?
- Under what circumstances?
- Where did this document—e.g., article, art work, cartoon—originally appear?
- What alternative interpretations might you offer based on this same document?
- For whom did they create it?
- What biases or other cultural factors might have shaped the message of this document?
- Why are you looking at it now?
- What question are you using this document to answer?
- Is this document consistent with what we now know of the historical record from that time?
- Whose point of view is this document representing?
- What other perspectives are represented through other documents from this time or event? How does their story compare with that of the others?
- What limitations—self-imposed or otherwise—might affect the validity of or ability to generalize beyond this information?
- How can I verify the information in this document?
- Are there perspectives (e.g., slaves, the poor, immigrants) that are not represented through these or other primary source documents? If so, who represents their story/experience—and why should I believe them?
- How is this document interpreted today—and if differently than in the past, why?
- What are the facts?
- What are the opinions (if comparing the primary source document against a textbook or article written later)?
- What criteria are most useful and appropriate to consider when evaluating the perspective or veracity of a primary source document?

Read
Plays

48

RATIONALE

Like poetry, drama sometimes gets slighted in the literature curriculum, yet it offers a wealth of opportunities for fun and learning. Because plays are written to be performed, not just read, they come with built-in strategies to help students read better. The structure and elements of dramatic texts offer useful guides, and the acting out of scripts forces students to work closely with the text to translate its words into the actions that make up the play. Many find favor with the "script" approach as opposed to the "scholarly" approach when teaching plays by Shakespeare, emphasizing the extent to which performance engages students' imagination due to the physical, intellectual, and emotional occupation of a role in the play. Plays also provide opportunities for the expression of a range of talents (e.g., artistic students can, as an option, create a series of sketches for the stage backdrops, including a written or spoken explanation of the decisions they made).

The man who writes about himself and his own time is the only man who writes about all people and about all time.

GEORGE BERNARD SHAW

WHAT TO DO

Perform plays using any of the following techniques according to your teaching objective:

- Have the class read specific segments aloud so they can hear and discuss the author's intentions and alternative ways of speaking/performing the lines.

- Have groups of students pantomime a scene, organize themselves into a tableau, or "freeze" midaction while the other members of the class discuss the choices and actions of the group performing (and interpreting) the text.

- Recast the text into modern form to make it more familiar; this could be done with language and/or costumes, but keep in mind that all interpretations must be anchored in the text (e.g., students always should be able to answer the question, "Where in the text do you find evidence to support that choice or interpretation?"). Other approaches could include recasting the

153

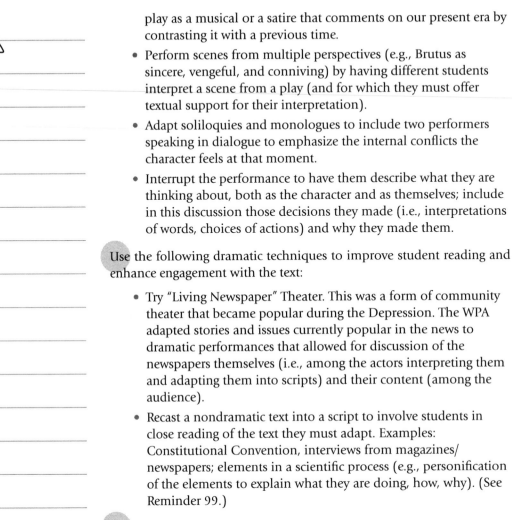

play as a musical or a satire that comments on our present era by contrasting it with a previous time.

- Perform scenes from multiple perspectives (e.g., Brutus as sincere, vengeful, and conniving) by having different students interpret a scene from a play (and for which they must offer textual support for their interpretation).

- Adapt soliloquies and monologues to include two performers speaking in dialogue to emphasize the internal conflicts the character feels at that moment.

- Interrupt the performance to have them describe what they are thinking about, both as the character and as themselves; include in this discussion those decisions they made (i.e., interpretations of words, choices of actions) and why they made them.

Use the following dramatic techniques to improve student reading and enhance engagement with the text:

- Try "Living Newspaper" Theater. This was a form of community theater that became popular during the Depression. The WPA adapted stories and issues currently popular in the news to dramatic performances that allowed for discussion of the newspapers themselves (i.e., among the actors interpreting them and adapting them into scripts) and their content (among the audience).

- Recast a nondramatic text into a script to involve students in close reading of the text they must adapt. Examples: Constitutional Convention, interviews from magazines/ newspapers; elements in a scientific process (e.g., personification of the elements to explain what they are doing, how, why). (See Reminder 99.)

When reading a play, look as a class at the interaction between:

- Language (arguably the primary source of energy in a play)
- Action (the physical expression of that energy, which is often mirrored in or commented upon by the language)
- Character (which plays often focus on as the central concern— e.g., what does the main character want more than anything else?)
- Visual details and imagery (especially as reflected in the setting)
- Stage directions (which offer sometimes crucial details as to how a scene should be read depending on how specific the playwright was in his or her directions)
- Form and function—e.g., how many scenes and acts and what

dictates the break between scenes and acts? For example, Shakespeare always has five acts that neatly conform to the traditional rising/falling/resolution pattern we associate with stories.

Decide what prior knowledge will be necessary for your students to have. Will knowledge about the history of Scotland help students read *Macbeth*? Will a unit on Shakespeare's era prepare them to read *Romeo and Juliet*? Or will a short unit on his language better meet their needs in learning how to read his plays?

Read Essays

RATIONALE

The essay has enjoyed a tremendous renaissance in the last decade. With this new interest has come a variety of forms as writers test and then define (for now) the boundary between the genres of real and imagined, true and not true. Certainly essays have a place in the curriculum of all subject areas. Many contemporary essays have the added advantage of being both timely and short, which allows us to copy them with ease, for our students to annotate.

WHAT TO DO

Have students determine which of the following traditional rhetorical modes best describes the essay they are reading and how that mode shapes the essay's meaning and message.

NARRATIVE

- Answers the question "What happened and when?"

- Emphasizes chronological order of events; use of transitional words helps such events to flow smoothly from one to the next.

- Point of view is important as it shapes the voice, tone, and purpose of the story.

- Mood is of fundamental importance as it directs the reader's response: Is this a fond memory of a loved one or an angry account of an event that left a lasting scar?

DEFINITION

- Answers the question "What is it?"

- Attempts to explain an important word or concept to the reader

- Uses negation to clarify what the word does *not* mean

- Might focus on the origins of the word as a means of establishing its meaning

DIVISION/CLASSIFICATION

- Answers the question "What kind is it?" or "What are its parts?"

- Arranges information into categories in order to establish and articulate the relationships between items in each category

- Contains distinct categories   (Exemplary Essay: "Friends, Good Friends—and Such Good Friends," by Judith Viorst)

PROCESS ANALYSIS

- Answers the question "How did it happen?"

- Explains how *to do* something or how something *was done*

- Addresses a specific audience

- Uses modes such as narration to explain process

CAUSE AND EFFECT

- Answers the question "Why did it happen?"

- Carefully examines what happened and why

- Contains clear, logical writing

- Uses descriptive writing to illustrate the relationship between the cause and the effect

ARGUMENTATION/PERSUASION

- Answers the question "Why should I want to do or think that?"

- Contains a thesis explaining what the essay will convince the reader to think or do

- Uses logic to make effective arguments

- Anticipates and addresses counterarguments

- Through argument focuses on logical appeal

- Through persuasion focuses on emotional appeal

COMPARISON/CONTRAST

- Answers the question "What is it (not) like?"

- Carefully establishes and develops similarities between two elements or sides

- Emphasizes the differences between the two elements or sides
- Establishes early on the basis of the comparison

EXAMPLE/ILLUSTRATION

- Answers the question "For example?"

- Depends on concrete, vivid examples that reveal the concept being discussed or the position advocated

- Contains active verbs that help the reader by showing exactly what this subject does   (Exemplary Essay: Nikki Giovanni's "My Own Style," in which she illustrates her way of living by describing specific objects and explaining how they exemplify her lifestyle.)

Read in Different Ways: To Think, to Study, to Gather

RATIONALE

We might not always remember that reading can itself be used as a tool, the text a stone on which we can sharpen the mind's blade. Reading as a prereading or writing strategy seems redundant, but offers readers a powerful means of improving and preparing for their reading. Computer programmers in the old days used to have to run a short program through the computer before loading the actual program; this preprogram prepared the computer to receive and read the primary program. Physics teacher Chris Balmy has his students do what he calls a "paradigm reading" prior to beginning a new unit. In this respect he is using the short text he provides to orient their thinking by establishing criteria and ways of thinking about a given subject.

The difference between journalism and literature is that journalism is unreadable and literature is not read.

OSCAR WILDE

WHAT TO DO

Encourage students to do the following:

- Read to think when they are:
  - Preparing to write or give a presentation
  - Preparing to read a larger work
  - Developing an idea or topic for a paper, project, or class
- Read to think by using the following texts to spur new ideas or extend current understanding:
  - Newsgroups
  - Web sites (including search engine results as a list of possible, related ideas)
  - Newspapers and magazines
  - Encyclopedias
  - Table of contents
  - Indexes
  - Abstracts

‣ Documentary or appropriate films

‣ Primary source documents

- Read to think by using a range of texts such as:

  ‣ Conversations (e.g., about racism, eminent domain, etc.)

  ‣ Case study

  ‣ Evidence

- Read imaginative literature to use and improve the imagination. Several students of mine this year confessed to me that they did not do well on the comprehension portion of the SAT test. This was confounding news, as they read voraciously: the *Wall Street Journal*, *New York Times*, several different magazines. What became increasingly apparent was that their capacity for imaginative, creative reading was undermined by their unbalanced diet of numbers, facts, and analysis.

- Read as an elaboration strategy designed to help you expand your ideas by seeing what others have written.

- Read to gather ideas by skimming through piles of books and magazines in order to glean articles of use or ideas that help to refine/revise your ideas.

- Read to study when you feel you are getting stale or have otherwise finished preparing. Reading through the book or another book can help to reinforce and expand your network of connections and knowledge about a subject.

SAMPLE ACTIVITY

READING TO THINK

Have students read a poem about a subject you will be reading about or are currently studying. In this case the poem might serve to expand or refine their thinking about a subject. An example of such a poem might be Roger Fanning's "Boys Build Forts," which traces the narrator's life through its many stages; such a poem would be ideal as preparation for reading *The Odyssey*, *To Kill a Mockingbird*, or many other novels.

TYPES OF PLACES	QUALITIES	VERBS (i.e., *place* as a verb)
• hiding • home • house • location • private • public • special • safe • secret • resting • paradise • area • imaginary	• home • private • public • safe • secret • imaginary • important • favorite	• appoint • hire • categorize • humiliate • identify • know • lay • under arrest • recognize • situate • arrange • happen
COMPARISONS • home vs. place • literal vs. symbolic meaning of • put in vs. make for yourself	**PHRASES** • find my place: where do I belong? • he doesn't know his place • home is a place where they have to take you in • I feel out of place here • place in my heart • new and better place • put someone in their place • she's going places! • your place or mine? • woman's place is in the kitchen • time and a place for everything • place in history • place in the sun	**CRITERIA (for organizing different ideas about place)** • what it does • what it means • what it is • where it is

FIGURE 50-1   This chart was done as both a note-making and brainstorming activity while students read a range of different essays and stories that had to do with the idea of place. They did it first as homework, then worked in groups to share and learn from each other's ideas.

Read for Style, Argument, Form, and Genre

RATIONALE

Students must read widely if they are to develop the range of textual skills needed to be powerful readers. Those who read newspapers and magazines fill themselves with information but can then lack the imaginative, cognitive powers readers develop by reading challenging literature and other more sophisticated types of texts. Readers must also learn to adjust their purpose when reading, knowing how to focus on one aspect of a text that might, for example, shape its meaning more than others.

WHAT TO DO

Remember that, just as jugglers can only juggle so many chainsaws at one time, readers can only handle so many tasks. Consider which of the following emphases would best meet your students' curricular and developmental needs at this time; the list includes reading for:

- Style
- Argument
- Form
- Genre
- Mood

Consider using or adapting the following techniques when studying style:

- Have students read for patterns; look for repeated use of devices or language structures. One way to do this is to have them organize their notes into columns—nouns, verbs, adjectives—and examine them for any patterns of sound or meaning.
- Ask students, "If you were to adapt this text into a piece of music, what instruments would you use and what would the music sound like?" This is a useful way of helping them to think about voice, mood, and style.

- Look for conspicuous features including but not limited to the following:
  - ◗ Typography
  - ◗ Language usage
  - ◗ Metaphors
  - ◗ Images
  - ◗ Arrangement or layout
  - ◗ Juxtaposition of ideas
  - ◗ Placement of image, idea, or word
  - ◗ Allusions
- Have them think about what tradition the author of the text is arguing with, working outside of, or honoring.

Know the different logical fallacies in the following list and teach them to your students so that they may better recognize them when reading an argument.

- *Appeal to Ignorance.* "Since no one has ever proved the claim, it cannot be true."
- *Appeal to Pity.* "You should do this because of my condition."
- *Jump on the Bandwagon.* "Everyone else is doing it, so you should, too."
- *Broad Generalization.* Based on the idea that everyone is the same, "everyone does this."
- *Circular Thinking.* Example: "I hate reading because books are boring."
- *Either-Or Thinking.* Leaves no room for the inherent complexity of the world, believing that everything can be reduced to a yes-or-no proposition.
- *Half-Truths.* Argument uses facts (selectively) to support the claim it seeks to prove.
- *Oversimplification.* Reductionist thinking is best exemplified by the statement, "There can only be one explanation."
- *Slanted Language.* Use of emotionally loaded language designed to distract people from the otherwise valid claims someone is trying to make.
- *Testimonial.* "If Mr. X, whom I have always respected, says it is a good product, then it must be. After all, he's an authority." Pay particular attention to the domain of the person's expertise: that is, are they an expert on the subject about which they are testifying?

STUDENT EXAMPLES

The following short analysis, written by sophomore Alex Dove, asked students to examine certain aspects of a story by Lynda Barry. The story was especially useful to the study of style because Barry uses a range of devices within it.

LYNDA BARRY ANALYSIS

1. There are no paragraphs in this story. That makes it different from most stories. She also uses a lot of capitals unlike other writers. The story is also written from a kid's point of view.
2. The lack of paragraphs makes the story harder to read because I do not know where to stop. The capital letters express the characters' feelings.
3. The first sentence—Keep Out!—is repeated so it had a greater effect on the reader.
4. The way she wrote from a teenager's perspective made it more realistic.

—*Alex Dove*

The following response, written by a senior in Advanced Placement English, exemplifies close reading and attention to style.

On the surface of Mr. Ciardi's elegy is a simple poem of a bunch of school kids' wild adventure on a runaway school bus. But c'mon, how many school buses just happen to drive by Cliff Houses with scenic views of the ocean? I interpreted the poem to be a commentary on the imminent destruction of the carefreeness of childhood and the upheaval of all the securities and beliefs that sheltered us when we were young.

The poem opens with the kids and the school bus merrily driving along, singing "Old MacDonald," the representation of youthful bliss and ignorance. Three different noises are associated with the actual singing. *Peep*—the sound young chicks make. *Oink*—the sound pigs make. *Moo*—the sound of cows. *Peep, oink,* and *moo* . . . all sounds of farm animals: farm animals born and raised to be mercilessly slaughtered, much like the children singing the song.

So anyway, the kids and the school bus reach the top of a picturesque cliff, which, to them, represents the pinnacle of their youth. The counter girls and the tourists are all decoys that trick the kids into thinking life is A-OK. But in reality, the school bus driver, the tourists, and the girls in pink aprons serving poison coffee are all in it together. The bus driver hits the top of the hill and "realizes" there are no brakes. With a *honk honk* here and a *honk honk* there, the bus driver is actually screaming to his partners in crime. "Ha ha! We got the little bastards!" Then he sends the bus over the cliff (adolescence) and into the deep blue sea (maturity). The tourists, they're just there to watch. They cannot tell how far they've sent the kids, even though they are in part responsible for it. The children were sent to their death, or even worse: adulthood.

SHAKESPEARE'S LANGUAGE:
A STUDY IN STYLE

Overview

The purpose of this assignment is to examine Shakespeare's use of metaphors—or, to put it another way, his metaphorical use of language. Please follow the directions and be prepared to explain your thinking to the class.

1. Underline all words in this passage that are (or are associated with) parts of the body.

2. Circle or highlight those words with religious connotations.

3. Note those words—e.g., *hand/hands*—that can be singular or plural and mark them "one" or "two."

4. Finally, go through and mark each word whose predominant sound is O or OO, or AH.

5. Having looked so closely at the text, what conclusions or observations might you make? Do you see any patterns that contribute to the meaning or effect of the play? Explain and illustrate with examples.

6. Write a paragraph in which you analyze Shakespeare's use of language. Helpful questions: What does he do? Why? Examples. How effective do you think it is?

7. Find the sonnet.

ROMEO:
> If I profane with my unworthiest hand
> This holy shrine, the gentle fine is this:
> My lips, two blushing pilgrims, ready stand
> To smooth that rough touch with a tender kiss.

JULIET:
> Good pilgrim, you do wrong your hand too much,
> Which mannerly devotion shows in this;
> For saints have hands that pilgrims' hands do touch,
> And palm to palm is holy palmers' kiss.

ROMEO:
> Have not saints lips, and holy palmers too?

JULIET:
> Ay, pilgrim, lips that they must use in prayer.

ROMEO:
> O, then, dear saint, let lips do what hands do;
> They pray, grant thou, lest faith turn to despair.

JULIET:
> Saints do not move, though grant for prayers' sake.

ROMEO:
> Then move not, while my prayer's effect I take.
> Thus from my lips, by yours, my sin is purged.

JULIET:
> Then have my lips the sin that they have took.

ROMEO:
> Sin from thy lips? O trespass sweetly urged!
> Give me my sin again.

JULIET:
> You kiss by the book.

FIGURE 51-1   Sample assignment I use to help students understand the way form and style contribute to meaning, in this case within *Romeo and Juliet*.

May be copied for classrooom use. Reading Reminders by Jim Burke (Boynton/Cook, a subsidiary of Reed Elsevier Inc., © 2000).

Ask Different Types of Questions

RATIONALE

Asking and answering questions places the reader in a more active role. They must create either meaningful questions based on reading the text closely or meaningful answers to these queries, finding support for their thinking in both the text and their own knowledge. Just as we use different types of tools for different jobs, so too must we use a variety of types of questions to help us think in different ways and at different levels about the texts we read. The ideas below will help you ask better questions and, more importantly, teach students how to ask these questions themselves so that they can increase their comprehension and degree of engagement. These ideas are useful in any class, for any level.

> I am a bad reader. I think most writers are bad readers. We just cannot immerse ourselves in a book. Our own thoughts get in the way; we start thinking what we could do if we had the book to write ourselves.
>
> ANTHONY BURGESS

WHAT TO DO

• Introduce students to these four types of questions (examples of each appear later) early on so that they can master and use them throughout the year. Each type refers to the place where the question's answer can be found:

  ▶ In the text
  ▶ Between the lines
  ▶ In their head
  ▶ In another place

• Have students develop questions they think will match these descriptions. Ask them to explain what each type of question means, or develop criteria for each.

• Share their questions and explanations, emphasizing those you think are particularly good questions and explaining why you think they are good questions.

• Give students these four questions (or make up four of your own for a text you are teaching) and ask them to identify them by type, explaining why they think they belong in that category:

  ▶ Where did Picasso live and work?
  ▶ What were the most important influences on his art?

▶ What do you think this painting shown here is about?

▶ What effect has Picasso's work had on the current generation of artists?

Another set of questions might be:

▶ What happened to Hamlet's father?

▶ How does Hamlet's relationship with his mother change after his father's death?

▶ Is Hamlet a coward?

▶ How is Hamlet different from and similar to the other characters (e.g., Antigone, McMurphy, Winston, and Gregor) we have studied this semester?

• Ask each group to explain the differences between the types of questions.

• Remember that the point is not to train them to use these specific types of questions so much as to use different types of questions to help them read the text more closely. Thus you should focus more on the type of answer their questions might yield and less on the exact language of their question, though this is also appropriate to discuss since it may be that the flawed response was the consequence of a poorly phrased question.

• Move students toward independence (i.e., the ability to ask their own questions) as quickly as possible so that you can concentrate on helping them ask better questions. The dense question strategy (see Reminder 14), a similar question strategy developed by Leila Christenbury, complements these other types of questions nicely. I have often used, with great success, the dense question model to have students prepare for and create their own culminating essay or final exams.

• Use the questions or allow students to develop them as tools for discussion or prompts for writing—or both, using one to support the other. For example, you could have groups each develop two of each type of question about a chapter, then pick the ones they think are the best, sharing these with the class and thereby inspiring an engaging discussion to which everyone can contribute ideas. An interesting alternative is to have groups generate questions for other groups to use in their own discussions or respond to in their learning logs.

• Use questions throughout the reading process instead of waiting until you reach the end. Questions are powerful tools that can help readers make meaning, especially if used while reading—and before—to get them thinking (see Reminder 54.)

Self-Select Books

RATIONALE

Obviously we cannot let students choose what they read at all times throughout the course of the year. Giving students some measure of choice about what they read increases their personal engagement and, by making reading a pleasurable activity, increases the likelihood that they will want to do it more. This approach can be used in a variety of ways for different purposes. Student choice is consistently identified as one of the key best practices in any balanced, effective reading program. Researchers consistently find that the more students read the better they read; thus another crucial argument for choice is to increase the sheer quantity of reading that students do by providing alternative contexts for reading in all subject areas. Finally, in classes where students inevitably read at all levels of ability, allowing them to choose their own reading individualizes instruction and allows each student to challenge themselves at the level most appropriate to their skill level.

My education was the liberty I had to read indiscriminately and all the time with my eyes hanging out.

DYLAN THOMAS

WHAT TO DO

- Let students exercise choice in the following ways:

  ▶ They can choose from a set of appointed texts (e.g., one of three speeches about World War II; any five poems from a book or anthology).

  ▶ They can choose their own books for their literature circles (see Reminder 7) or book groups.

  ▶ They can choose any book they want for their sustained silent reading (see Reminder 1).

  ▶ They can choose from a list of approved books (e.g., any book from a list of AP-level literature texts).

  ▶ They can choose any book to read within a certain genre (autobiography) or according to specific criteria (e.g., AP-level).

- Evaluate their reading using any of the following methods or a combination of them:

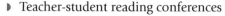

> ▶ Teacher-student reading conferences
>
> ▶ Informal observation of their discussions with others about the book
>
> ▶ Written responses to the reading (see Reminder 100)
>
> ▶ Class discussions
>
> ▶ Booktalks

• Teach students how to choose books by modeling for them and discussing how you choose your own books.

• Develop a classroom library with books you know or students tell you to get; their proximity increases the likelihood that students will read them and allows you to act as a reading mentor, saying, for example, "Hey Sandra, this book is one I think you'd find interesting based on some of the things you said in class today").

• Let them choose a variety of types of reading over the course of the year:

> ▶ Have them read any two magazines about the same subject (e.g., fashion) and write a comparative evaluation of the two.
>
> ▶ Have them read a newspaper they like over the course of a week (online editions are acceptable), making notes about the paper's editorial stands on issues and supplying examples to support their findings.
>
> ▶ Have them read a Web site dedicated to a specific subject appropriate to the class (e.g., a site devoted to smoking for a health class) and evaluate its content in light of what you are studying (see Reminder 42).

• Grade them on completion, not quality or length of the book. Depending on the class or the context, students should be free to choose whatever they want within the parameters you define. If your emphasis is entirely on the grade they will earn, students will inevitably choose the easiest book and do the safest assignment.

• Provide opportunities for readers to talk with each other about what they choose to read.

STUDENTS' COMMENTS

The following are students' remarks about choosing their own books.

> I really enjoy reading a book of my choice. Books that are required to be read are usually not as interesting as reading books of your own choice. These last few weeks have been really helpful in finishing my book.

—*Jason Stamer*

FIGURE 53-1   Robert Farella developed a new interest in reading when he realized there were books written about the subject he loved most: football.

I picked *The New Birth Order Book* off the shelf and skimmed the table of contents. Amongst the seventeen chapters stood the usuals, introduction, different aspects of birth order, and I was all set to turn the next few pages and start at the beginning. It was then that something caught my eye, "Chapter Nine: Born Last but Seldom Least: A Closer Look at the Baby of the Family." I thought, maybe I will just read that chapter first and then go back to all of the rest. So I turned to page 167 and began the first paragraph. "First of all, I want all you babies of the family to know I'm on to you. I know you have just skipped the first eight chapters and started right here. I understand. Like any last born, I would have done the same thing." I was shocked, speechless, and amazed. I was caught out by an author I'd never met. From that point on I ate up every word of the book.

—*Hannah Tucker*

I figured out that I love boats, the sea, and being out on the water. I have to admit that I do not read much. But I found something that I am interested in, a very interesting book about a sword fishing fleet [*A Perfect Storm*] and a huge storm comes by and wipes out half of the fleet.

—*Chris Wolfe*

Take a moment to reflect on your reading and teaching. You may find the following discussion points useful, or you can come up with your own:

• Write a summary of the last section. Include in this summary three main ideas—techniques, strategies, tools—that relate to your own classes.

• Which reminders from the preceding section might help you the most?

• Looking ahead to the next section, consider its title and, before you begin reading, create your own list of reminders for this topic. After checking yours with mine, discuss which of these reminders—from your list and mine—will help you and your students the most.

Use Various

Strategies

When I find a well-drawn character in fiction or biography, I generally take a warm personal interest in him, for the reason that I have known him before—met him on the river.

—MARK TWAIN

Carolina, Maritza, Loren, and Janine discuss the books they are reading for SSR. Such discussions offer important opportunities for students to learn about other books from friends.

Successful readers not only have an array of strategies to choose from, they know when and how to use them. The strategies that help one student better understand a history textbook do not necessarily help another, nor do they necessarily offer the support that student needs to read and understand a novel or poem. Thus we must use and help students to master a range of strategies, discussing as part of that process when, why, and how to use each one. Students, by reflecting on their own reading, will eventually identify those that help them most. Taralyn Lewis, for example, finds visualization an important aid to her reading: "I didn't understand how the main character was able to see death. Once I started reading, I got really into it. I imagined that it was actually going on in my head so I could understand it better and it was like I was right there in the backyard with them."

How we visualize can depend on the experiences we draw from and the type of text we are reading. Angelina Tufo, a sophomore in my class, was in all the school's drama productions, so when she read Neil Simon's *London Suite*, she "was paying attention to the play and trying to set it on a stage." She then realized, by monitoring her reading, that at some point she "was concentrating too much on visualizing the set rather than concentrating on the story line of the play." Overall, however, her technique helped her: "I was visualizing the play being performed on stage and when I watch plays they go by fast. As I was reading, I was watching it on stage in my head." While using our imagination to see and hear what we are reading, other strategies, discussed in this section, help also. Jenna Goldberg, using the strategies we discussed in class, wrote, "I have decided to make a prediction of what I think is going to happen through the rest of the book. I think that Harry [Potter] is going to cast a spell upon the Dursleys. Boy, do they deserve it! I also think that when Harry goes to his witchcraft school he is going to be the most popular because of who he is and he will stay in the nice rooms at school. Maybe he will even get the same room his parents stayed in."

Throughout this section I emphasize the importance of moving students toward independence as readers. This means that they must have time to learn and practice a range of strategies in their reading of a variety of texts. At the heart of the reader's enterprise is the need to make connections: between themselves and the book, the characters, the world at large. Students should be encouraged to use those strategies that best help them do this. The following paper shows Monica Garcia using a range of approaches to help her understand a very difficult book, Maxine Hong Kingston's *Woman Warrior*. Monica evolved a strategy over the course of the semester that I would call a call and response: she would find quotes she engaged with and write her responses. She naturally gravitated, without my guidance, toward dialogue journals, a tool that helped her, through written conversations, to make connections between the book and herself, her past and her present, her life in Mexico and her life in America, all of which allowed this transitional ESL student to read a difficult book successfully. (Note that the underlined text indicates quotations from Kingston's book.)

While I was reading I noticed that the narrator and I have so many things in common. Some of this common things were in how their parents educated her and her believes. "<u>In China your father had a sister who killed herself. She jumped into the family well.</u>" When I was living in Mexico and I was ten or eleven years old. My mother had four sisters and six brothers. But about five years ago, one of my uncles was killed and we have to come to the United States. But of course there were another problems that we have in Mexico beside the death of my uncle. My sister, my brother and me felt so bad and did not want to go anywhere and wanted to die because he was the uncle that visited us and we loved him so much. "<u>She couldn't have been pregnant, you see, because her husband had been gone for years. No one said anything. Now that you have started to menstruate, what happened to her could happen to you. Don't humiliate us</u>." Since I was a little girl my mother and father have told me what is wrong and what is good for my body, health and reputation. They taught me how to respect people so that people could respect me. And they also taught me that if I do something wrong they were going to be the ones who will be affected beside me and that they will felt bad and will suffered for the bad thing that I could have done. "<u>All the married women blunt-cut their hair in flaps about their weddings they displayed themselves in their long hair for the last time</u>." My mom have told me that when she was going to marry with my dad. All the women who were engaged there were not allow to see their fiancées again until the day they suppose to get marry. And right now there are women that live with their fiancées before they get marry. "<u>Death is coming. Death is coming.</u>" When I read this sentence I think of dying and I am really afraid of die and I don't want to. "<u>When we children girls listened to the adults talk story, we learned that we failed if we grew up to be but wives or slaves.</u>" My mom have told me that the women didn't born to be slaves to any man or to be born that any men can abuse women. The women have to study to have a better life if she get divorce or separate from her husband. "<u>She reached down to touch the hot, wet, moving mass, surely smaller than anything human, and could feel that it was human after all—fingers, toes, nails,</u>

175

<u>and nose. Do you think you can bear to stay with us for fifteen years? We can train you to become a warrior? What about my father and mother? I asked. I learned to move my fingers, hands, feet, head, and entire body in circles. I walked putting heel down first, toes pointing outward thirty to forty degrees, making the ideograph 'eight,' making the ideograph 'human.' Knees bent, I would swing into the slow, measured 'square step,' the powerful walk into battle."</u> When my uncle die my mother taught me how to fight the horrible things that were happening to me during those first years that I really missed my uncle because he was not there when I need him anymore. When he die I couldn't stop thinking about him and I didn't want to be alive anymore because I felt with a hole in my mind and in my heart that he have left. And still right now I missed him so much. My mom taught me how to get over with all my depression and I didn't have to go away from her, or my family or my house. But now I know that this things happened in order other people came to this world, but with him it was unfair because he was too young to die.

Monica's mechanical difficulties reveal someone who is still learning to master the language, but more importantly her insights demonstrate the power of her strategies to overcome obstacles to her comprehension. Most of all, Monica's writing reminds me of all the reasons why reading is so valuable: it helps us make sense of ourselves and others, understand our past and the present.

Use Question the Author (Q & A)

54

RATIONALE

This method helps students from various grade levels and with different reading abilities comprehend confusing texts and increase their engagement. The approach asks the reader to be active, to function in the capacity of a "reviser" of the original author's text, especially in those places where confusion creeps in. The ultimate goal of the method is to increase the capacity and independence of readers as they graduate from teacher-supported texts. The purpose of this approach is to make students aware of the choices authors make while writing and, by examining them through the queries explained below, understand how authors convey meaning through words and structures.

> It is a very great thing to be able to think as you like; but, after all, an important question remains: *what* you think.
>
> MATTHEW ARNOLD

WHAT TO DO

Planning

Evaluate the text through students' eyes, determining what areas of the text might pose problems.

Keep in mind the three primary outcomes of the planning session; students should ber able to:

1. Identify key concepts and potential problems.
2. Segment the text into related chunks to allow for focused attention on its content, form, and function.
3. Develop what Beck et al. (1997) call "queries." These generally fall into the following categories:

   - Initiating
     - What is the author trying to say here?
     - What is the author's intention?
     - What point is the author trying to make?

   - Narrative
     - What situation is the character in now?
     - Given all that we know about the character so far, what do you think he will do next?

177

> ▶ How has the character changed from the beginning of the story?

> ▶ What events along the way inspired or caused these changes?

- Follow-up

> ▶ What does the author mean when she writes . . . ?

> ▶ Does the author explain her reasons clearly and effectively?

> ▶ To what extent did the author achieve what he or she set out to accomplish?

Discussing

Think about the students' role. Students are responsible for running the discussion, using their queries (and others provided by the teacher if necessary) to focus their conversation. Beck et al. compare a text to a maze that students must learn to navigate themselves if they are to arrive at the end (i.e., understanding). In pairs, groups, or with the whole class, the students should have time to talk about the different turns they took in the textual maze and the questions they used to help them make those decisions.

Think about the teacher's role. In the earlier stages of using this method, the teacher may need to be more directive, but aside from teaching them to use QtA, the teacher's role is to facilitate the discussions and monitor their understanding of the text. The teacher's primary role is to pose initial queries based on their initial planning, then query students' thinking throughout the process, posing questions designed to challenge their thinking and help them achieve greater clarity and depth. Beck et al. identify six types of discussion moves: marking, turning back, revoicing, modeling, annotating, and recapping. All of these work toward the same end: helping students and teachers pay closer attention to crucial aspects of the text.

Teaching

Keep in mind that one essential requirement of this method is that students learn about "author fallibility" so that they realize that as readers they can challenge what the author says and the means by which the author says it. Throughout the QtA process, teachers and students should be thinking out loud, narrating their decisions and thoughts so that others can see how they arrive at their interpretation of the text.

Use ReQuest
(Reciprocal Questioning)

55

RATIONALE

Reciprocal questioning (ReQuest) teaches students to develop their own questions and to know when to ask them. They must use the habits of inquiry—questioning, comparing, clarifying, wondering, predicting—if they are to become active and thus effective readers. Working within the supportive and structured environment of the classroom, students can read with increasing independence if they learn the types of strategies that ReQuest helps them develop. As students learn to ask their own questions, they also bring greater purpose and individual control to their reading experience, since they are able to delve into those aspects of the text that intrigue them for individual, personal reasons. Thus the method can help increase students' engagement with the text.

People want to know why I do this, why I write such gross stuff. I like to tell them I have a heart of a small boy—and I keep it in a jar on my desk.

STEPHEN KING

WHAT TO DO

- Use ReQuest by following these steps:

    1. Select a passage for the students to read, choosing the text based on the degree to which students can practice making predictions. The text can be expository or narrative, so long as there is some string of events that the reader might use to predict a change or other outcome.

    2. Reflect on your own reading of the passage, so that you are ready to discuss with students how they arrived at their interpretation of the text.

    3. Have the students read the passage and write down questions that come to mind about it, questions that might yield information useful in making predictions. They can practice this step in class with short passages of text in order to master the technique; you can then have them use it at home on longer passages from their assigned reading.

    4. Once students have their questions written down, have them enter into discussion in one of the following formats: teacher-student conference, pairs, small groups, or full class.

179

5. Begin discussion by having a volunteer pose one of their questions to the group or class. This student is then responsible for calling on someone to answer the question.

6. The student who responds to the question chooses the person who will pose the next question to the group, and so on. Students who have already contributed cannot be called on a second time. Ideally, you will have time to work through the entire class so that everyone is able to participate.

- Disallow students from "passing" when they are called on; if they don't know an answer, students should make an effort to respond to the question. One of the aims of this activity is to teach students how to speculate in response to questions that they do not know the answer to. If they are at a complete loss, try saying, "What would you say if you *did* know the answer?" This or a similar line is surprisingly effective because it gives students permission to take a risk.

- Remember that the teacher's role in this activity is to help students refine or rephrase their questions as necessary. They need to learn that answers will only be as clear as the questions that prompted them. The teacher should intervene to help the class recognize how a question might be improved or why it is a particularly good question, as well as to encourage students who have difficulty responding. In the early stages of using this technique, it may be useful to generate a criteria of good questions and discuss exemplars. The teacher should also model the development and application of good questions.

- Though the steps above comprise the recommended approach, be flexible in the early stages of using this or any technique. Students need time to master new strategies; for this particular activity, they may need to develop elaboration and reporting skills discussed in Reminders 93 and 94.

- Scaffold your teaching so that passages and queries become more sophisticated as students become more familiar with this approach.

Use Concept Cards

RATIONALE

Struggling readers lack the capacity to put it all together when reading a complicated text. The concept card strategy, which I learned from Joan Rossi, helps them grasp the big picture while also serving to develop their note-taking skills. This technique is especially useful when students are reading textbooks or other informational texts.

To call forth a concept a word is needed; to portray a phenomenon, a concept is needed.

ANTOINE LAURENT LAVOISIER

WHAT TO DO

- Give students the following instructions:

    1. *On the front* of a 5 × 8″ index card, write down the chapter (or section or book) title (e.g., "The Golden Age of Greece").
    2. Skim the chapter, looking only at the headers, subheaders, sidebars, bold words, pullout quotes, and first sentences of each paragraph.
    3. *On the top of the back* of that same card, *in pencil*, write down your prediction of what you think the chapter is about.
    4. Make a list of five to six items (using single words or short phrases) predicting what will happen or what the text is about based on your quick review of it.
    5. Read the assigned text.
    6. Go back to the index card and check your predictions against the actual text.
    7. Erase any wrong predictions and replace them with correct descriptions of what the text is about.

- When they have finished the assignment, collect the cards and check them for accuracy and completion.

- Teach them to use the cards as study aids and measure their reading performance according to how well they do on a reading test you prepare for them.

- Hold conferences with students in which you discuss how closely their predictions matched what they ultimately found out.

Discuss with them why and how they made their predictions, and model as appropriate other ways they might have approached this task.

• Consider having students use these note cards to write a paper that allows them to integrate and thus reinforce their knowledge about the text.

Use Repeated
Reading

RATIONALE

Repeated reading helps readers at all levels read texts they find difficult. It is used in more controlled ways in the lower elementary grades, but from upper elementary through high school it provides useful support to readers who find themselves challenged by the demands of a particular text. The strategy not only increases comprehension but raises readers' confidence and engagement with the text. It is especially beneficial to remedial readers who need to improve their fluency and comprehension.

> The great sin is to assume that something that has been read once has been read forever. . . . Nobody reads the same book twice.
>
> ROBERTSON DAVIES

WHAT TO DO

Familiarize yourself with the following approach, which I learned from Sheridan Blau, whom I thank every time I use it:

- Choose a short text that can be read three times by everyone in a relatively short period of time (e.g., ten minutes or less).

- *First Reading*: As you read, underline any word or phrase you do not understand using a specific color or pattern (e.g., straight line). When you finish reading it the first time, give yourself a comprehension score of 1–10, 10 meaning you understood it perfectly.

- *Second Reading*: Read it again, underlining what you do not understand with a different color or pattern (e.g., dotted line). Again, evaluate the extent of your understanding using a scale of 1–10.

- *Third Reading*: As before, underline with yet a different color or pattern, then evaluate your comprehension. Finally, write down one question about the text, a question about one aspect of the text you still do not understand.

- *Follow-up*: In small groups, share your questions and try to answer them for each other. When you have finished the discussion, have a full-class discussion that begins by considering those questions people were still unable to answer.

Use repeated reading to accomplish a variety of ends:

- Read for different purposes (e.g., for style, for argument, for character)
- Find and improve retention of factual information about a given topic
- Develop, improve, or reinforce comprehension and other reading skills using a variety of progressively more demanding texts
- Increase awareness of and appreciation for the role practice and repetition play in all learning, including sports, music, and reading
- Improve speed and overall fluency, as well as comprehension and confidence

Consider the following variations:

- Repeated reading done aloud. Poet Robert Bly says a poem must be heard several times at a sitting in order that people begin to hear and understand it.
- Mixed reading. Begin by reading aloud, then read the same text silently, then read it aloud again.
- Read along while the teacher or a classmate reads aloud.
- Use a series of texts (e.g., more than one poem or excerpt) so that students learn to apply the strategies and skills to a range of materials, thereby increasing their confidence and capacity.
- Keep in mind that texts for this activity must be within reach of the reader's current ability (i.e., roughly 85% accuracy rate on the first reading) or it will be ineffective.
- Keep reading and practicing the strategy at the same level of difficulty until the student shows mastery of that level or type of text, then move on.
- Pair up students for collaborative repeated reading in which they follow the steps just outlined above but discuss with each other their performance and evaluate each other for comprehension.

Use the PreReading Plan (PReP)

RATIONALE

The PReP technique, developed by Judith Langer, teaches students to generate what they know about a subject and to elaborate on and evaluate that information. This makes it a productive method, since it not only improves their reading performance but strengthens their thinking skills and independence. The method also helps teachers assess students' prior knowledge and ability to communicate that knowledge. Studies have also found that this method helps students realize what they know before they read more about a subject and thus improves their sense of efficacy (i.e., they realize they *do* know things that are not always apparent to them).

> One can be amused or excited by a book that one's intellect simply refused to take seriously.
>
> GEORGE ORWELL

WHAT TO DO

Define your role. Throughout the process the teacher acts as a model or master reader, showing students how to generate information (i.e., brainstorm ideas), modeling questioning and discussing the subject, and demonstrating intellectual risk-taking. The teacher's role during the first stage of PReP is to encourage and inspire contributions and thinking, *not* to edit or otherwise critique students' ideas.

Follow these two steps:

STEP ONE: CLASS DISCUSSION

- Prior to the class discussion the teacher identifies the concepts they want their students to discuss.
- Determine the best method for stimulating an effective discussion about the ideas, including whether students should work in pairs, groups, or as a whole class.
- Discuss initial associations.
    - What do you think about . . .
    - What might happen if . . .
    - What do you think you already know about . . .
- Reflect on the initial associations.
    - How did you come up with that idea or interpretation of the passage?

> ▸ What other associations come to mind when you think of this concept?

> ▸ Do you see any connections between this and our previous studies?

- Reformulate their knowledge and revise their understanding.

> ▸ What new ideas come to mind about . . .

> ▸ What do you realize is *not* true or important about this subject, which previously seemed so?

> ▸ How has your understanding of or perspective on this subject changed as a result of your reading and discussion?

STEP TWO: ANALYZE STUDENTS' IDEAS FROM STEP ONE

- Develop with students or provide for them yourself the criteria by which the ideas from step one should be assessed. Tierney and Readence (2000) describe the three guidelines by which Langer suggests the teacher can determine if students' understanding of the material at this point is complete, partial, or inadequate:

> ▸ *Complete Prior Knowledge*: Their questions and responses show sophisticated integration and synthesis of ideas within the passage and other material being read and discussed. Exemplary responses might include analogies and examples from the text or other readings in this or other classes.

> ▸ *Partial Prior Knowledge*: Students make vague references to the text or ideas recently discussed, perhaps trying to draw from personal experiences that are remotely related but not helpful.

> ▸ *Inadequate Prior Knowledge*: Students know only the surface details of the passage, including the literal meaning of words but not their connotative meaning. They lack the prior knowledge needed to read the text successfully.

Keep in mind that all readers function at the levels just described depending on the complexity of the text, the way in which they are asked to read it, and their prior knowledge and experience.

After evaluating what the students know, determine the most effective means by which to develop students' prior knowledge. Possible options include direct instruction; individual or small-group conferences with those in the "Inadequate Prior Knowledge" category; reading a supplemental, more accessible text to prepare them to read the required text; further class discussion.

Use the Directed Reading and Thinking Activity (DRTA)

RATIONALE

This stategy works best when students can make predictions about the text they are to read. The strategy improves close reading and supports readers at all levels. The method works well for readers at all grade and ability levels as well as with a range of texts. It also allows readers to self-assess their level of understanding prior to moving on or, should the results reveal inadequacies, returning to the confusing parts for further clarification.

The king was pregnant.

URSULA Le GUIN, FROM *THE LEFT HAND OF DARKNESS*

WHAT TO DO

• Have students, after skimming the text, make some predictions about its meaning, main ideas, or other information. This means looking at the headings, graphics, tables, maps, and pullout quotes to activate schema and orient their mind to this particular text.

• Ask students to use the Cornell Notes form in Appendixes 7 and 22 to take notes under three headers: Preview, Notes, and Review. All predictions and initial questions should be written down under Preview.

• Have them take notes while they read the text, noting down any examples or other details that support their initial predictions or provide evidence that demands they revise those predictions. All evidence and examples should be listed under Notes on the Cornell sheet.

• Ask them to review their notes and the text, and then write a summary of the text under the Review heading on the Cornell sheet. This synopsis should be in their own words and should include examples from the text that support their conclusions.

• Note that DRTA can be used with a class or group. In this case, ask the following questions:

   ‣ What do you think a story with this title might be about?
   ‣ What do you expect to happen in this story?
   ‣ Which of your classmates' predictions do you agree with?

• Have students discuss these predictions, their assumptions, and the means by which they arrived at these conclusions.

• Have students read the text in chunks, stopping as directed to test their predictions against what they have read so far. Such questions as "What do you think will happen next?" or "Were you correct in your initial predictions?" are useful at this point.

Use
SQ3R

RATIONALE

SQ3R (Survey Question Read-Recite-Review) is primarily used with text-books or articles with headings. It provides a systematic way of approaching informational texts prior to actually reading the text. It is thus a technique to improve comprehension of new material or difficult texts by helping students develop an initial mental schema about what the article discusses. It is also described as a crucial study skill that can be used with a number of subjects and is not limited to reading, since these skills—questioning, reflecting, reviewing—help us with other types of text besides print.

> The adult relation to books is one of absorbing rather than being absorbed.
>
> ANTHONY BURGESS

WHAT TO DO

- Remember that SQ3R stands for the following activities that students must do:

    ▸ *Survey*: Skim through the assigned reading, paying attention to any major textual or graphic features (e.g., pullouts, headings, tables, bold words) that might give them a quick sense of the content and its categories. Readers should give extra attention to the introduction, and the opening and concluding paragraph(s).

    ▸ *Question*: Turn all the chapter or section headings into questions that they can answer as they read. If, for example, the subheading is "The Importance of Caste in India," they should ask themselves questions like, "What is important to know about caste in India?" or "How does caste affect the lives of people in India?" They should form these questions as they skim and then revisit them and attempt to answer them while reading the actual text.

    ▸ *Read*: Read the assigned passage, revisiting and trying to answer the questions they developed in the previous step. They should revise the questions as necessary or ask new ones as they arise during their reading.

    ▸ *Recite*: Retell the text (see Reminder 71) to themselves or others immediately after they finish reading it so they can process it and begin to make deeper connections. This retelling should be in their own words.

▶ *Review*: Revisit their questions and skim the chapter once again to firm up any connections they have made, asking themselves as they skim what a particular section is about and how that relates to the other sections. They might note those questions they were unable to answer and, after reflecting on why they could not answer them (e.g., not enough information, not well-phrased questions, never saw anything related to the question), put the question to the class or their group.

• Keep in mind that when students finish using this strategy, they are ready to take their thinking to the next stage, to augment their understanding. Possible next steps include jigsaw or group discussions, class discussion, and written reflection in their learning log in which they discuss how they learned what they learned (see Reminder 8).

• Remind students that this and many of the other techniques discussed in this book can help them read other types of texts—images, tables, graphs, Web pages, articles—better if they internalize these questions and habits.

Use the KWL Strategy

RATIONALE

This method, familiar to many, prepares students to read expository texts about subjects that may pose some difficulty. The KWL method (the acronym comes from the key words in the phrases What you *Know*/What you *Want* to know/What you *Learned*) helps them activate the knowledge they already have while making them aware of what they need to know to read the assigned text. It is a method that students can learn to use independently and master in various settings. Central to this technique is the KWL organizer, which you will find in Appendix 11. A student example is included at the end of this reminder, as well. KWL is a process that mirrors what we always should do as readers, so this technique is one of the more highly recommended ones to use when reading textbooks or other informational texts.

Indeed he knows not how to know who knows not also how to unknow.

SIR RICHARD FRANCIS BURTON

WHAT TO DO

Teacher Preparation

• Decide if this method is appropriate for your students and this text. While the method is very effective if used properly, it can be detrimental to struggling readers who tend to discount what they already know and, after reading, may register confusion and resent that they were not given the kind of support to read it successfully.

• Identify those ideas and concepts that students must get from the reading and structure the subsequent work so as to ensure they achieve this understanding.

Brainstorm Session and Preliminary Discussion

• Using the board or butcher paper, have students brainstorm everything they know (or think they know) about the topic you are studying. Your role at this point is to help push them without critiquing or otherwise responding to what they suggest.

• Have students use the worksheet (see Appendix 11) to organize their ideas and take down notes from what has been recorded on the board.

• Invite students to discuss what confuses them or seems ambiguous.

• Have the class, together or in groups, determine the categories of information students should expect to apply to the subject they are preparing to read about. For example, if they are reading an article about *Time* magazine's Person of the Century (Albert Einstein), what categories might they expect the information to fall into (e.g., influences on his thinking, consequences of his ideas, criteria for his selection, who else was nominated)?

• If you don't have them working in groups, now is an opportune time to have them pair up and discuss what they have come up with so far. During this time you can move around the room to clarify and evaluate as you are able.

Reading Session and Discussion/Reflection

• Based on the preceding class work, ask students to identify those things they would like to find out about through the reading. These then become the questions they will ask as readers.

• Have them read the assigned article, taking notes in the What I Learned column of the KWL organizer as they read, and comparing what they learned against what they knew and wanted to learn to see if they match up or reveal new insights.

• When they finish reading, have them complete their notes in the What I Learned column, then discuss their findings in groups or as a class, adding to their notes as they uncover new connections or gather new information.

• When they complete their discussion, have them fill in the final column: What I Still Need to Learn (or want to know more about). This will help them keep their attention focused when they read next time; it also helps them read better by making them more interactive readers, who read with a clear purpose.

Possible Variations

Keep in mind that many readers have adapted this method for their own purposes, some of which are worth mentioning. Some suggest a fourth column that asks the reader to identify what they want to learn next or need to know now. Still others ask students to include in a fourth column suggestions about how they can find out what they want to know or how they found out what they learned.

KWL Organizer

What I Know	What I Want to Know	What I Learned
World War I was between Germany and Russia and many other countries. Many people were fighting and many people died in this war. It caused a lot of problems to another nations also. This was a very scary situation. They were using weapons such as guns and other weapons. The course of this battle died in 1000000 people. There were many people dead.	Why did or Why was there a World War I? Why was it called the World War I? Who were really involved? Which countries fought in this world wars? What was the reason for the countries to fight? How did affect the countries? Did it affect other nations? Did it affect my family? Was everything disturbed because of the World War I?	World War I, sometimes known as the "Great War," followed forty years of relative on the European continent. From the end of the Franco-Russian war, the great powers in Europe (France, German) Russia, England and Austria-Hungary) did not confront each other directly rather, they formed protective alliances and argued over colonial possessions. Verdun: 315,000 French 280,000 German Same: 800,000 total 19536000 Estimated wounded soldiers

Possible Categories for Information: Whose involved, How many people died, How many people were killed, causes of the death, significant battles, weapons.

Summary/Response/Still Need to Know
World War I, sometimes know as "the Great War" followed forty years of relative peace on the European continent. They were friction: The Austrains and the Russians were constantly in conflict, the French and the Germans were beset by mutual distrust, and although France was Britain's historical enemy, the British were more alarmed by the growth of the German navy.

FIGURE 61-1 Nitya Bandla used the KWL organizer to help her prepare to read Remarque's novel *All Quiet on the Western Front*. Such activities are especially helpful to students who are new to the country and thus need added knowledge about the books they will read or the subjects they will study.

62 Use the CRITICS Procedure

RATIONALE

There are three classes of intellects: one which comprehends by itself; another which appreciates what others comprehend; and a third which neither comprehends by itself nor by the showing of others.

NICCOLO MACHIAVELLI

Developed by English teacher William Welker, the Critical Reading Instruction That Improves Comprehension Skills (CRITICS) procedure helps students determine the credibility of what they read. The CRITICS method trains readers to distinguish, through direct instruction, between fact and opinion when reading any text. Though the procedure focuses on printed texts, the same procedure and habits can be adapted to read other types of text such as Web sites, commercial and news media, and film. Students' access to the Internet makes these skills more essential than ever.

WHAT TO DO

Help students establish the criteria by which a fact and opinion can be identified. Before giving students those criteria you developed, give them a set of examples to use as tools to generate and test their own. When they are finished, or if they get stuck, give them your list (such as the one following) to help them get unstuck or to check their own criteria:

- Facts are:
  - Observable
  - Verified by repeated use/experience across time
  - Testable
  - Unemotional
  - Concise statements that use clear language
  - Uncontestable
  - Supportable (e.g., reliable data is available to support the fact)
  - Opinions are:
    - Emotional
    - Debatable
    - Described using terms that emphasize or intensify

- ▶ Linked to words like *think, feel, assume, contend, suppose*
- ▶ Overly generalized, implying that all people think or feel the same way

Once they have a set of criteria to use, consider having them apply that knowledge in the following situations. Have them:

- Create an anticipation guide (see Reminder 63) consisting of statements about the subject they will soon be studying. They must use their criteria to determine whether each statement is a fact or an opinion.
- Use the criteria as a secondary tool when working with anticipation guides. For example, after students complete a guide like the sample included with Reminder 63, have them then reread the statements in the guide and explain why they are fact or opinion.
- Evaluate and complete multiple-choice anticipation guides, supporting their answers with evidence based on the criteria (e.g., "It's an opinion because they use the words *feel* and *believe*.")
- Take their knowledge to the next level of understanding by writing fact and opinion statements in response to the texts they are reading. They must then identify whether their statements are fact or opinion and use the criteria to support their assertion.

Develop the habit of asking students during discussion whether their comment is a fact or an opinion so as to extend and reinforce their knowledge of the CRITICS approach and critical thinking in general.

63 Use Anticipation Guides

From the moment I
picked up your book
until I laid it down I
was convulsed with
laughter. Someday I
intend reading it.

GROUCHO MARX

RATIONALE

Anticipation guides prepare students to read by activating their prior knowledge and asking them what they think about certain ideas. The strategy inspires lively discussions that not only prepare students to read but allow them to see how their ideas and beliefs compare with those of their classmates, the author, and society at large.

WHAT TO DO

Decide on the ideal configuration for this activity according to your desired outcomes: individual, small group, or full class.

Use anticipation guides to:

- Activate prior knowledge and schema
- Get students thinking
- Engage them in thoughtful discussion
- Prepare them to read texts or content about which they know little if anything
- Challenge students' preconceived notions about a subject, author, or idea
- Examine attitudes toward a subject; assumptions or knowledge about that subject; understanding of that subject.

Before you create an anticipation guide, decide whether you want students to: identify, evaluate, or determine. Consider the following examples of possible response options:

- Strongly Disagree . . . Strongly Agree (with the statements)
- Likely . . . Unlikely, or Certain . . . Impossible (probability as it relates to an event or person)
- True . . . False (with gradations in between)
- Check the names of all to whom this would apply (when evaluating a range of people, countries, or organizations according to certain criteria)

Read the anticipation guide I developed for use prior to the class's reading of *Macbeth*. Note the steps I followed in its use:

- Put students in groups of five to six (such larger groups yield energized discussion and make consensus a bit more elusive).

- Have them develop criteria for evaluating an act or person.
- Have them read through the anticipation guide scenarios and, using their criteria, reach unanimous decision as to whether each one is evil or not.
- When finished, ask students to revisit their criteria and evaluate how successfully it accommodated their decisions (e.g., was there one scenario to which their criteria did not seem to apply?).
- Have them report back to the class for class discussion.
- Ask them to begin reading the play.
- Have them revisit the anticipation guide during and after their reading to see if their criteria still seem appropriate in light of what they now know.

SAMPLE ACTIVITY: *MACBETH* ANTICIPATION GUIDE

Directions Rate each statement according to the Strongly Agree/ Strongly Disagree continuum and explain your choice on a separate piece of paper. Then, in your group, discuss each statement; you must reach consensus on your rating. Finally, you must ask two people outside of class to rate these statements and discuss their choices with you. These two people may not be high school students; they must be at least nineteen years old.

People will do whatever is necessary to achieve their goals.

STRONGLY DISAGREE   DISAGREE   DEPENDS   AGREE   STRONGLY AGREE

Ambition is good (i.e., a positive, desirable trait).

STRONGLY DISAGREE   DISAGREE   DEPENDS   AGREE   STRONGLY AGREE

All leaders are ambitious.

STRONGLY DISAGREE   DISAGREE   DEPENDS   AGREE   STRONGLY AGREE

It is impossible to be ambitious and maintain your integrity.

STRONGLY DISAGREE   DISAGREE   DEPENDS   AGREE   STRONGLY AGREE

Ambition, lust, greed, and desire all mean the same thing.

STRONGLY DISAGREE   DISAGREE   DEPENDS   AGREE   STRONGLY AGREE

Everyone is capable of lying, killing, and betrayal; in other words, of being evil.

STRONGLY DISAGREE   DISAGREE   DEPENDS   AGREE   STRONGLY AGREE

The world is just: if you do something wrong you will be punished for it.

STRONGLY DISAGREE   DISAGREE   DEPENDS   AGREE   STRONGLY AGREE

Our nature (i.e., our character) is fixed; try as we might we cannot change who or what we are.

STRONGLY DISAGREE DISAGREE DEPENDS AGREE STRONGLY AGREE

Our fate is predetermined; we cannot alter our own destiny.

STRONGLY DISAGREE DISAGREE DEPENDS AGREE STRONGLY AGREE

If someone kills someone because someone else coerced them, the person who did the killing is not responsible for the murder.

STRONGLY DISAGREE DISAGREE DEPENDS AGREE STRONGLY AGREE

STUDENT EXAMPLE

Students were required, after completing this anticipation guide, to assess their responses and draw conclusions. Standards documents in most every subject area will emphasize the importance of being able to read a variety of types of documents and make inferences based on the content. The following sample comes from a student who was concurrently enrolled in my English class and a transitional ESL class:

> People will do whatever is necessary to achieve their goals depending on the goal they are trying to achieve. Let's say a student wants to get straight A's in his/her report card. This guy will achieve his/her goal by studying really hard, doing his homework and paying attention to all his/her classes. That way he won't hurt anybody for his ambition of achieving his goal and he will because of his effort. But for example let's take a man that is willing to achieve his goal no matter what, the only problem is that he wants to become the president of us, but he has never taken a class about law. He may have power and a lot of money, but that is not enough for him, he has this greed of becoming the leader of a country. This person will become very evil and start killing people that gets into his way, his desire would make him lose control of his own mind. For this man it would be impossible to have his integrity.

Is this student ready to read and discuss *Macbeth*? You bet!

Use
Think-Alouds

RATIONALE

Thinking aloud is the process of allowing others to see *what* you think by narrating *how* you think as you read a text or discuss an idea. We often send our students out the door with the directions, "Read this chapter and jot down some thoughts about it in your notebook." Taking notes is simple for us: we know how to think about what we read and what such thinking looks like. Students often do not know what good thinking about their reading looks like, so we must constantly model it for them and ask them to model it for us so we can shape their performance through feedback.

Another important outcome of this procedure, especially when the teacher uses it to narrate their own thinking/reading process, is the realization of how messy reading actually is; students glimpse this through the teacher's false starts, guesses, revisions, questions, and so on, all of which give students permission to read this way.

If you would tell me what you think, then I could answer better.

FIFTEEN-YEAR-OLD STUDENT QUOTED IN ROBERT COLES'S *THE CALL OF STORIES*

WHAT TO DO

- Use think-alouds to:
    - Demonstrate what students should do and how they should do it
    - Reflect on what they read
    - Help them comprehend their reading
    - Develop their internal reader (the reader's equivalent to a writer's internal critic)
- Use think-alouds in a variety of configurations, such as:
    - Teacher to students
    - Student to teacher (in conferences or class discussion)
    - Students to students
    - Author to readers (via interviews with authors or the teacher's summary of an author's remarks taken from an article)
- Think aloud:
    - On paper
    - In your head

> ▶ In a group

> ▶ As a class

• Keep in mind that think-aloud strategies are not a sequence but a set of habits of mind common to all effective readers which, if used well, can help readers make sense of a wide variety of texts in different media and of varying complexity. When we use the think-aloud technique, we:

> ▶ Predict

> ▶ Describe

> ▶ Compare

> ▶ Make connections

> ▶ Monitor and correct

> ▶ Question

> ▶ Clarify

> ▶ Apply previous or new knowledge

> ▶ Identify what's important

> ▶ Troubleshoot and problem solve

> ▶ Speculate

• Use examples from your own discipline to show them what each of these behaviors looks like when reading in your subject area. I prepared a sheet, which appears at the end of this chapter, that I give my English students that acts as both exemplar and checklist for them to use while reading. We review it as a set of possible responses to the upcoming reading and a checklist of available techniques that they should be using. When they return to class the next day, for example, I might ask them to get out their think-alouds in their learning log (see Reminder 100) and, after sharing them with a partner or their group, discuss which methods they used and why. If possible, we would compare one student's speculation with another's to see not only how they used the technique but what they speculated about.

• Think-alouds also provide the teacher a running record of students' thinking and comprehension, thus allowing you to assess their performance informally, but structure the culminating assignment so as to allow them to use their think-alouds (e.g., for an essay on a topic they create based on their own think-alouds).

• Use this technique when assigning reading to a class so that you can model for them how you want them to read it. This clarifies their purpose and directs their attention, which will help them read more effectively.

SAMPLE ACTIVITY—THINK-ALOUDS: *THE ADVENTURES OF HUCKLEBERRY FINN*

Note: The think-aloud is a strategy that helps you better understand what you read by forcing you to think about what you read *as you read it.* The think-aloud might be personal or philosophical, addressed to the author or yourself. While doing a think-aloud, you should give yourself permission to interact with the text by doing any or all of the following:

Speculating

Example: I think that Huck's father is going to come back into the picture since Huck has all that money.

Guessing

Example: I guess Miss Watson is just the Widow Douglas's sister; she probably came to live with her after Mrs. Douglas's husband died.

Wondering

Example: Things back then don't seem so different than they do now. I wonder if it's true when people talk about "the good ol' days." In *Huck Finn* I see examples of people having drinking problems, being racist, kids being reckless or "adventurous," and other things that don't seem too different from today. I wonder if things were really better "back then"— . . . or do we just think they were?

Observing

Example: Religion seems to have meant more to people back then. I'm not sure why that is, but it seems like today we move too fast through life to think about these things. I also notice that it is often women who are portrayed in older books as religious. Men often seem to think religion is foolish, at least that is what Twain implies.

Arguing

Example: I don't think that Twain was racist at all, as people argue today. He uses the language of his time. But also, if you look at it, he introduces Jim right away as a character who gains our sympathy and interest. And Huck is just as superstitious as Jim is, so the idea that Jim is a caricature doesn't ring true since Huck acts much the same way. Maybe that's just the way they were in the South—if you weren't superstitious you were religious.

Philosophizing

Example: Things seem so much simpler when you're a kid. All they have to worry about is what game or adventure is next. Yet even this doesn't seem to be enough, since Huck Finn ends up "lighting out" for other experiences that he thinks will give him more satisfaction. Like most other Americans, he is restless.

STUDENT RESPONSE: MARIA PEREZ'S *HUCK FINN* THINK-ALOUD

I used the previous example as a handout in Maria's class to clarify terms and show students what I expected. Because I had clearly established standards for thinking, reading, and writing, Maria was able to produce the following think-aloud:

> Now that Huck has spent more time with Jim he is getting to know him better. Huck is realizing how smart Jim is. Huck always thought blacks were dumb, but by talking to Jim he's finding out otherwise. Huck feels that with everything he tells or asks Jim, Jim always has a good response. Jim always leads a good conversation and Huck is always amazed.
>
> *I notice* that Huck before doing something adventurous says Tom Sawyer would do it. So *I'm guessing* that he looks up to Tom. Huck seems to want to be like him. He wants adventure just like Tom always did. But *I think* that the adventure that Huck wants and goes after will get him and Jim into trouble. Jim gets real uncomfortable when Huck does something adventurous. *I wonder* if adventure is what is going to get them both caught.
>
> Every time that Huck gets off the river something interesting happens. Like the guy the town wanted to hang. *I think* that it was good that he told them what he did. It made them think. They should learn not to be nosy and mind their own business. I personally hate it when I have a problem with a person and then everyone gets involved and a bigger problem starts from that little problem. For example, with me, I'm kind of on a river. Everything is going good and then I meet a guy and I get off that nice calm river. I get into trouble and suffer the consequences. Then I get back on that calm river. I do good in school, get along with my friends and family, and am very happy.

Use Reciprocal Teaching

RATIONALE

This strategy, developed originally by Annemarie Palinscar and Ann Brown, has proven consistently successful with a wide range of students in diverse settings. It also adapts itself well to all subject areas and reading levels. It is particularly useful for informational and content area reading, though certainly it works with literature, also. It is an approach that lends itself to schoolwide implementation, allowing teachers in all subject areas to anchor their teaching in the same strategies and terms. The four skills—predicting, clarifying, questioning, and summarizing—allow readers to effectively monitor their own reading.

> The whole art of teaching is only the art of awakening the natural curiosity of young minds for the purpose of satisfying it afterwards.
>
> ANATOLE FRANCE

WHAT TO DO

• Using a short text that can be read quickly, model the four key activities of predicting, clarifying, questioning, and summarizing. Narrate your own thinking and actions out loud so that students understand what you are doing and why you are doing it.

• In a full class setting or small groups (note that this activity is ideally done as a small group in which the teacher also participates), take turns leading the discussion of the text being read and discussed. The group leader is responsible for facilitating the discussion and ensuring that the appropriate types of questions are asked. Reading selections should not be long—the point is to use texts to facilitate discussion.

• Note that questions fall into two main categories: what the text says (surface questions) and what the text means (deep questions). Surface questions, posed by the appointed leader, are formed through:

  ‣ Summarizing
  ‣ Paraphrasing
  ‣ Telling what happens
  ‣ Clarifying surface details
  ‣ Finding out: who, what, where, and when

Deep questions, which depend on a working knowledge of the surface details, allow the group leader to take the readers into the meaning of what they read. The leader asks such speculative questions as:

- What do you think will happen next based on what you already know?

- Why do you think that will happen next?

- What do you think about this idea, event, issue?

- How effective or successful was the author in conveying their message?

- How does this relate to your ideas, experiences, and values?

- How does this relate to the other texts you have read, issues you've studied, or people and cultures of the world?

- What gaps are there in this perspective of the world or this argument?

- Using these questions, helping students to recognize whether questions are surface or deep questions, groups help themselves better understand the text at hand while simultaneously strengthening their reading skills.

Ask Questions to Understand Stories

. . . .

66

RATIONALE

Stories invite the reader to ask certain types of questions at certain times depending on the nature of the story. The following list of questions, which students should learn to ask themselves as they become more independent, conscious readers, can be used to guide independent reading, journal writing, or group discussions.

I think a writer has a responsibility to comment on our culture, to read other writers.

JOYCE CAROL OATES

WHAT TO DO

Have students ask themselve the following:

- Who is telling the story?
- What is the narrator's point of view; i.e., is the story being told as it happens? recalled from past events? as an internal monologue? dramatic monologue?
- To what extent can you trust the narrator?
- What do you know about the characters?
- What do these things tell you about the characters?
- What is the relationship between the setting and the characters/story?
- What are people in the story *not* talking about?
- If there is more than one narrator, what is the relationship between them and what purpose do these multiple narrators serve?
- What shape or diagram best describes the action and/or structure of the story?
- How would it change the story if . . . e.g., the narrator changed from first to third person? the point of view changed from one character to another? the narrative started before/after the crucial event? a different narrative structure (e.g., journal format, internal monologue) was used? the narrator changed from man to woman (or visa versa)?
- How would you describe the voice and how it influences the tone of the story: e.g., formal or informal?

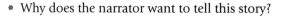

- Why does the narrator want to tell this story?
- What is the narrator's attitude toward their subject/characters/story?
- What, if anything, is influencing the shape and function of the text/story? (e.g., cultural tradition such as Native American story circle? different genres such as Cisneros's allusions in *The House on Mango Street* to folk and fairy tales?)
- Why does the author _____? (e.g., shift time frames, change narrators, incorporate different types of texts—poems, letters, diaries—within their story)
- How does the character change in response to their experiences in this story?
- What are the sources of conflict or tension in the narrative?
- How do your perceptions of the character(s) change as the story progresses?
- Does your answer to the question "What is this story about?" remain the same throughout your reading? If not, at what point does it change?
- What factors most influence your response to and interpretation of this story? (e.g., past experiences you've had? cultural bias? gender? socioeconomic status? other?)
- How does the historical setting/context affect this story's outcome/meaning/style?
- What must you know in order to understand this story?
- What is the relationship between this and other works by this author—or other writers/works in this genre?
- Which character do you most identify with and why?
- What would _____ be saying/thinking in their head as _____ talks about _____?
- Why did the author tell the story as they did? (e.g., in first person, from that character's point of view, from present looking back? What was their "authorial intent"?)
- If a character has some condition—physical, psychological, emotional—what effect does that have on the story and our perception of the character?

Make
Predictions

67

RATIONALE

In *Between Hope and Havoc* (1995) Frank Smith writes, "We make sense of the world by anticipating what the world is likely to be like. Without predictions, there can be no comprehension; we understand what we anticipate." In short, predicting means making a guess about what will happen next or down the line based on the reader's interpretation of evidence provided within the text. Such active engagement with the text characterizes effective readers and is thus an essential skill to develop in all students.

I think I did pretty well, considering that I started out with a blank piece of paper.

STEVE MARTIN

WHAT TO DO

• Teach students to look for specific words that signal some predictable outcome. For example, if the text uses such phrases or words as *but, in contrast,* or *however,* then the reader knows to look for some kind of contrast of differences. If the reader encounters words like *also, in comparison,* or *similarly,* they know to look for a comparison or similarities.

• Model for students how you use this habit when reading by thinking aloud during a demonstration reading.

• Interrupt a read-aloud or discussion of a text and ask the class or a student what will happen next based on all they know at this time. Press further to find out why they think that will happen.

• Use segments of films they have not seen (e.g., foreign or independent films) and pause them at crucial moments to ask what they think will happen next and why they think that.

• Discuss why an author might use predictable structures throughout a story, then violate those structures later (i.e., do something different from what he did earlier).

• Discuss the types and characteristics of information students can reasonably trust when making predictions. These might include:

  ▶ Word choice (e.g., "Since the description of this character includes the word *beneficent* I will predict that he is a good man and will do the right thing")

207

> ▸ Dramatic structures (e.g., "At this point in the story there will be some resolution of the conflict, since I'm about to move into the final act.")

> ▸ Students' previous experience (e.g., with situations similar to those described in the text, with other texts written by this author or about such events)

> ▸ Students' prior knowledge (e.g., about how people act under such circumstances, about this particular historical period or event)

• Distinguish between predicting what will happen later in a text based on current information and predicting how the text does or will function to create a certain effect in the reader (e.g., "I predict that the identity of the one who committed the crime will be kept a secret until the end, since that is what will create the tension that draws the reader through the text"). (See Reminder 77.)

• Have students use a three-column organizer (Appendix 22). In the left-hand column have them write down events that happen, and in the middle column what they think will happen, adding a short explanation of why they think that will happen and identifying the cause. As they read the text, have them check their predictions against what really happened to evaluate the validity of their predictions. In the third column note any discrepancies between what they thought would happen and what actually did.

• Use predictions as the basis for a class discussion, asking at every turn, "Why do you think that will happen?" or "What do you think that would cause to happen if your prediction came true?"

• Have students make predictions based solely on the title, the cover, blurbs, or the names and descriptions of the characters, supporting their assertions with any available evidence.

SAMPLE SEQUENCE: *MACBETH* NOTES

Directions   Take notes as you read/work through a scene from the play (appoint someone to take notes for your group). Your notes should include the following:

• The name, identity, and role of each character in the scene (e.g., Macbeth, thane of Cawdor, relative of the king, great soldier in the king's army)

• What happens (summary of the action)

• Why it happens

• The implications, consequences, or meaning of the event in the current scene and in the future (e.g., because *X* happened, we predict that *Y* will happen, which may cause *Z* to happen if *A* does not change)

• The event(s) that students in class should add to their *Macbeth* time lines, complete with the brief summary (each group will provide these for the rest of the class to help them complete their time line)

Here is one group's response.

Characters

Porter: A drunken doorman for the king

Macbeth: Scottish general who is conflicted about killing the king and taking over the crown and title thane of Cawdor

Macduff: A Scottish noble

Lennox: One of the Scottish nobles

Summary

The drunken porter is making believe that he is a guardian to the gates of Hell. He opens the gate to Macduff and Lennox, who wish to talk to the king. They talk, then Macduff leaves and when he returns, he announces that the king has been killed.

Why It Happens

Macbeth kills the king because he obviously wants to become the king.

Cause and Effect

Because Macbeth killed the king, he is going to be punished if caught. Because the king is gone, fighting is going to be going on about who the new king should be.

The Event Everyone Should Add to Their Time Line

Macbeth kills the king.

We used notes like these to facilitate our discussion and prepare for a writing assignment in which students explained why, for example, they thought the killing of the king was *the* most important event in the given scene (and why Shakespeare chose to have this event take place off-stage).

Keep a Journal

RATIONALE

Through engagement with others, literature lets us imagine what it would be like to be different.

DENIS DONOGHUE

Journals provide students with a place to do their thinking as they read and discuss what they read. They allow for a wider range of informal but productive responses to reading, thus allowing teachers to ask for more writing without necessarily having to evaluate it all.

WHAT TO DO

• Have students keep their journals out during class so they can stop and take notes, think, or revisit other writings.

• Encourage them to use the journal (aka response log, dialectical journal, daybook, double-entry journal) for any and all of the following reasons:

> ▶ To think
> ▶ To elaborate on their thinking
> ▶ To make connections between this and other texts or ideas
> ▶ To synthesize their different ideas and understandings at a critical juncture in the reading process or the text
> ▶ To develop lists of questions to ask of themselves, the text, their classmates, the teacher, or the author
> ▶ To respond to questions from the teacher, classmates, or the text

• Use the journal in all subject areas to improve student engagement, comprehension, and cognitive capacity.

• Have students use journals to:

> ▶ Prepare for discussion
> ▶ Take notes for a paper
> ▶ Plan a presentation on the text
> ▶ Synthesize reading or discussion of a text

• Instruct students to keep in mind the difference, as they read, between *taking note* and *making notes*. The first approach is passive; they write down the main ideas as they appear. The second is interactive; they not only jot down main ideas but write down connections, insights, questions, observations.

- Provide examples of effective journal writing for a specific assignment.

- Evaluate and respond to journals in a variety of ways depending on your objective:

  ▶ As you walk around the room while they work on an assignment

  ▶ While they work in groups, each student responding to the others' journals (see Reminder 81)

  ▶ Using a rubric that identifies those characteristics of good journal use in your class. This allows for efficient but informative assessment that can improve subsequent use of the journal.

- Have students try using any of the following techniques in the journal to improve reading performance:

  ▶ *Notes and quotes.* In this approach, students find or are given specific quotes from a text that are essential to their understanding of it. They write down the quote on the left-hand side, then write their response to these quotes on the right-hand side.

  ▶ *Three-column organizer* with the following headings: What it is/What it means/Why I think that. Students enter in those details or symbols or observations from the text they are reading, supporting their interpretations with details or quotes.

  ▶ *Cornell Notes format.* This provides room for subsequent response to initial readings. (see Appendixes 5, 6, and 7).

STUDENT EXAMPLES

This is Andrea Wong's journal response to Maya Angelou's "Phenomenal Woman," which I used as part of a larger junior-class unit on *The Scarlet Letter*.

> Maya Angelou is so sure of herself. She walks with her head held high and many don't understand her. She is a phenomenal woman of grace who passes everyone by, women, men, children. . . . She is outstanding in what she does. I wish I had this much confidence in myself. She smiles widely and does not allow anything to bring her head down. She is Maya Angelou, a phenomenal woman, phenomenally.

This sample response log entry from Eric Martin for *Huck Finn* came from the same class later in the year.

> *Chapter 3:* This chapter reminded me of an important lesson of childhood. When we were young, our imaginations ran wild and we would often mistake imagination with reality. The boys all got their hopes so high up because they were going to rob diamonds and see 400 elephants. But when they came charging down the hill they were faced with plain old reality. It's great to have a creative imagination, but you shouldn't expect those things to occur in real life.
>
> *Chapter 6:* The life that Huck lives with his father seems a very good one. No rules, no manners. If you're hungry, go fishing. If only Huck had a good father. Strange, how adaptable the boy is. At first he couldn't stand living with the widow, or going to school, but he got 'round to liking it. He even says that he got used to living with his Pa, and that it was nice, except for the cowhiding. If I were the boy I would hate everything about living with my father if he beat me. Huck is good at looking at the good things he has.

Annotate
Texts

RATIONALE

Having students annotate or otherwise mark up texts is one of the most powerful ways of turning them into active readers. Knowing how to annotate in a way that will improve their reading and overall academic literacy is essential to students as they encounter increasingly sophisticated texts that they use for a wide range of purposes (e.g., research). We must not leave this teaching to any one subject area but instead use the natural context of our own classes (e.g., history) to instruct them in this important technique.

He listens well who takes notes.

DANTE

WHAT TO DO

Recall that there are different types of annotating: mental and marginal. When we write, our internal critic says, "Oh that's a brilliant idea," or "There's a better way to say that." While reading, we have another internal voice that responds both personally ("Oh, that reminds me of when I went fishing that time!") and critically ("I see why the writer would organize the story that way but I don't think it works.") Sometimes we cannot actually write on the page, in which case we can make annotations either in our heads or in temporary places such as on Post-it notes we stick to the pages of the book. Written response in journals and logs is another form of annotating a text.

Keep in mind that annotations should, when assigned, address a skill or specific type of content. The discipline of reading for a purpose and annotating the text with this purpose in mind is critical if students are to learn to train their attention on specific details of texts.

Have students use annotation in the following ways, all of which will help them to pay closer attention to the text and thus read more effectively. (Note that each example depends on the student having a photocopy of the text to allow for such work.)

- *Coding the text.* Depending on the purpose of the reading, students develop (or are given) a set of coded symbols to use throughout the text. This exercise is more directed than most but is useful if a specific set of skills or ideas are being taught. For example, if a teacher were teaching the students the parts of an argument, the reader might identify by coded letters or symbols each component of the argument as it appears in the text.

- *Revealing patterns.* Annotations might focus on grammatical patterns, sound patterns, imagery, or structural design of the text. Annotations in the form of underlines and marginal comments are most appropriate.

- *Underlining meaningful passages.* As a tool for discussion and a step toward greater independence in reading, students are given the text and told to mark it up as they wish. The next step is to ask what they marked up and why, using their annotations as an entrée into a critical reading discussion.

- *Collaborative annotation.* Photocopy a text (see the example of the Wilfred Owen poem shown in Figure 69-1) and give each student a copy. After they read and annotate their copy, putting their name on the top, they pass it along to another member of their group or the class who then rereads the text and adds their own remarks, questions, or observations about meaning, patterns, or design. When everyone in the group has completed the cycle, they then compare and draw conclusions from their comments, which the group then reports to the class or writes about in a short reflection.

- *"Publishing" annotations.* Presenting one's ideas is a form of authentic publication. I sometimes photocopy a poem or passage onto transparencies and have groups annotate the text right on the overhead transparency. They then must get up and present their annotations using the overhead. The Wilfred Owen example included here was presented on an overhead and used to teach the class how to approach the text.

Keep in mind that annotations lend themselves to being discussed in class. Such discussions are more about *how* to read than the text itself, since they put the readers in the metacognitive role of reflecting on and explaining their own reading process as applied to the text.

Morgan Price 2°

who?
(the commercials?)

"Dulce et Decorum Est"° *by Wilfred Owen (1893-1918)*   ° *"It is sweet and fitting."* (Latin)
1918

WWI

Bent double, like old beggars under sacks,
Knock-kneed, coughing like hags, we cursed through sludge,
Till on the haunting flares we turned our backs
And towards our distant rest began to trudge.
Men marched asleep. Many had lost their boots
But limped on, blood-shod. All went lame; all blind;
Drunk with fatigue; deaf even to hoots
Of tired, outstripped Five Nines* that dropped behind.   *5.9-in. caliber shells

the men are all young soldiers, but he compares them to older, worn men; they've grown up fast; 'are taking care of themselves
forced into early maturity by brutality of men's action
(5)
seen things & done things far beyond their years; aging them too fast.

describes what happened to all the men; they became used to the sounds; torture
became immune to horrors of war
Like rehearsed motion

Gas! Gas! Quick, boys!—an ecstasy of fumbling,
Fitting the clumsy helmets just in time;   (10)
But someone still was yelling out and stumbling,
And flound'ring like a man in fire or lime. . .   → *compares gas to fire; gas causes fire*
Dim, through the misty panes* and thick green light,   *window of gas mask
As under a green sea, I saw him drowning.

→ *compares gas to a sea*

In all my dreams, before my helpless sight,   (15)
He plunges at me, guttering, choking, drowning.   → *last moments of gassed soldier*

nightmare & waking up in cold sweats. You never forget.

If in smothering dreams you too could pace
Behind the wagon that we flung him in,
And watch the white eyes writhing in his face,
His hanging face, like a devil's sick of sin;   (20)   *describes face as so twisted that it looks like a devil sick of sin, but a devil would never be sick of sin; this man has now entered hell; there is no turning back*
If you could hear, at every jolt, the blood
Come gargling from the froth-corrupted lungs,
Obscene as cancer, bitter as the cud
Of vile, incurable sores on innocent tongues,--
My friend, you would not tell with such high zest   (25)
To children ardent for some desperate glory,
The old Lie: Dulce et decorum est
Pro patria mori.*

amount of sin witnessed in war comparable to sin witnessed by the lord of sin
A Devil wouldn't be sick of sin, it's an image so beyond our comprehension just like this death. We can't even imagine it.

it's a nightmare
their whole thought process
compared gas poisoning to other diseases, and it's worse
you can't forget

if you had experienced this, you wouldn't tell all these young children it's an honor to die for your country; not that gratifying & wonderful

The old lie
"It is sweet and fitting to die for one's country."

Hide truth from public, too horrible to share.

Close Reading Activity:

1. Read the poem.
2. Note your first reactions to any aspect of the poem.
3. Pass your paper to the person to your right. Add your responses to the previous reader's responses; that is, react to their comments.
4. Keep reacting, in writing, to each other responses until you get back your original paper.

FIGURE 69-1   Seniors in Elaine Caret's AP English class first annotated Owen's poem on their own, then, as shown here, they discussed the poem and integrated their annotations into one sheet as a means of looking more closely at the text and making their thinking visible to others.

70 Take Good Notes

RATIONALE

Taking good notes is not only an essential skill but a powerful tool for readers. Taking notes makes the student a more active reader, forcing them to evaluate whether a quote or idea is important enough to write down, or how it relates to what they already know or have noted. You can use note taking in a variety of settings for different reasons. While you or others read aloud, for example, students can take notes to help them listen more closely and minimize distracting behaviors. In short, note taking is one of the most useful strategies and skills students can use to record, organize, remember, and respond to what they read.

WHAT TO DO

Encourage students to take notes

- While reading
- During lecture
- As someone reads aloud
- During presentations
- While participating in group and/or class discussion
- While watching a video used to support their reading of a printed text

Teach them to take notes

- In outline format (see Reminder 83), both formal (e.g., alphanumeric format) and informal (e.g., bullets)
- Using the Cornell system(s) (see Appendixes 5, 6, and 7)
- In clusters or webs
- In lists
- Using quick-write responses to reading

- In graphic formats (e.g., maps, graphs, time lines)
- In margins (i.e., as annotations *on* the text; see Reminder 69)
- Using a combination of all the above according to the reader's needs or teacher's goal
- With the aid of a tape recorder (for students with special needs)

Explain that they should take notes

- To synthesize (see Reminder 84)
- To summarize (see Reminder 84)
- To remember (see Reminder 84)
- To use in or help them write a paper on the text they read
- To organize
- To reflect
- To review
- To evaluate their understanding or their thinking process

Familiarize students with the Cornell note-taking system (see Figures 70-1 and 70-2). The Cornell system and its different variations all share a similar format: they involve using a page divided lengthwise into two sections (one-third column on the left side, two-thirds column on the right). Some methods require or encourage students to use an additional box at the bottom of the page to sum up or respond to the ideas on that page. The two-thirds column, which I'll call the note-taking area, is used during reading to identify essential information, jot down questions as they occur to the reader, and record any other information that might be of use later. The one-third column, which I will refer to as the connections column, allows readers to return to their notes and make essential or more sophisticated connections. Questions readers posed while reading might be answered or refined in the connections column. Also, readers might add additional reference information (e.g., "See also page 43 in *World of Difference* re: Gandhi's methods"). Included here are two student examples of note-taking using the Cornell method.

Identify for students the reason they are taking notes and the uses to which these notes will be put. This orients them to the type of information they should look for and the way they should note it. For example, if they are taking notes while reading an essay on the life cycle or the idea of leadership in *Julius Caesar*, they should know to specifically identify quotes by, first, using quotation marks, and by including the page and line numbers if appropriate.

217

Remember that, ideally, students should learn to take notes in different ways for different purposes early in the year in order to achieve initial mastery of this skill. Then as the year unfolds the teacher should encourage students to adapt these skills and styles as the student chooses. Subsequent discussions or evaluations might include asking students why they decided to take their notes in that particular format and to reflect on how effective it was for a given assignment.

Cornell Note Taking Form

Connections/Observations

Elements of a sonnet

What purpose does rhyming serve?
Is it a poem if it doesn't rhyme?

the rhyming words seem to be related· time/prime, night/ (black)/white

Reading Notes

14 lines: 3 quatrains,
          1 couplet

Quatrain: 4 line unit
              in a poem

Couplet: last two lines rhyme

Rhyme structure : AB
example: AB
        time (a)   CD
      → night (b) CD
        prime (a) EF
        white (b) EF
                   FG

Themes: Time
    Examples: count the clock 12:1
             tells the time 12:1
             the wastes of time 12:10
             past prime 12:3
             barren of leaves 12:5
             white and bristly beard 12:8
             erst 12:6

Qs to ask when reading a poem
  •any images?
  • How is it made?
  • What are they trying to tell me?
  • Is there a key example they want me to understand?
  •what do certain words mean?

Summary/Analysis How to read a sonnet/poem:
The first thing to do is just read it straight through.
Then look up any words you don't know or understand.

FIGURE 70-1 Students in my sophomore class took notes on initial comments about sonnets to help them understand the poetic form as well as to develop the skill of note-taking. We talked as much about how to take notes as how sonnets worked.

Connections/Observations	Reading Notes
·Why do they split them into prokaryotes and eukaryotes?	Kingdom of Organisms ·· based on their cell structure all living organisms are either prokaryotes or eukaryotes
·Why are they only 5 kingdoms?	· Look @ p238 Tbl. 10.1 summarizes major differences ·5 kingdoms
· How can we be sure how old earth is?	1. Prokaryote ----prokaryotes 1 2. Plantae ---- plants (eukaryote) 4 3. Animalia---- animals (eukaryote) 5
·What exactly is Millers Apparatus?	4. Fungi ----fungi (eukaryote) 3 5. Protista---- algae, protoza, slime molds, etc. (eukaryote 2
· What are stromatolites?	·Origin of Diversity ·· life began 3.5 billion years ago ·· micro fossils - stromatolites of western Australia about 3.5 b.y.o · Earth 4.6 billion years old ··· early atmosphere composed of volcanic gases: CH_4, amonia gas, methane gas, H_2, hydrogen gas Look @ p 245 Fig. 10.20 Millers Apparatus

Summary/Analysis

FIGURE 70-2   Following the direct and modeled instruction on note-taking with sonnets, I required students to demonstrate their understanding through independent application of the skills in a different class. Here is Erica Cook's example from her science class.

71 Retell the Text

RATIONALE

I should but teach him how to tell my story.

WILLIAM SHAKESPEARE, OTHELLO

This strategy provides an opportunity for the reader to process what they have read by organizing and explaining it to someone else. Retelling texts, whether they are expository or narrative, develops students' story grammar, because they must learn to identify what is crucial in the text and how the sequence of that information determines its meaning. The activity challenges them to remember information and events, making them interact with the information from a variety of perspectives: their own, their audience's, and the author's. Retelling also reinforces good reading, because to do it they will have to read the text repeatedly, getting more fluent each time. Finally, retelling is its own form of assessment, since the students' performance confirms that they read it and reveals the extent to which they truly understood what they read. Research suggests that this technique increases both the quantity and quality of what is comprehended.

WHAT TO DO

• When introducing this strategy, clearly explain to students how to do it and why, then model the technique for them. While demonstrating how to do it, the teacher should also comment on how he or she determined what to include in the retelling, why they performed it a certain way, or why they used a particular technique (e.g., outlining) in retelling the text.

• Have student read through the text several times to identify and then internalize the elements that are most important. Using one of the graphic organizers included here (see appendixes) or their own system to organize the information, students must then decide how to deliver the retelling using their own words and style. Whether using storytelling techniques or a formal description, they should look for places to provide emphasis and use such devices as transition words. They may find it useful to prepare visual aids for themselves and/or the class.

• Consider beginning with shorter, easier texts and, as students develop competence, move on to longer or more complicated texts.

- Consider having students do their first retellings in writing, in less formal settings such a journal; as they learn to identify the important elements and sequence them in effective ways, students can do retellings in pairs, progressing to small groups and the entire class when they are ready.

- Assess retellings based on audience understanding and appreciation. Allow time for follow-up discussion of content and delivery. Consider developing a rubric for the assignment that the teller and the audience can use to guide their discussion and thereby improve the reteller's performance.

STUDENT EXAMPLES

In the following example, taken from her learning log, Laurel Hackleman retells Gary Soto's poem "The Levee" in order to better her understanding.

> At seventeen Fresno was the worst place to grow up. I hated it so much because there was nothing to do but drive around. Oftentimes I thought about putting nails under a neighbors car or putting my fingers in the box fan. The only thing that would comfort me was to drive out to the levee and watch the water. It was something that would always be constant. I would listen to the radio and if the song wasn't on I would talk to myself. Stepping on leaves and counting shadows would supply maybe a few minutes of entertainment.

Freshman Stacey Saber uses retelling (in writing) to help her grasp the opening of Homer's *Odyssey*:

> As I sat on the soft, white sand, looking at the crashing dark blue sea, I longed for my mortal, yet beautiful wife, and my home in Ithaca which I had left seventeen years ago to fight the Trojan war. Calypso, the beautiful yet seductive goddess, who does not compare to my wife, has held me prisoner on this remote Island with the hopes of me falling in love with her. My wife and I have too strong a bond between us for it to break for another woman. I sometimes thought I should give up hope, yet I know in my heart that my loving wife is still faithful to me as I am to her. The Gods liked me yet I was still prisoner. There was only one God who loathed me, Poseidon, for blinding his son Polyphemus.
>   After my eighth year held captive, Athena, a wonderful goddess, went to Zeus, concerned about me. Athena told Zeus

her thoughts on my predicament, she felt sorry for me, being the kindhearted goddess that she is. Zeus carefully thought this matter over, and made a good decision. He sent his messenger son Hermes to Calypso. Hermes commanded Calypso, who was now convinced I loved her selfish personality, to free my aching soul, to find my true love, my wife. Calypso did not like this idea, although she thought I would stay with her on the isolated island even when permitted to leave.

As I wept on the secluded island, Calypso dramatically approached me and announced that I was free to leave her and the island. I had already suffered enough and was more than ready to leave. So, I braved the glistening blue ocean, and its soaring waves for seventeen torturous, yet optimistic days. On the eighteenth day Poseidon wanted revenge on his biggest enemy, me. A land-destroying storm swept over the ocean and seemed to erupt with the loud crashing clatter of lightning and thunder. I thought I did not have a chance, the winds were just too strong for my mortal, yet godlike, self. Luckily for me a sea goddess had pity on me and saved me from the terrible storm. I grabbed onto her flowing, white veil and she guided me to land, where Poseidon could not reach me.

Perform
the Text

RATIONALE

Performance of a text develops readers' capacity for imagination and interpretation. Performing a text also offers useful ways to help all students get inside the text to understand its structure, language, characters, and meaning through close engagement and manipulation. Through occupation of different roles—dramatist, director, characters—students learn to read the text for different purposes and to anchor their thinking in the text. Performing a text, whether a play that has already been written or a script students have created themselves (by adapting a story, a poem, a textbook chapter, or a historical document), offer students the ideal way to think in threes: they can hear/see it, perform it, and read it.

A book is meant not only to be read, but to haunt you, to importune you like a lover or a parent, to stick in your teeth like a piece of gristle.

ANATOLE BROYARD

WHAT TO DO

• Have students engage in Word for Word. Named for a dramatic troupe, this technique requires taking a literary text, usually a short story, and adapting it into a dramatic script, complete with stage directions. Every word of the original text is traditionally included, even the dialogue attributions ("he said") and expository description. The actors can divide the script up so that several different people speak lines from the same sentence to make for a richer arrangement of voices or for certain dramatic effect.

• Have students annotate a text for performance (e.g., code it for how to deliver lines [e.g., yell], what to do [e.g., pause], or who should speak) to force closer reading of the text.

• Keep in mind that dramatic interpretation offers, through movement or reading aloud, opportunities to perform a text from multiple perspectives to better understand the author's intentions, the characters' desires, or the text's meaning. Such interpretation can extend to all curriculum areas: by having students perform a historical encounter or even a scientific process ("OK, everyone in this row is an X chromosome . . . ") students must look closely to the script for the answers to such performance questions as "Who am I?" "How am I supposed to act?" "What do I want most?" "Under what circumstances is this action taking place?"

• Don't limit performace to dramatic action: musical interpretations of texts can, if thoughtfully executed, allow students to explain certain aspects (e.g., mood, structure, action) of a text. Similarly, don't limit performance to words: pantomime and tableau offer other viable and appropriate means of performing a text.

• Keep in mind that all performances of a text should remain anchored in the text. In short, whatever form the performance takes, students should be able to answer the question, "Where in the text do you find evidence that this is what they felt, did, or thought?" This will ensure that students actually read the text they are performing (and potentially adapting or interpreting) closely and accurately.

• Have students recast the text into a different context for performance: for example, take a novel, a play, or a historical event they are studying (e.g., *Lord of the Flies*, the Constitution) and adapt it into a trial which requires that all witnesses and lawyers draw their evidence, ideas, and other information from the text (and other approved supplemental materials).

• Have students perform a text as a teacher, a character (in the text), a historical persona, a narrator, journalist, or invented persona.

• Use the text as a jump-off point for a theatrical simulation that will help them better understand their reading.

• Have the class read aloud using one of the following techniques:

  ▶ *Choral reading.* This demands that one person or group read a portion of the text while others read a different segment. In the interplay between the two (or more) voices there emerges a dramatic tone that reveals something useful about the text they are trying to understand.

  ▶ *Reader's Theatre.* This requires that dramatic energy be invested in the delivery of lines and facial expression to evoke character.

STUDENT EXAMPLE

The following example was created by a group of students who were reading *The Scarlet Letter*.

CHAPTER 10
THE LEECH AND HIS PATIENT

SETTING: Roger Chillingworth and Mr. Dimmesdale's house in town

Physician:	This man pure as they deem him—all spiritual as he seems—hath inherited a strong animal nature from his father or his mother. Let us dig a little further in the direction of this vein.

Mr. Dimmesdale:	Where, my kind doctor, did you gather those herbs, with such a dark flabby leaf?
Physician:	Even in the graveyard here at hand. They are new to me. I found them growing on a grave, which bore no tombstone, nor other memorial of the dead man, saved this ugly weed, that have taken upon themselves to keep him in remembrance. They grew out of his heart, and typify, it may be, some hideous secret that was buried with him, and which he had done better to confess during his lifetime.
Mr. Dimmesdale:	Perchance he earnestly desired it, but could not.
Physician:	And wherefore, not since all the power of nature call so earnestly for the confession of sin, that these black weeks have sprung up out of the buried heart, to make manifest an unspoken crime?
Dimmesdale:	That, good sir, is but a fantasy of yours, there can be, if I forebode a right, no power, short of the divine mercy, to disclose, whether by uttered words, or by type or emblem, the secrets that may be buried with the human heart. The heart, making itself guilty of such secrets, must perforce hold them, until the day when all hidden things shall be revealed. Nor have I so read or interpreted Holy Writ, as to understand that the disclosure of human thoughts and deeds, then to be made, is intended as a part of the retribution. That, surely, were a shallow view of it. No; these revelations, unless I greatly err, are meant merely to promote the intellectual satisfaction of all intelligent beings, who will stand waiting on that day, to see the dark problem of this life made plain. A knowledge of men's hearts will be needful to the completest solution of that problem. And I conceive, moreover, that the hearts holding such miserable secrets as you speak of will yield them up, at that last day, not with reluctance, but with a joy unutterable.
Chillingworth:	Then why not reveal them here? Why should not the guilty ones sooner avail themselves of this unutterable solace?

73 Draw the Action

RATIONALE

Students must develop the ability to see what they read, to "build envisionments" of the information. This strategy allows for alternative learning styles but also provides a different route for engagement—some kids who don't like to read love to draw. The strategy's primary value is that it develops a new strategy and a different way of thinking about text and how it functions, since students must translate the words into a different form (symbols, images, time lines).

WHAT TO DO

• Consider that this activity can be done in a variety of ways, as a full-scale art project (e.g., drawings detailing the French Revolution, the life cycle of a cell, etc.) or as a functional "drawing to think" assignment that is assigned, completed, and presented/submitted during the period. The latter is beneficial in that it deemphasizes the drawing talent—students understand that the point is to get their ideas across. The teacher also might pass out butcher paper and have students draw the action in, for example, *Romeo and Juliet* to help them see how the text's design relates to the action and the characters. Depending on your setup, you can do this in stages, drawing the action in the play, for example, act by act, using the story map to visually narrate the action for basic comprehension (what happens) and to facilitate class discussion about the patterns and themes that arise and return throughout the play. Options include but are not limited to charts, graphs, maps, flowcharts, time lines, webs, and illustrations.

• Have students do the assignment on overhead transparencies; one means of assessment could then be to have the individual or group "publish" their work on the overhead, in an informal presentation. This allows others to see how their peers think and how they approached the same assignment from potentially different directions.

• If you can, have students post their drawings on the wall. This not only celebrates their creation but more importantly provides you with readily available tools to refer to in subsequent discussions, making of your class walls a living, evolving text that teaches as it honors.

STUDENT EXAMPLES

Nickola Shakhour brings her personal style to drawing the action (see Figure 73-1). Steve Gomez's sequence from *Macbeth* (see Figure 73-2 a, b, and c) also clearly demonstrates how much insight art can bring to reading; moreover, because he was able to use his artistic talent, Steve brought to this piece of work a measure of interest and commitment that he might not have mustered had he been limited to writing.

FIGURE 73-1   Nickola Shakhour's cartoon both summarizes and shows insight into Shirley Jackson's story "The Lottery."

FIGURE 73-2a

FIGURE 73-2b

Steve Gomez's images reveal how much insight
students can bring to a text when given a range
of response options.

FIGURE 73-2c

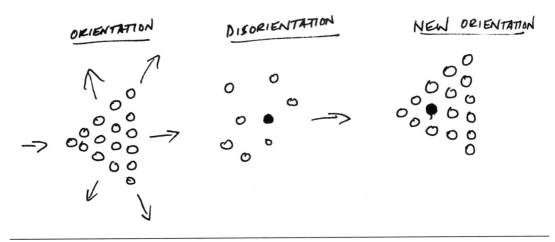

FIGURE 73-3   This simple graphic allowed us to examine what was happening within Marquez's story "The Most Handsome Drowned Man." Asking students to represent the action of the story using pool balls allows them to see things in a different but useful way.

The third example is quite different. I came up with this idea when my students read a series of stories in which a person comes into a community and really shakes things up. Using the analogy of billiard balls getting broken up with a cue ball allowed us to think about the action in useful ways. (See Figure 73-3.) We could look at the resulting diagram and ask who the cue ball represented, and how his actions affected everything else.

74

Chunk the Text

RATIONALE

My friend Carol Prater says, when we are doing a big project (like writing our book *I'll Grant You That*), that we need to "eat the chocolate elephant one bite at a time." This is an apt metaphor to apply to difficult texts. The chunk-the-text strategy allows students to read with greater independence since, using it, they can break a text into meaningful but shorter units. When I was learning Arabic, all the words sounded like one long word until I learned to see and hear the gaps between the words and to break the sentences into smaller, more manageable units.

WHAT TO DO

Depending on the nature of the text—i.e., length, type, structure, genre—determine if you can or need to chunk it down by:

- Paragraph
- Stanza
- Scene
- Line
- Sentence segments (if the text features long, complicated sentences)

Introduce the notion of chunking by using simple, accessible texts in different genres and following this sequence:

- Introduce with examples and rationale for when, why, and how to use
- Model using a text similar to the one the class will read
- Guide them through an initial practice and evaluate the degree of mastery before moving on to independent application of the technique
- Have students apply the ideas and techniques on their own and follow up with evaluation of their work to determine mastery or the next instructional step to get them closer to mastery

Have students evaluate the decisions they make when chunking so that they extend their awareness of what they do as they read.

Chunk the text by rewriting or annotating it into discrete units to see the ideas more clearly. Consider this example excerpted from Lincoln's Gettysburg Address. The chunks are represented in the form of a restructuring of the speech into a found poem (i.e., I recast the speech as a poem).

> Four score and seven
> Years ago our fathers
>   brought forth a new nation,
>   conceived in Liberty, and
>   dedicated to the proposition that
> All men are created equal.
>
> Now we are
>   Engaged in a great civil war, testing
>   Whether that nation, or any nation so
>   Conceived and so
>   Dedicated, can long endure.
> We are met on a great battlefield of that war.
> We have come to dedicate a portion of that field,
> As a final resting place for those who here
> Gave their lives
> That that nation might live.
>
> * * *
>
> We cannot dedicate
> We cannot consecrate
> We cannot hallow—this ground. The brave men,
> Living and dead, who struggled here
> Have consecrated it, far above
> Our poor power
> To add or detract.
> The world will little note, nor long
> Remember what we say here, but it can
> Never forget what they did here.

Or this example from Macbeth:

> If you can look into the seeds of time,
> And say which grain will grow and which will not,
> Speak then to me, who neither beg nor fear
> Your favours nor your hate.

First Witch   Hail!
Second Witch   Hail!
Third Witch   Hail!
First Witch   Lesser than Macbeth,   and greater.
Second Witch   Not so happy,   yet much happier.
Third Witch   Thou shalt get kings,   though thou be none:
So all hail, Macbeth and Banquo!

Take a moment to reflect on your reading and teaching. You may find the following discussion points useful, or you can come up with your own:

• Write a summary of the last section. Include in this summary three main ideas—techniques, strategies, tools—that relate to your own classes.

• Which reminders from the preceding section might help you the most?

• Looking ahead to the next section, consider its title and, before you begin reading, create your own list of reminders for this topic. After checking yours with mine, discuss which of these reminders—from your list and mine—will help you and your students the most.

Develop Their Own

Reading Capacity

The artist speaks to our capacity for delight and wonder, to the sense of mystery surrounding our lives: to our sense of pity, and beauty, and pain.

—JOSEPH CONRAD

Students use images to explain what is happening in a particular scene in *Macbeth*.

My objective throughout the course of this book is to develop in teachers the ability to teach students to read well and to independently develop their capacity as readers. Capacity is something that must not only be developed but maintained and enhanced. Just as the poet Rilke wrote that each time he began a new poem he felt himself a beginner (because every poem presented its own unique set of challenges to him as a poet), so we come to each text and read it as if for the first time. Our success with texts depends on our capacity to persevere in the face of potential frustration or confusion, to navigate the page with confidence and intelligence.

We want our students to be able to respond the way sophomore Erica Cook did when she wrote, "I think I have made real progress this semester. I can concentrate a lot better now. The focus and determination to read well are all there. I don't even take my eyes away from my book when I'm distracted. I block out everything but my book." Avram Lum, a sophomore in that same class, wrote about another crucial capacity, saying that early on writing about and explaining what he read was difficult, that he "had trouble making my thoughts come out well. I had my ideas straight but writing it out was hard for me. I have since improved my ability to think and write about what I read." For many of my students, the capacity to simply focus their attention and take themselves seriously as readers remains the first serious challenge; as one student reminded me, their mind is often elsewhere: "See my book was ordered last week so I don't have a book right now. It's probably better like this anywayz, my mind is some where else right now. See I got sprung of some stupid *beep* for a long time and I'm finally getting over her, so my head is all screwed up right now." Another student, Jason, remarked, "Today I was only distracted by one small problem, I had a hangnail and it took me about five minutes to get it out." Sometimes these personal and organizational challenges lead to interesting encounters with books: "I didn't bring my usual book today because I left it on my floor at home so I randomly selected *Cowboys Are My Weakness* off the shelf. It is a chick book about her experiences with cowboys or so I thought. However, I soon realized that it was about men and women's different views, aspects, and opinions on certain situations."

The most important capacities we can develop in our students are the belief in the value of reading and their ability to read any text they encounter. As Alejandro wrote, "A good reader is a person who can pick up almost any piece of literature and read and comprehend it. As an experienced reader, I can read a lot of different types of books and comprehend them. Also, good readers can find books they like to read fast. I have more difficulty finding books that I like because I don't have as much confidence as a really good reader."

The reminders in the following section all strive to help you develop just such confidence in your students as they move toward independence and mastery.

Read Different
Types of Text

75

RATIONALE

Good readers are able to read a text in different ways for different purposes; they can also read a variety of types of text (e.g., poetic, literary, informational, persuasive). Students must develop the same capacities, reading texts of different types and levels of difficulty. They must learn when, how, and why they must adopt new strategies toward texts; indeed they must learn that different types of texts require different or at least adjusted reading strategies depending on the demands they make on the reader. It is also worth noting that readers go through stages, as Linda Robinson (1998) reminds us:

> Understanding how a reader's purpose for reading shifts as she becomes a more mature reader helps teachers understand their students' reading behaviors. For instance, an eighth grader may choose to reread *Stuart Little*, a book she read in unconscious delight as a third grader, but she will not read it aesthetically to analyze how E. B. White created his characters and established a believable fantasy. It explains how two students reading Robman Philbrick's *Freak the Mighty* might respond to the question "What did you like about this book?" so differently that a teacher might wonder if they read the same book.

If you read a biography, remember that the truth is never fit for publication.

GEORGE BERNARD SHAW

WHAT TO DO

• Use the Types of Text list (Appendix 43) as a guide to the different types of text—e.g., genres and subgenres—to include in your class.

• Integrate the following examples into your curriculum to complement the textbook you use:

   ▶ Poetry

   ▶ Essays

   ▶ Newspaper articles

   ▶ Speeches

   ▶ Web sites

- ‣ Letters
- ‣ Novels
- ‣ Biographies

- Use these different types of texts to help your students:
  - ‣ Acquire or improve textual skills (see Reminder 77)
  - ‣ Expand their understanding of the subject
  - ‣ Read from a range of perspectives about the same subject
  - ‣ Increase or maintain student attention and engagement

- Make the different types of text talk to each other by comparing—in writing or through discussion—what they say, how they say it, what they mean, how they mean it, how they work (individually and comparatively).

- Read them in different ways at different times. For example you might use different types of text to:
  - ‣ Read aloud to your class to begin or end the class with a biography or story that somehow relates to your curriculum.
  - ‣ Read aloud or have them bring in and read to the class articles from the newspaper to supplement your current discussion or allow for discussion of current events.
  - ‣ Prepare them to read other, more sophisticated texts.
  - ‣ Make room for the imagination in the classroom (e.g., use of historical or issues-related fiction).

Write to
Improve Reading

76

RATIONALE

In his book *Textual Power* Robert Scholes (1986) argues that no reading of a text is complete until the reader makes their own text from it. This might be done in any of a number of ways: discussing what we read, translating the ideas into some visual explanation or response, or writing. We might write to summarize or clarify, to extend or commence our thinking about the text. Writing is inherently active; to write is almost certainly to think. To paraphrase a remark the poet William Stafford made about poetry, writing invites a certain type of attention. The use of writing as a means of thinking, of forcing readers to pay attention through interaction with the text, should play a key role in any balanced curriculum, across subject areas.

> Those big-shot writers . . . could never dig the fact that there are more salted peanuts consumed than caviar.
>
> MICKEY SPILLANE

WHAT TO DO

- Encourage students to use writing before, while, and after they read to help them make sense of the text. Such writing can be informal, taking the form of:

    - Journal entries
    - Quick writes
    - Notes
    - Annotations

    More imaginative forms of written response include:

    - Letters (written to or as if the student were a character in the text)
    - Poems
    - Personal essays (about experiences related to the text)
    - Scripts
    - Short stories

- In their writing about texts, encourage students to:

> ▶ Paraphrase
> ▶ Imitate
> ▶ Speculate
> ▶ Predict
> ▶ Make notes (and thus connections)
> ▶ Reflect

• Keep in mind that writing provides valuable opportunities to develop students':

> ▶ Elaboration strategies, as students respond to questions and prompts the teacher provides and internalize the habits of inquiry
> ▶ Thinking skills, as the act of writing about a text requires that readers make meaning
> ▶ Verbal articulation, as students use their writing as a script to help them discuss their ideas more confidently
> ▶ Textual intelligence, as students use writing to examine and respond to different aspects of the texts they read—this might take the form of imitating, recasting, or reflecting on the texts
> ▶ Imaginative capacity, as students occupy the role of writer/creator, one which invites them to see the inherent creativity in all types of writing

STUDENT EXAMPLES

The following response from Courtney Neale shows her using—and developing—her writing ability to engage with and better understand *The Adventures of Huckleberry Finn*.

TRANSITION BETWEEN ADOLESCENCE AND ADULTHOOD

The book *Huck Finn* is a story about a young boy and a runaway slave. The book tackles a number of different issues including race, abuse, and the act of growing up and challenges you face while doing so. Mark Twain does an incredible job writing from the point of view of Huck a young boy between the ages of 12–14.

One issue that Huck deals with is that of his father. Huck is in constant fear of his father possibly coming back. His father was an abusive drunk who beat Huck anytime something was wrong. I feel that this among many other situations forced Huck to become more grown up and leave the stages of Childhood. He had to try to hide this from other people and though not very successful it forced him to come up with elaborate stories on what happened.

When Huck's father finally came back and took Huck away this also pushed him further into adolescence. He had to basically live on his own. His father was there but was always drunk. Huck had to constantly try to keep away from his father's fists. Finally Huck agreed he wasn't going to stay there anymore. He devised a plan to escape from his father's clutches. He faked his own murder and ran away and set sale on the river. Now to plan and fake your own murder isn't a normal issue for a young boy to face. It forces him to grow up and step outside himself, so he could make it look like it really happened. He had to be grown up about what he was doing. He no longer had someone to rely on and help him.

The last step of completely transferring to adolescence was when Huck was finally off on his own. He no longer could turn to anyone for help. Everything he did to survive was done on his own. He couldn't afford to screw up and possibly lose control. If this at all happened he was stuck because he couldn't go to town, they thought he was dead, and he was alone. This pushed him into adolescence more because the level of responsibility he took upon himself is way too much for a child.

Today kids make many transitions and have many different things to push them to do so. But one that is the most significant I feel is the transition from middle school to high school. During this time you discover more about both whom you are and what you want to be. Not to mention you are struggling more to be accepted by society and/or friends. Kids at these ages are very judgmental and I feel that this transition can either make or break an individual. You can get in the rut of being depressed, lonely, and not accepted, or you could take what you learn about yourself and put it into effect. Figure out your place and stay there. Find your group of friends that accepts you for you and your fine don't pretend to be something your not.

Here we see sophomore Shawna Nelson's poetic response to our discussion of Macbeth's insomnia.

AWAKENING NIGHT

Darkness burrowing
like a mole that tip
toes around my pillow
and steals the hushed
casket embracing my
restless soul. My eyes
that throw away all
my days, unshaded
in all deep thought;
forgetfulness. The
sound of waves and
bees murmuring in strange
winds and seas. Sky is
always pure as water.
Leisurely I prance through
sand and live out my
memories by night. I've
thought of all my turns,
and still I lay sleepless.
From heaven I am torn
in a heart beat into a whole
brand new day to live out my dreams
during the day and in remembrance
in the night I play.

Develop Textual Intelligence

77

RATIONALE

Contemporary texts include a wide range of features. Thanks to computers, texts are designed in new and sometimes complicated ways. Different writers and publishers use different devices and structures. "Textual intelligence" is my term for the skills involved in evaluating and knowing how to read the various types of text.

The last thing we find in making a book is to know what we must put first.

BLAISE PASCAL

WHAT TO DO

- Teach students to ask the following questions when they encounter a new text, especially one with complex or unfamiliar design features:

  ▶ How is the author/publisher using typography? (e.g., what does it mean when a word is in **boldface** and when it is in *italic*?)

  ▶ What genre best characterizes this book? (e.g., *Angela's Ashes* reads like a novel due to novelistic devices, but it is a memoir)

  ▶ What questions do I need to ask when reading such a text?

  ▶ How is language working in this text? (e.g., why is the writer using this particular style?)

  ▶ How is the text designed? (e.g., is it broken up into small units, each one identified by a bold subheading?)

  ▶ What is the best way to read this type of text in this context?

  ▶ What is the relationship between the main body of text and the peripheral texts (e.g., words, images, graphics, illustrations) that also appear?

  ▶ What devices or features is the writer using to convey or influence meaning in this text?

  ▶ Where do I look to find the main ideas in the text and in each section/paragraph?

  ▶ What words (e.g., transition words) signal crucial moments?

  ▶ What support does this particular text offer me as a reader? (e.g., sidebars, indexes, glossaries, notes)

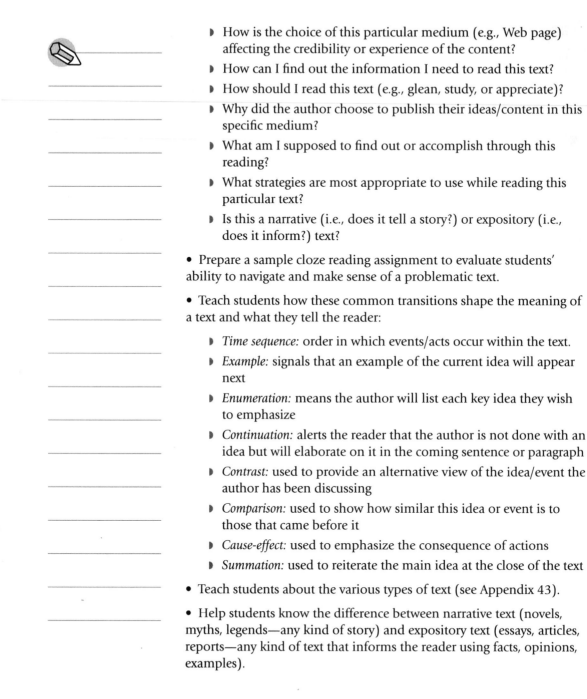

> ▸ How is the choice of this particular medium (e.g., Web page) affecting the credibility or experience of the content?

> ▸ How can I find out the information I need to read this text?

> ▸ How should I read this text (e.g., glean, study, or appreciate)?

> ▸ Why did the author choose to publish their ideas/content in this specific medium?

> ▸ What am I supposed to find out or accomplish through this reading?

> ▸ What strategies are most appropriate to use while reading this particular text?

> ▸ Is this a narrative (i.e., does it tell a story?) or expository (i.e., does it inform?) text?

• Prepare a sample cloze reading assignment to evaluate students' ability to navigate and make sense of a problematic text.

• Teach students how these common transitions shape the meaning of a text and what they tell the reader:

> ▸ *Time sequence:* order in which events/acts occur within the text.

> ▸ *Example:* signals that an example of the current idea will appear next

> ▸ *Enumeration:* means the author will list each key idea they wish to emphasize

> ▸ *Continuation:* alerts the reader that the author is not done with an idea but will elaborate on it in the coming sentence or paragraph

> ▸ *Contrast:* used to provide an alternative view of the idea/event the author has been discussing

> ▸ *Comparison:* used to show how similar this idea or event is to those that came before it

> ▸ *Cause-effect:* used to emphasize the consequence of actions

> ▸ *Summation:* used to reiterate the main idea at the close of the text

• Teach students about the various types of text (see Appendix 43).

• Help students know the difference between narrative text (novels, myths, legends—any kind of story) and expository text (essays, articles, reports—any kind of text that informs the reader using facts, opinions, examples).

TRAGIC DECISIONS

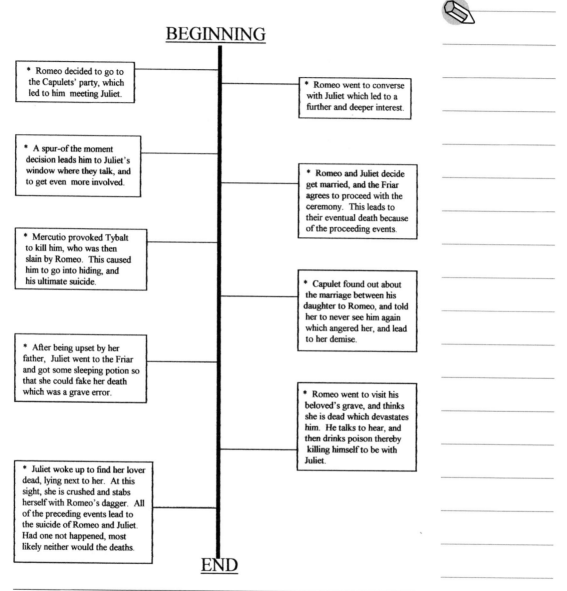

BEGINNING

* Romeo decided to go to the Capulets' party, which led to him meeting Juliet.

* Romeo went to converse with Juliet which led to a further and deeper interest.

* A spur-of the moment decision leads him to Juliet's window where they talk, and to get even more involved.

* Romeo and Juliet decide get married, and the Friar agrees to proceed with the ceremony. This leads to their eventual death because of the proceeding events.

* Mercutio provoked Tybalt to kill him, who was then slain by Romeo. This caused him to go into hiding, and his ultimate suicide.

* Capulet found out about the marriage between his daughter to Romeo, and told her to never see him again which angered her, and lead to her demise.

* After being upset by her father, Juliet went to the Friar and got some sleeping potion so that she could fake her death which was a grave error.

* Romeo went to visit his beloved's grave, and thinks she is dead which devastates him. He talks to hear, and then drinks poison thereby killing himself to be with Juliet.

* Juliet woke up to find her lover dead, lying next to her. At this sight, she is crushed and stabs herself with Romeo's dagger. All of the preceding events lead to the suicide of Romeo and Juliet. Had one not happened, most likely neither would the deaths.

END

FIGURE 77-1 Victor showed and improved his understanding of the structure of *Romeo and Juliet* by creting this decision time line.

Montague

1. Romeo Montague
2. Romeo is the son of old Montague, friend to Mercutio and Benvolio, and husband to Juliet
3. He is somewhat of a loner and an outcast from the group. Although he is this, he can also be described as a lover, and a romantic. At times, friendly, impulsive and excitable.
4. Romeo is, along with Juliet, the main character. Had he not been keen on visiting Juliet, they would most likely not be married, and there would be no story.
5. Romeo is to Old Montague what Juliet is to Capulet, because they are the only son/daughter of the two most powerful people.

1. Mercutio
2. He is the kinsman, and friend to Romeo.
3. Mercutio is somewhat outrageous, and negligent in his actions; he does not think ahead. Very sarcastic, he will do anything for a laugh from his "group".
4. Because of his careless behavior, he winds up getting slain by Tybalt, which leads to more events later on.
5. Mercutio is to Tybalt what Montague is to Capulet—both are mortal enemies.

Non-partisan

1. Friar Lawrence
2. He is a friend to both the Capulet family and the Montague family.
3. The Friar is a man who cares about other people. He is generous, and non-discriminating.
4. In the play, Friar Lawrence acts as a liaison between the two lovers (families) as a liaison. Were it not for the friar, the couple would not be wed, or for that matter—dead. He is the one who gives Juliet the sleeping potion, and triggers their suicide.
5. Friar Lawrence is to Romeo what the nurse is to Juliet, because the nurse is in close contact with Juliet and the Friar talks a lot with Romeo.

1. Nurse to Juliet
2. She is the life-long nurse to the Capulets, a friend to Romeo, Juliet and acts as a go-between for the two parties.
3. She is a very joyous and happy person who genuinely cares about Juliet's well being.
4. Because of the nurses caring, and kind nature, she makes arrangements for the marriage.
5. The Nurse is to Juliet what Benvolio is to Romeo, because they are both intimate friends.

Capulet

1. Juliet Capulet
2. Juliet is the daughter of Capulet, friend to the nurse. And wife to Romeo.
3. She is a kind person, who found a true love at a very young age. She is a lover, and a romantic just as is Romeo.
4. As I said before, she and Romeo are the main characters. Basically everything revolves around them, and their relationship. With her love for Romeo, she decides to fake death, which leads to the double suicide.
5. Juliet is to Paris as Romeo is to Rosaline, because Rosaline was Romeo's first lover, and Paris was "in line" ahead of Romeo.

1. Tybalt
2. He is the nephew to Capulet, and "protector" of Juliet.
3. Tybalt is one who stays loyal to the Capulet name. He lets nothing happen that would, in anyway, tarnish its image. He shows no mercy for those who bear the name Montague.
4. In the story, Tybalt acts as a catalyst—by killing Mercutio, he causes Romeo to kill him, who is then put into exile etc.
5. Tybalt is to the Capulets what Mercutio is to the Montagues because they are both "leaders" of the families' youth.

FIGURE 77-2 Victor elaborated on his decision time line by explaining the different moments and their importance.

Read at
Different Levels

RATIONALE

Students are quick to read only at the literal level, saying, for example, that a story is "about a boy who gets lost in the woods with only a hatchet" instead of a story about persistence or courage. Using a variety of types of text in our class not only prepares students to read different texts in different ways but at varying levels and for different purposes. I once heard an elementary school teacher say when speaking with a literature professor: "I teach the kids to see what is there; you teach them to see what is not there." Students need to be able to do both.

WHAT TO DO

Keep in mind that reading at different levels means examining the difference between:

- Literal and symbolic (aka figurative) texts
- Easy and frustrating texts
- Different implied and possible meanings

Recognize that some students are good at playing the symbolism game: like little kids learning to speak, using a few words to refer to many things, these students overgeneralize, assuming everything is a symbol. As Flannery O'Connor wrote, however, an object must first be able to function within a story as the object it really is. Only by surrounding it and thereby investing the object with symbolic value does the writer, often through repeated allusion, transform something (or some place or person) into a symbol.

Use a graphic organizer to help your students examine a text for different levels of meaning. Consider the following example, in which students reading a poem were asked to fill in three columns: What it is/What it means or represents/Why you think that. In this case the text is a poem, but this organizational structure (the three columns and three categories) could easily be adapted to any other subject area or type of text.

> A book consists of two layers: on top, the readable layer . . . and underneath, a layer that was inaccessible. You only sense its existence in a moment of distraction from the literal reading, the way you see childhood through a child. It would take forever to tell what you see, and it would be pointless.
>
> MARGUERITE DURAS

When reading, ask students the following questions:

- What happened?
- Why did it happen?
- What does this event imply about the character, the era, or the author?
- What is the object (or place or person)?
- What role does it play in the text?
- What does it mean to the author or characters?
- Why do you think it means that?
- Complete this sentence: _____ represents _____ since . . .
- On what level or in what way am I supposed to read this text?
- What objects or concepts does the author keep circling back to? For example, in William Golding's novel *Lord of the Flies* he refers to "the scar" nearly twenty times in the first three pages. Its repeated use combined with its menacing meaning demands that the reader think more carefully about just what the scar is and why the author keeps referring to it.

STUDENT EXAMPLE

WHAT IT IS	WHAT IT REPRESENTS/MEANS	WHY YOU THINK THAT
Rocks like the teeth of a dinosaur	From childhood; represents kids' imagination	It is what kids do: pretend things are something else
Honeycomb	Sweet, home (for bees), frail, important, his parents' home	Compares his home to what happens to the bees' home
Furnished house	Fun, past with his parents, very important to him	His parents died, and that's the thing his parents left for him
Chest open	He feels that he is dead	His closest relatives were died; he doesn't want to live at all
Mildew	Something like people in an army, an enlist-man	The mildew which wears marching boots
Bound to fall apart	Everybody is going to die	This is the rule in this world; fall apart is like living far apart from others
Desolate sound	Strange, peace	If you can hear the sound of the wind, it should be a silent place; I can't tell what the sound of the wind is because it is so strange.

FIGURE 78-1 Annie Au-yeung used the three-column graphic organizer to help her think more analytically about the poem "Boys Build Forts."

Read from a Variety of Perspectives

79

RATIONALE

Literature offers us the chance to see the world through the eyes of the Other. Men can read a book written about or from a woman's perspective, or someone can read something written from the point of view of a person with a different experience. This quality doesn't just apply to literature: science and history, health and business classes offer the same opportunities to read imaginatively (from the perspective of a customer, a consumer, someone in history, or even an atom). Such imaginative reading, if cultivated, enables the reader to appreciate and understand their subject in general and the text in particular at a much deeper level.

Reading is the sole means by which we slip, involuntarily, often helplessly, into another's skin, another's voice, another's soul.

JOYCE CAROL OATES

WHAT TO DO

Encourage students to engage in the following activities:

Discussion

Ask such questions as

• How might someone from a different background or perspective than mine read this text?

• How might that different perspective affect their reading?

• If one of the peripheral characters in the book were to read this passage, what would they have to say to or about the author?

• What would they say about the scene or character(s) being described in it?

• How do I read this differently today, knowing what I know, than people did when it was originally written?

Writing

• Rewrite a scene, using all proper conventions for that genre, from two other perspectives. Examples might include writing from the perspective of the author, yourself, another character, an expert in that field, a different era, or a different gender, race, or culture. Change the voice, tone, and diction as you think necessary.

• Write in your journal about the different ways this could be read, even if some of them are silly: think outside the lines!

• Recast the text in form, function, and perspective (see Reminder 99).

Performing

• Modern adaptations of Shakespeare often have someone of a different class, culture, or race play a crucial role in order to let the play offer yet more insight into another's condition. Adapt a scene from a poem, play, or novel to use or represent someone other than the writer originally intended. (Discuss and/or write about how this occupation of the Other affected them afterward.)

• Read the text with different accents or mannerisms to examine how this might change the meaning or action in the scene.

Thinking

Use the following graphic organizers to help you make connections or generate ideas from other perspectives:

• *Conversational roundtable* (Appendix 4): write a different character or perspective in each of the four boxes and in the middle write the subject of their conversation. In each of the four boxes write down examples or characteristics of their different responses to this subject. At the bottom of the page write a synthesis of your thinking.

• *Venn diagram* (Appendix 24): If you are working with two different perspectives, brainstorm or list the different characteristics of each perspective on each side then identify those common attributes in the middle section of the diagram.

• *Think in threes* (Appendix 21): It is easy to fall into the trap of either/or thinking. Try always to explore at least a third perspective on the subject so that students can learn to occupy more than one point of view on any given subject.

STUDENT EXAMPLES

The following writing sample is from freshman Mike Woods's character journal. In this assignment, and James Windsor-Wells's subsequent

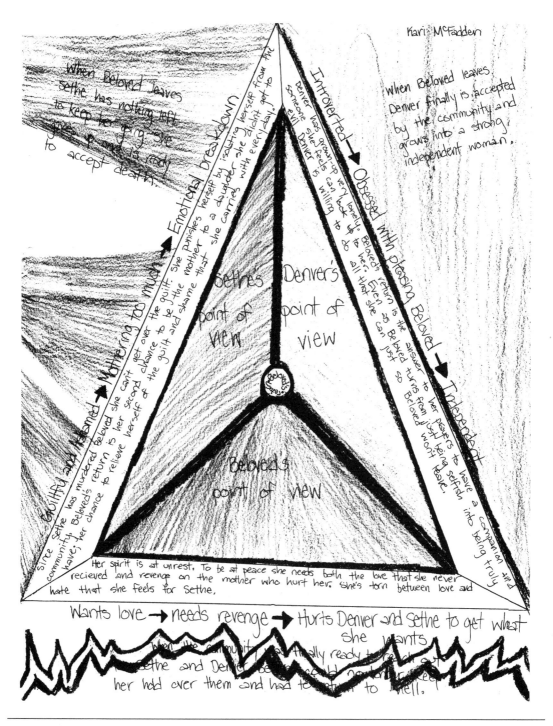

FIGURE 79-1   Kari McFadden's "think in threes" graphic organizer helps her examine and reveal the complexity of Toni Morrison's novel *Beloved*.

example, also, the students had to write as if they were one of the characters in the novel.

MIKE WOODS'S *LORD OF THE FLIES* Journal

Today during the meeting everybody was talking RESCUE RESCUE RESCUE!!! I was interested in getting rescued but I didn't see the urgency. I was calmly participating, just pitching in on the important issues like food and hunting, when someone suggested we build a fire. I wanted to do something and I was beginning to grow a bit antsy and when somebody suggested that we build a fire I jumped to my feet because I was ready to show off my leader-like qualities such as craftsmanship.

I led the way as the other boys and I assembled a grand ol' heap of old logs, branches, and other items that would aid the flames. I set the standard of hard work and almost everybody else followed but that fat Piggy strolled his big fat duff down to where we was constructing the heap without doing any work.

Ralph the "intelligent chief" didn't have a smidge of a thought on how to do a fire. I knew that you needed to rub a few sticks together but I hadn't done it before. Nobody really knew how to get a fire going. Once Piggy got his fat duff up to the heap I was hit by my very own smarts. I brilliantly thought of using his specs to get the fire going.

I ran over and grabbed his specs. The second I laid hand on the specs he started to wail like a little crybaby. He was the one who was so preoccupied with being rescued. Anyhow I retrieved his specs and I got the fire going, and Ralph the "leader" couldn't. Once the fire was going we got more wood. Rest and hunger claimed the boys and drew them, allowing the fire to halt.

Thereafter we fell into a vast bundle of arguments. We decided to have a permanent fire maker. That portly boy Piggy is starting to drive me bonkers. He is always whining like a little girl. "I got the Conch and I'm speaking." Then that fat bastard tried to blame me for the fire going out. He's so concerned with shelters in 90 degree weather. Then Ralph and Piggy started going on about how a boy's dead when he's probably just missing.

James Windsor-Wells took a different approach to the *Lord of the Flies* character journal:

The fire raged on, crushing innocent creatures,
angry at anything in sight.
Raging on and on because it was raped by power,
Risking without knowing the risk.
SMASH, CRACK, BOOM, SNARL,
the fire was only doing its job.
The fire had no pity, no control, or wisdom,
It was us, we were bathing in shame.

We hold in our hands miles of salt,
millions of acres of cinnamon,
and all the other ingredients to life sitting before us
eager to help us on our journey,
But we don't know how to make culture of life,
We only know to sit and watch,
and some of us don't know we have to make anything at all,
knowing too well to take it for granted.
We are running out of time, out of life,
we must learn, control.
Our food is getting cold,
It needs salt and cinnamon,
But too much of either will ruin the whole thing.

80

Develop Prior Knowledge

. . . .

RATIONALE

When I want to read a good book, I write one.

BENJAMIN DISRAELI

If we take time to develop or access knowledge of certain things before reading, we will read it faster, be more engaged, understand it better, and remember it longer. Obviously we *have* to know certain things about a text if we are to understand what we read. Helping students realize this, and the different types of prior knowledge that can help them, is one of the most important lessons we can help them learn.

WHAT TO DO

- Develop students' knowledge about:

    ▶ The subject (e.g., child development)

    ▶ The discipline (e.g., science/biology)

    ▶ The textual structures and conventions (e.g., scientific report)

    ▶ The cultural/historical context

    ▶ The author(s) of the text

    ▶ The language and general vocabulary used in the text

- Point out at every possible opportunity how good readers access this information. You can do this by modeling your own practice for them (e.g., "This is how I orient myself before reading a text: I ask myself these questions . . . ")

- Keep in mind that prior knowledge can be obtained in any or all of the following ways:

    ▶ Teacher can provide it through direct instruction

    ▶ Students can glean it through related readings or discussion

    ▶ Through active, even directed imagining of ideas

    ▶ Through students' own experiences or past studies

    ▶ By brainstorming ideas, facts, and questions about a subject about which you are preparing to read

    ▶ Via clues available to them through the text—e.g., sidebars, pullouts, table of contents, graphic illustrations

- Remember that the reader must not only develop or call up prior knowledge, but evaluate its accuracy and its ability to help them read a given text.

  ◗ Have students preview a text to awaken their existing knowledge and establish an outline of the text in their heads.

  ◗ Keep in mind that, because prior knowledge is associative—i.e., I am thinking of *A* to help me better understand *B*—good readers will bring to this reading their expectations about how the text functions based on their previous experiences. Discussion, due to its give-and-take nature, allows for a more associative mode through which our past experiences and readings can yield useful information about how to read such texts or a particular author.

  ◗ Develop prior knowledge as an individual, group, or a class by brainstorming questions, facts, and associations related to the text. This validates what everyone knows since someone is bound to have something to contribute. Janet Allen calls this the "community knowledge bank" in which the class pools its intellectual resources prior to the actual event or reading.

  ◗ Have students make predictions based on what they think they know and support these predictions with whatever they can find.

  ◗ Have them use the KWL graphic organizer (see Reminder 61) to identify what they already know and want to know.

STUDENT EXAMPLE

The following questions and answers came in response to the simple question, "What do you know or want to know about Shakespeare?"

- *Romeo and Juliet*

- Why does he use such weird words?

- It's hard for me to understand what he writes.

- Where did he come up with the ideas for his plays?

- What's so great about his plays?

- I like the romantic tragedy *Romeo and Juliet*.

- How could Shakespeare invent so many words?

- Why were people scared of Shakespeare?

- How old is Shakespeare?

- What age in history did Shakespeare live in?

- Why are we required to read Shakespeare?

253

81 Use Written Conversations

RATIONALE

Written conversations offer students the chance to discuss a text through writing with one or more students. The strategy also invites more imaginative applications such as a conversation with the author, characters, or some other entity. They provide opportunities for students to interact and, through these interactions, to deepen their understanding of the text. The idea is to provide a range of discussion techniques that help second-language learners and students with special needs while simultaneously making room to challenge all students.

WHAT TO DO

Have your students try the following activities:

- *Journal share.* Students write in their journal (or on a sheet of paper) in response to a text or based on observations they've made of some object or process (e.g., in a science class). When they are done writing, ask them to trade with another student; this student then writes in the partner's journal, responding to what they wrote. Have them trade once again with another person; this person then responds to both of the previous entries. Return the journal to its owner and ask them to read and then synthesize the different contributions to this written discussion.

- *Chat room.* Have them imagine that a sheet of paper is a blank computer screen and that everyone in the class is part of an online chatroom. This means, for example, that they cannot talk. After reading a text, they write their ideas, explanations, response, interpretations, or whatever on the sheet. They pass it around to others (all should be anonymous) who then pass theirs around and in this way the class keeps writing, responding, and passing the "computer screens" around until you feel they understand or need further guidance. Then have each person write a synthesis of their simulated online discussion.

- *Fictional conversation.* Have them make up a conversation between any or all of the following: themselves and the author; themselves and a character; a famous thinker from a given field (e.g., Freud, Einstein, FDR) and a character or author; characters from different stories. Tell them to use appropriate dialogue format and style.

- *Sustained conversation.* Two (or more) students can make the commitment to participate in an ongoing written conversation through e-mail or a threaded discussion; this will then be presented as evidence of their reading performance.

- *Snowballs.* This technique, developed by Kate Kinsella, asks students to write down their ideas, questions, or responses on a piece of paper which they then crumble up and throw around the room until everyone gets one. That person then opens it up, reads it, responds to it, then crumbles it up again and throws it for additional response.

- *Before/during/after.* Use any of the previously described activities before (to orient them to the text and activate prior knowledge), during (to clarify, synthesize, understand), or after (to summarize, apply, or interpret).

STUDENT EXAMPLE

One option that interests many students is to take their conversation into writing and onto the computer for an online discussion. This opportunity has several benefits: time, interest, motivation, individualization.

ONLINE CONVERSATION: *THE KITCHEN GOD'S WIFE*

MJoli: So what do you think about *Kitchen God's Wife?*

GirlPwr: I thought it was a novel not only about the life of a Chinese woman, but also about the importance of knowing your roots.

MJoli: Oh yeah, I forgot about the roots part. Pearl knowing her mother's background?

GirlPwr: Right, I think she will now be able to understand why she disliked her childhood.

MJoli: Whose childhood?

GirlPwr: Pearl's. Do you think their relationship will be closer?

MJoli: After she hears the story? I suppose . . . but it might drive it further apart. Maybe something . . . will be said that she doesn't want to hear.

GirlPwr: That's true. She may not want to hear it, but she is better off understanding her family.

MJoli: Sometimes it is strange to hear your parents' stories. Why? Can't some things be left in the dark?

GirlPwr: Then both of them will go through their lives feeling like they are hiding something.

MJoli: Yes, but does Pearl need to know her mother's history? What good will come of it?

GirlPwr: At least now maybe Pearl will feel as if she is truly loved. Trust and friendship is based on knowing the details of someone's life. Didn't she feel that from the beginning? It isn't like Winnie ever was mean to her . . . Nothing different from another mom and daughter relationship.

MJoli: Hey. Good point. I know all of my friends' pasts . . . as much as they will tell me anyway.

GirlPwr: Winnie and Pearl never developed a trust, so both weren't informed of the most influential points in each other's lives.

MJoli: Yes . . . I suppose somehow the "not knowing" created a wall between them.

GirlPwr: I really don't believe it is. Winnie really hasn't caught up the happenings of Pearl's life.

MJoli: But a little wall is there . . . that natural wall that prevents us from becoming best friends with our parents.

GirlPwr: Yea! What secrets does Pearl have? Winnie was very inquisitive about Pearl's past loves, and the way she felt for her father. I think Winnie wants to know what Pearl thinks of motherhood because it would be an opportunity to prove that she was not a terrible mother.

MJoli: Why do you say that? What makes you think that?

GirlPwr: Well, Winnie was trying to prove herself as a good mother toward the end of her story.

MJoli: How? I think I missed that part . . .

GirlPwr: If Pearl says she is having a problem with her daughter, then Winnie can say, "I went through the same thing with you."

MJoli: Oh yeah. Good eyes.

GirlPwr: Do you think you'd ever want to be best friends with your parents?

MJoli: No. I want them to be my parents . . . to do parent things.

Use Shared Inquiry

RATIONALE

Developed and still used today by the Great Books Foundation, this technique focuses on using questions to drive thoughtful conversations about meaningful literature. The method can be easily adapted to reading in any of the subject areas. The Great Books Foundation describes it as "a distinctive method of learning in which participants search for answers to fundamental questions raised by a text. The search is inherently active; it involves taking what the author has given us and trying to grasp its full meaning, to interpret or reach an undestanding of the text in light of our experience and using sound reasoning."

> If one cannot enjoy reading a book over and over again, there is no use in reading it at all.
>
> OSCAR WILDE

WHAT TO DO

Have group leaders, who might be parents, teachers, or appointed students, complete the following steps prior to beginning the shared inquiry:

- Read the selection twice, during which time you should make notes that

  ▶ Raise essential questions

  ▶ Highlight interesting or important issues

  ▶ Identify and discuss your own insights while reading

- Identify those issues central to the text's meaning or message. These might include issues that challenge readers' assumptions or allow for alternative interpretations

- Use these issues to help you generate a set of matching interpretive questions that might address:

  ▶ Character motives

  ▶ Author's use of language or imagery

  ▶ Important details, words, or phrases

- Sort out and sequence the questions in such a manner as will provide for an engaging and successful conversation. Cluster the questions into sets, beginning with the one that will most likely engage and challenge but not frustrate them.

Once the discussion begins, review and discuss the four guidelines for shared inquiry discussions:

1. Only those who have read the selection can participate in the discussion

2. The discussion shall be limited to the selection that everyone read

3. Opinions must be supported by evidence from the text

4. Leaders may only ask questions; they may not answer them

Have students prepare for the shared inquiry discussion by reading the selection twice and taking notes. The Great Books Foundation suggests, especially in the initial stages, that leaders share their notes with participants, using them as exemplars so that students know what sorts of things to note and observe.

Keep in mind that the leader's role throughout the discussion is to:

- Facilitate discussion, encouraging students to talk and ask each other questions

- Ask questions that will clarify ideas being discussed

- Help students make connections to the text and their own experience

- Help students formulate questions about the ideas and content

- Redirect the students' attention to the text as the primary source for the answers or evidence to support their thinking

- Encourage the participants to challenge the leader's assumptions and questions, asking them to offer their own questions instead

- Ensure everyone participates in the discussion

- Pose follow-up questions to clarify, support, synthesize, elaborate, or develop a new line of inquiry

Engage in follow-up activities including:

- Using notes and insights from the discussion as the basis for further conversations about other, related texts

- Writing a paper that draws its supporting evidence and insights from the discussion

- Training students to run these discussions so they can internalize these habits and skills

Outline What
They Read

RATIONALE

Outlining is one way for a reader to take more structured notes while reading. The technique of organizing information into categories that make sense to the reader helps focus that reader on the important ideas and details that support those ideas within the text. Outlines can be used in other ways to develop readers' textual intelligence (see Reminder 77), particularly as it relates to structural design and the way information is organized.

Planning to write is not writing. Outlining a book is not writing. Researching is not writing. Talking to people about what you're doing, none of that is writing. Writing is writing.

E. L. DOCTOROW

WHAT TO DO

• Have students take notes in outline format while reading an expository text (e.g., an article, textbook, or essay) that is difficult but very structured so they can see the obvious structure. When they are finished, have students get into pairs or small groups and compare their outlines as a tool for discussion and a means of evaluating the precision of their comprehension. Provide correction and clarification as needed to individuals or the whole class.

• Use outlines in one of the following ways specifically to improve students' textual intelligence through manipulation and discussion:

   ▸ Give students an article and a blank outline form (See Appendix 14) to complete as they read. When they finish, give them the same outline form completed (by yourself) but with all the elements scrambled and no identifying information (e.g., numerical or alphabetical cues). They must work through the information and reorganize it according to the guidelines of the blank outline you provided them. They should do this either individually, then collaboratively, or collaboratively; in either case, they must be able to explain their decisions about sequencing.

   ▸ Give a group of students a completed outline of a text they read, cut up into strips which they must manipulate to achieve what seems the more logical order. They must be able to explain their decisions about sequencing based on their reading of the text.

- Use outlines to develop and improve their categorical thinking so that while they read they can make connections and impose order on what they read, seeing how it relates to other ideas in the same category. As a prereading activity, you might brainstorm the possible ideas or connections to the article they are about to read. Such attention to categories will help them to make sense of what they read.

- Avoid the overly regimented thinking of one outline by developing alternative outlines (see "think in threes" graphic organizer) that focus on different categories. This technique challenges students to view a text from multiple perspectives and to realize that authors conceive of a text from a variety of angles.

- Have them think in bullets. This more informal outline strategy downplays the importance of using the numerical and alphabetical clues provided by outlines and asks readers to use the more egalitarian bullet as a means of quickly organizing the ideas without respect to sequencing. This page itself is an example of such an outline.

- Use outlines as tools to prepare them to read, to write, to discuss; use them to establish the mental habit of organizing as you read, which is one among many ways of interacting with what you read to better understand it.

- Teach them to read the table of contents in a book or chapter, especially in a textbook, as an outline which the chapters will complete. This focus allows them to see not only how the book works but what it will be about, through such prereading techniques (e.g., read the chapter outline as described in both the table of contents and the headers to the chapter).

- Use the index, too, as another form of outline that can help you read a textbook better: the index reveals the main categories and reveals many connections, both subtle and essential, between the content in the book. To the extent that one realizes how to read an outline they can then navigate the index easily, using the information to help them read better.

STUDENT EXAMPLE

OUTLINE: GULF WAR SYNDROME PROJECT

I. Background of topic

   A. The Gulf War

      1. War fought by U.S. against Iraq in early 1991

      2. Reason: Control of oil

    3. 670,000 troops sent; U.S. easily defeated Iran

  B. Gulf War Syndrome

    1. Ever since war ended, soldiers have been becoming sick—Gulf War Syndrome

    2. Symptoms of Gulf War Syndrome

      a. Gastrointestinal dysfunction

      b. Severe fatigue

      c. Chronic headaches

      d. Joint aches

      e. Memory loss

      f. Skin rash

      g. Diarrhea

    3. Now estimated that 80,000 veterans have Gulf War Syndrome; 6,526 have died

    4. Increasing amount of veterans are getting sick

      a. Symptoms may not appear for 5, 10, 20, or 30 years

  C. Cause of Gulf War Syndrome

    1. Specific cause is unknown

    2. Believed to be caused by exposures to toxic chemical weapons or biological weapons

      a. Chemical weapons—toxic gas or substance

      b. Biological weapons—germs, bacteria or virus

      c. Many believe Gulf War Syndrome is caused by a combination of things

    3. Some believe Syndrome is caused by antinerve agent pill called PB.

      a. Supposed to protect soldiers from chemical weapons

      b. Was not approved by FDA (food and drug administration)

      c. PB issued to nearly all soldiers who were sent to the Gulf and $2/3$ of the soldiers took it for certain periods of time

84 Summarize and Paraphrase

RATIONALE

The ability to summarize varying amounts of information is crucial for adult success in most fields. Being able to take an entire article, poem, or book and sum it up in a sentence or a short paragraph helps readers to better understand what they read. This active process whereby the reader extracts the main idea(s) and sums up their importance becomes a habit in more proficient readers. It is not a skill we are born with, however; good summaries must be precise and contain specific types of information that the novice often overlooks. In their important book *Reading for Understanding: A Guide to Improving Reading in Middle and High School Classrooms* (1999), Ruth Schoenbach et al. identify four essential strategies that readers must master: questioning, summarizing, clarifying, and predicting.

WHAT TO DO

• Model this technique for students, explaining the process as you go (e.g., what questions did you ask to help you create the summary?)

• Use this method in different mediums or contexts:

WRITTEN
  ▸ Journals
  ▸ Reports
  ▸ Essays
  ▸ Written conversations
  ▸ Think-alouds

SPOKEN
  ▸ Discussions
  ▸ Presentations
  ▸ Think-alouds

ALTERNATIVE FORMS

- ‣ Multimedia presentations
- ‣ Visual summaries
- ‣ Graphs
- ‣ Charts
- ‣ Video
- ‣ Graphic organizers

- Instruct students to ask these questions when summarizing a text:

  - ‣ Who did what?
  - ‣ Where and how did the event(s) take place?
  - ‣ What caused the action?
  - ‣ What was the consequence of the action?
  - ‣ What changes occurred between the beginning and the end of the passage you read?
  - ‣ What are the crucial moments? (Why are they crucial?)
  - ‣ Does this text operate on multiple levels? If so, how can you succinctly describe these levels in your summary?
  - ‣ What was the sequence of the events?
  - ‣ Is this event/action different from what happened in the past?

- Inform them that words to consider when writing a summary are: *describe, classify, explain, discuss, state, outline, illustrate, define, compare, contrast.*

- Alert them to transitional words authors use to signal information they will want to include in their summary (see Reminder 90).

- Have them write a five-minute paper about the subject based on their reading. Have them write this paper in the Cornell note-taking format so that they can return later to make additional notes and connections in the available space.

- Use the index card summary. At a transitional moment (e.g., between chapters or stages), pass out 3 × 5″ cards and ask students to explain what they just read to another in their own words.

- Check for accuracy. Whether using the 3 × 5″ cards or another technique, you need to check their summaries for accuracy. The summary or paraphrase offers useful information about their comprehension: e.g., if their summary is too general, simple, or plain wrong, you know that you should not proceed to the next chapter or stage.

- Use exemplars from previous assignments or other classes to show them what a successful and unsuccessful performance looks like. If you have time, use these exemplars or several from the current assignment to develop criteria for good summaries. These guidelines, if made available up front, will help students produce more complete, precise work.

- Make sure they include in the summary crucial events, people, actions, features, characteristics, themes, developments, qualities, authorial information (e.g., perspective, biases, intentions). Students can also include comparisons, connections, opinions, and speculations about what might have happened or what will happen depending on the assignment guidelines.

- When summarizing, have students:

  ▶ Preread the text, getting a quick sense of it and its main ideas

  ▶ Annotate the text (using underlines or highlighter if possible; otherwise with Post-its, notes, or outlines), keeping in mind what information will be useful to them when summarizing it

  ▶ Distinguish between information and details—details are generally left out to make room for crucial information

  ▶ Write a paragraph-long summary organized around the key information

  ▶ Write the same summary in one sentence

  ▶ Trade summaries and, imagining they had never read the text that was summarized, explain why they would or would not be able to understand what it was about based on this summary

  ▶ Add information or write down questions on their partner's summary that will help them improve it

  ▶ Return the summary to the original writer and have them use the new information—questions, suggestions, details, expanded knowledge from reading others' summaries—to revise their previous summary

  ▶ Use signal words, at least while learning how to write summaries, to guide them and provide more structure to the reader: *first, then, finally*

- Have them ask the following questions: What happened? What is essential to tell? What was the outcome? Who was involved? Why did this happen? Is that a detail or essential information?

STUDENT EXAMPLES

SUMMARY OF SSR BOOK, CHRIS CRUTCHER'S *CHINESE HANDCUFFS*, by David Lee

People go through rough times in their life and sometimes it's hard for them to communicate with others about their problems. Oftentimes, not sharing your problems with others could very well lead to bigger problems in your life ahead. As one learns to deal with their problems, one will understand the importance to talk and share problems with others.

The two main characters in *Chinese Handcuffs*, Dillon and Jennifer, have especially hard times talking with others about the problems they face in their lives. Dillon saw his brother die right before his own eyes. The shock causes Dillon to occasionally write letters to his brother, talking about how life would be different with him still alive. Dillon's dead brother is practically the only person he talks and reveals his problems to. Jennifer never got any attention from her mom. Even more traumatically, she found out her sister had been raped. Worse yet, the rapist was her mother's boyfriend and warned Jennifer that if she told anybody what happened, her family's lives would be in danger. This secret shuts down Jennifer's ability to talk to others, as it eats away at her insides. The traumatic death of Dillon's brother and the hideous rape of Jennifer's sister causes our two main characters to be verbal castoffs in society.

This story about two teenagers facing problems with communication makes me realize how everyone goes through the same sorts of problems; I used to think that I was the only one in the world with problems. Both characters had parents who rarely paid attention to them, getting into situation after situation with no one to support them. Both Dillion and Jennifer went through huge problems, which they didn't want to or couldn't share with others. For Jennifer, if she told anyone of her problem, there would be consequences. For Dillon, he was simply shut down by the death of his brother and couldn't face the real world.

It's hard to talk about your problems to others, especially when your parents don't listen. I'm faced with that problem from time to time. I would go up to my parents and explain that I have a problem at school or in my life. Although they claim that they are always open and listening, they would always yell at me for getting into stupid situations. My situation is very similar with Jennifer, who's mother struggles to listen and sometimes doesn't try at all. When Jennifer found

SUMMARY AND COMPARISON OF ESSAY "DREAM HOUSES"	
"DREAM HOUSE"	**OLD HOUSE**
• In the woods	• One bathroom: tub no shower
• Back wall made of glass	• Rooms small
• Huge stone fireplace	• Basement: divided into father's
• Large rooms	music room and kids' playroom
• Low-slung pine beams on	• Small ranch-style
upper floor	• Foil wallpaper over the stove
• Bathroom: massager shower,	• Paneling downstairs
white, everything matching	• Ceiling that buckled
• River with a small island	• "Make do house"
• Fox fur on the path	• Everyone gathered in the
• Can't find the light switch	bathroom to talk, even if
• Feels like a motel	people were using it!

FIGURE 84-1 Students used the feature analysis graphic organizer to summarize and compare ideas within an essay about houses.

out that her sister had been raped, she couldn't face telling her mom. After reading this story and re-evaluating my life, I realize that it is a good idea to be more interactive with your friends and parents so they can be there in your time of need.

It is necessary to provide teenagers with all the support they need in order for them grow up healthy. This story showed me that when you keep your feelings to yourself, you will get no where in this life. Both characters struggled to face their problems, but, as the story went along, they were able to conquer and get past those problems by talking and interacting with others. It doesn't matter what kind of problem it is, big or small, you need to talk it out with a friend or a parent. It is much easier to solve the problem when you have someone helping and supporting you.

Expand
Vocabulary

85

RATIONALE

Students cannot read what they don't understand. Assuming that their reading continually grows more demanding—in its use of language, sentence structures, and concepts—we need to prepare them by introducing them to the necessary words and teaching them the strategies they need to expand their own vocabulary. Reminder 20 looks specifically at helping students approach words they do not know; this reminder focuses on bulding on the vocabulary they already have.

WHAT TO DO

- Follow these guidelines for teaching vocabulary:

  ▷ Teach the words that are most useful now and in the future

  ▷ Teach the words they need before reading; review them after they are done; reinforce them when they come up in subsequent readings

  ▷ Teach word structure and its relationship to the word's meaning: e.g., *scribe; script; subscribe; postscript; scribble*

  ▷ Examine word relationships: antonyms, synonyms, analogies, associations

  ▷ Examine the different uses of words: connotative versus denotative meaning

  ▷ Examine words in their context within the poem, story, chapter

  ▷ Provide multiple exposures to these words in different contexts over time

  ▷ Help students activate their prior knowledge when learning new words

  ▷ Make connections between new words and concepts, and those they already know

- Expand students' vocabulary using the following strategies:

  ▷ *Reading, reading, reading:* the single best way to expand vocabulary.

Words don't deserve that kind of malarkey. They're innocent, neutral, precise, standing for this, describing that, meaning the other, so if you look after them you can build bridges across incomprehension and chaos.

TOM STOPPARD, FROM
THE REAL THING

267

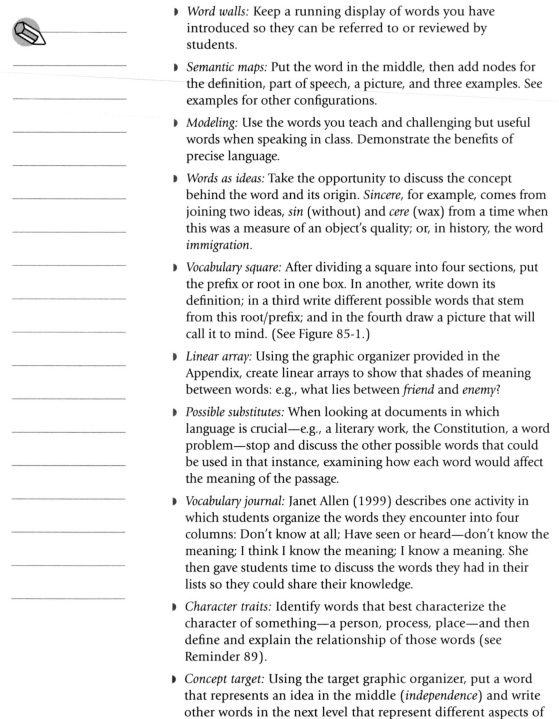

- *Word walls:* Keep a running display of words you have introduced so they can be referred to or reviewed by students.

- *Semantic maps:* Put the word in the middle, then add nodes for the definition, part of speech, a picture, and three examples. See examples for other configurations.

- *Modeling:* Use the words you teach and challenging but useful words when speaking in class. Demonstrate the benefits of precise language.

- *Words as ideas:* Take the opportunity to discuss the concept behind the word and its origin. *Sincere,* for example, comes from joining two ideas, *sin* (without) and *cere* (wax) from a time when this was a measure of an object's quality; or, in history, the word *immigration.*

- *Vocabulary square:* After dividing a square into four sections, put the prefix or root in one box. In another, write down its definition; in a third write different possible words that stem from this root/prefix; and in the fourth draw a picture that will call it to mind. (See Figure 85-1.)

- *Linear array:* Using the graphic organizer provided in the Appendix, create linear arrays to show that shades of meaning between words: e.g., what lies between *friend* and *enemy*?

- *Possible substitutes:* When looking at documents in which language is crucial—e.g., a literary work, the Constitution, a word problem—stop and discuss the other possible words that could be used in that instance, examining how each word would affect the meaning of the passage.

- *Vocabulary journal:* Janet Allen (1999) describes one activity in which students organize the words they encounter into four columns: Don't know at all; Have seen or heard—don't know the meaning; I think I know the meaning; I know a meaning. She then gave students time to discuss the words they had in their lists so they could share their knowledge.

- *Character traits:* Identify words that best characterize the character of something—a person, process, place—and then define and explain the relationship of those words (see Reminder 89).

- *Concept target:* Using the target graphic organizer, put a word that represents an idea in the middle (*independence*) and write other words in the next level that represent different aspects of this word/concept; in the third round of the target write either synonyms or antonyms, definitions or explanations.

- Keep in mind the different types of vocabulary:
  - Subject-specific (scientific terms; see glossary of literary terms in Appendix)
  - Transitions
  - Metacognitive words (to provide a way of discussing *how* they think about what they read or how they arrived at a particular understanding)
  - Utilitarian words (high-frequency words)
  - Multiple meanings (words that have multiple meanings, often as a result of being able to function as both verbs and nouns)

STUDENT EXAMPLE: ERIC MARTIN CHARACTER STUDY

The assignment included with Reminder 89 requires students to come up with adjectives to describe a literary character, then to explain how that word fits by drawing examples from the text. Eric's example below illustrates this assignment well.

> *Superstitious*: Early in the book Huck was in his room and he killed a spider. He says that "it was bound to fetch him some bad luck," so he stands up and turns around three times and crosses his breast every time. Then he ties up some locks of his hair to keep witches away. Synonym: *worrisome*. Antonym: *religious*.

Vocabulary squares were the cornerstone of my vocabulary study during the semester I wrote this book. They worked well, providing a reasonable balance between number of words and ability to process them. The students responded well to the assignments and the words were always related to ideas we were studying or stories we read. Alice Lee's, shown in Figure 85-1 (page 270), is a wonderful example.

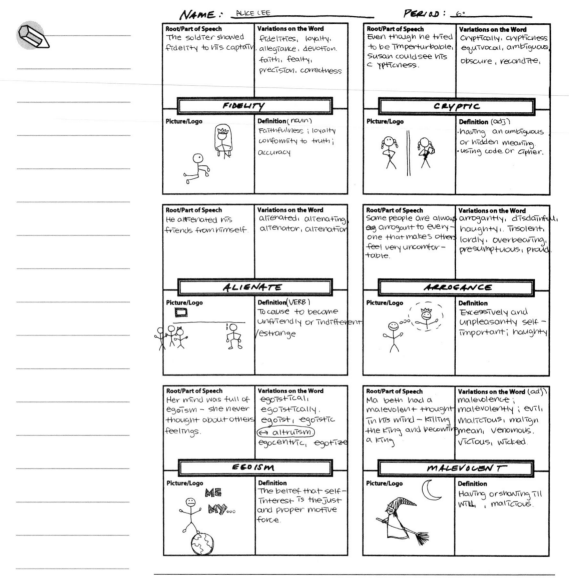

NAME: ALICE LEE   PERIOD: 6°

Root/Part of Speech	Variations on the Word
The soldier showed fidelity to his captain.	fidelities, loyalty, allegiance, devotion, faith, fealty, precision, correctness

FIDELITY

Picture/Logo	Definition (noun)
	Faithfulness; loyalty conformity to truth; accuracy

Root/Part of Speech	Variations on the Word
Even though he tried to be imperturbable, Susan could see his crypticness.	cryptically, crypticness, equivocal, ambiguous, obscure, recondite,

CRYPTIC

Picture/Logo	Definition (adj)
	• having an ambiguous or hidden meaning. • using code or cipher.

Root/Part of Speech	Variations on the Word
He alienated his friends from himself.	alienated, alienating, alienator, alienation

ALIENATE

Picture/Logo	Definition (VERB)
	To cause to become unfriendly or indifferent /estrange

Root/Part of Speech	Variations on the Word
Some people are always arrogant to everyone that makes others feel very uncomfortable.	arrogantly, disdainful, haughty, insolent, lordly, overbearing, presumptuous, proud.

ARROGANCE

Picture/Logo	Definition
	Excessively and unpleasantly self-important; haughty.

Root/Part of Speech	Variations on the Word
Her mind was full of egoism – she never thought about others' feelings.	egotistical, egotistically, egotist, egotistic (↔ altruism) egocentric, egotize

EGOISM

Picture/Logo	Definition
ME MY...	The belief that self-interest is the just and proper motive force.

Root/Part of Speech	Variations on the Word
Macbeth had a malevolent thought in his mind – killing the King and becoming a King.	(adj) malevolence; malevolently; evil, malicious, malign mean, venomous, vicious, wicked.

MALEVOLENT

Picture/Logo	Definition
	Having or showing ill will, malicious.

FIGURE 85-1   Alice Lee shows how much can be accomplished using the vocabulary squares graphic organizer.

Make the Foreign Familiar

86

RATIONALE

While related to Reminder 95, this page is dedicated to a different problem that plagues many readers: trying to understand content that they have never read or otherwise encountered before. As we read more articles and books about other cultures, by people with very different experiences than our own, or about subjects we have not previously studied, we need techniques to help us understand what we read. This is particularly true for students whose lack of capacity in this area can get them into serious trouble when, for example, they encounter information on the Internet or in textbooks, which can be warehouses of the unfamiliar. Finally, to paraphrase a poet, always look to make the familiar strange so that you might know the pleasure of discovering that aspect or idea anew each time.

No passion in the world is equal to the passion to alter someone else's draft.

H. G. WELLS

WHAT TO DO

• First help your students determine why the information or ideas are foreign to them. Are they words from a different language, specialized terms from a discipline they do not know, or a story the likes of which they have never heard before? Then, help them, as the mind is naturally inclined to do, find the familiar within the foreign by asking themselves such questions as:

> ▶ What might I compare this with in order to better understand it?

> ▶ Does this remind me of anything with which I am already familiar?

> ▶ Can I compare this to any experiences of my own?

> ▶ What word might have an equivalent meaning (e.g., when reading another language, a new discipline, or an author like Shakespeare)?

> ▶ What category most completely accommodates this idea? (If they cannot immediately tell the category, have them back up to a larger category until they find one that describes it, then work back toward the specific.)

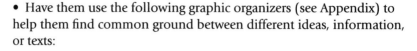

• Have them use the following graphic organizers (see Appendix) to help them find common ground between different ideas, information, or texts:

  ▶ Venn Diagram
  ▶ Feature Analysis
  ▶ Conversational Roundtable
  ▶ Target Diagram
  ▶ What Confuses Me Most
  ▶ Think in Threes
  ▶ What's the Big Idea?

• As they examine the foreign idea, object, text, or information, have them try to gather the following details:

  ▶ What are its qualities?
  ▶ What are its attributes?
  ▶ How does it behave?
  ▶ What does it want?
  ▶ What motivates it to act?

• Have them improve their understanding of the foreign by:

  ▶ Writing their way into the text from their perspective (Reminder 77)
  ▶ Translating it into modern language, different terms, or their own ideas
  ▶ Summarizing the text (Reminder 85)
  ▶ Recasting the text from one form, medium, or perspective into another (i.e., one that is more familiar to them and might help them better understand) (Reminder 99)
  ▶ Drawing the action (e.g., diagram, cartoon, storyboard, picture, plot) (Reminder 74)
  ▶ Performing the text (Reminder 73)
  ▶ Brainstorming with others in a group or a full class those ideas or possible meanings that will help them read the text

STUDENT EXAMPLES

"THINK IN THREES"

Natalia wrote the following explanation of her "think in threes" process:

> There is more than one answer to every question. A lot of
> people just think of only two sides to a question or a conflict;

FIGURE 86-1   Natalia Nicholson shows how the "think in threes" graphic organizer can expand students' thinking even as it helps them make sense of difficult texts like *Beloved*.

they cannot think beyond. This assignment helped me and can help others set up a way to think beyond the "black and white" point of view. The first thing I did was write out my question, then I thought about all the possible answers that could go along with my question. Of course there was the obvious "Yes" and "No," but then I had to think and use my knowledge from the book in other sections of the triangle under the answers. The last part of the triangle allowed me to put specific examples and quotes which further supported each answer. On the outside I used symbols to represent some of the ideas and to support what I had written. The organized brainstorming sheet allowed me to think in threes instead of the obvious answers.

SAMPLE ACTIVITY

ANTIGONE Anticipation Guide

Overview   Perhaps the most striking aspect of this play is the range of moral dilemmas it poses and the extent to which these dilemmas apply to our own society today. Such concepts as justice, shame, and piety continue to be central issues in our society's discussions about itself. Please bring the full measure of your intelligence to bear on the following moral dilemmas and the initial quotes from your reading of the play.

Moral Dilemmas   Explain what you would do in each situation and why you think that would be the right thing to do. Write the answers on a separate sheet of paper to turn in.

1. You are with someone who decides to commit an illegal act. By staying you implicate yourself in the crime as an accomplice even if you sit there; by leaving you risk the loss of that friend and a reputation as a Judas in the eyes of friends.

2. You are with friends one night at someone's house. You decide to log onto the Internet. While on the Internet you find a site that houses stolen credit card numbers you could use safely for shopping on the Internet or by phone.

3. While participating anonymously in an America Online chat session about teen issues, you learn that someone you know at school has AIDS. What would you do with that information? Why?

4. You get caught by the police in front of your school on the night they TP'd the school. You are a Service Commissioner. You are brought into the principal's office the next day, along with the others

who were also caught. The principal asks you to tell him who else was there. You know who was there. He tells you if you cannot offer him names you can no longer be in the Service Commission. What do you do? Why?

5. It is the end of your junior year, the year colleges pay the most attention to. Your friend asks you if you want a copy of the final exam in your American History class. It has all the answers. It ensures an A on the exam and thus the promise of that illusive A you could not otherwise obtain no matter how hard you tried. It could mean the difference between going to San Francisco State University and University of California at Santa Barbara. What do you do? Why?

6. You are my aide and I ask you to go down and pick up some copies in the office. In the back room where all the copies are stacked, you see a copy of the American History final exam. There is no one around. What do you do? Why?

7. You are standing in front of your parents, Mr. Crane, and Mr. Cheney, having been accused of cheating on the American History final exam. You did. They know you did. They promise only to give you an F for the exam (which means you would still pass) instead of suspending you if you tell them how you got it and who stole it in the first place. You know the answer. Your parents are watching. . . . What do you do? Why?

Know the Difference
Between Fact and Opinion

RATIONALE

It is essential in our information-saturated world that all students be able to determine whether information is true or not, whether it is fact or opinion. The following assignment is one I developed as part of a larger unit on reading for truth.

WHAT TO DO

Give students the following assignment.

Directions   The purpose of this assignment is to further develop your ability to determine the credibility of a range of texts. In this exercise you will find statements, advertisements, images, and obituaries. Throughout the exercise it is essential that you reinforce the habit of asking such questions as "Why do I think that?" or "How do they know that?"

fact (noun)

1. Information presented as objectively real.

2. A real occurrence; an event.

3. (a) Something having real, demonstrable existence.   (b) The quality of being real or actual.

4. A thing that has been done, especially a crime.

5. Law: The aspect of a case at law comprising events determined by evidence.

Synonyms: *certainty, truth, verity, reality, actuality, gospel, data.*

o•pin•ion (noun)

1. A belief or conclusion held with confidence but not substantiated by positive knowledge or proof.

2. A judgment based on special knowledge and given by an expert.

3. A judgment or an estimation of the merit of a person or thing.

4. The prevailing view.

5. Law: A formal statement by a court or other adjudicative body of the legal reasons and principles for the conclusions of the court.

Synonyms: *belief, judgment, idea, thought; impression, notion, fancy, assumption; conviction, view, stance, position, attitude.*

1. How do you explain the difference between the "truth," a fact, and an opinion? Please provide an example to illustrate your point, taking time to explain your example.

2. What questions do you need to ask to determine whether a piece of information is a fact or an opinion?

3. After reading each of the following statements/excerpts, please indicate whether you think each one is a fact (F) or an opinion (O). (Briefly explain why you think this.)

____The San Francisco 49ers are the best team in the history of football.

____The San Francisco 49ers won more Super Bowls than any other team.

____Children exposed to violent television programming are more likely to engage in violent behavior immediately after watching such shows.

____Television is bad for kids.

____It is programs like *Doom* that are to blame for the Littleton massacre.

____America has a short attention span: it will forget about Littleton by the end of June.

____More kids in America die from physical abuse every 15 minutes than died in Littleton.

____The Ford Mustang is the most popular American-made car.

____The Ford Mustang is the best car made in America.

____ALPHARETTA, Ga.—Rick Rood, who as "Ravishing Rick Rude" was one of professional wrestling's biggest stars in the 1980s and early 1990s, died April 20. He was 40. Rood was found unconscious at his home. He was resuscitated, but died later at a hospital. Autopsy results were pending. In the ring, Rood played a womanizing, conceited bad guy who would often finish off opponents with the "Rude Awakening," a neck-breaking takedown. He was injured in a 1994 match with the wrestler Sting in Japan and then retired. Since then, he had been a manager and commentator for Extreme Championship Wrestling, the World Wrestling Federation and, most recently, Atlanta-based World Championship Wrestling.

___1986 Ford Maverick w/ new tires and AM radio. Lime green metallic paint. 240k miles on it. Excellent condition. A classic. Great first car for teen driver! Call 342-8892.

4. Write a short piece titled "How to Know a Fact When You See One," or "How to Spot an Opinion with Your Eyes Closed." Be sure to provide examples to illustrate and to explain how these examples support your ideas.

Note: I might include some photographs and advertisements—e.g., the Apple Computer "Think Different" ads—here and ask students to explain what is fact and what is opinion about them.

STUDENT EXAMPLE

Alison Grites on how to identify a fact:

One way to know a fact from an opinion is to think about what you already know about a subject, and see if what you are being told coincides with what you already know about something. If you think something is too outrageous to be a fact, it is probably an opinion or false. Another way to know that something is a fact is to hear it first person. Gossip starts when one person tells something, then that person tells someone, and so on. If you eliminate the middleman and go right to the source, you are more likely to get factual information.

Understand Narrative Design

88

RATIONALE

According to Madison Smart Bell in his book *Narrative Design* (1997) "Form is of primary importance, always. [Everything else] . . . is always subordinate to form." To think about narrative design is to develop textual intelligence and to refine students' story grammar, a faculty that serves them well as readers.

> I try to leave out the parts that people skip.
>
> ELMORE LEONARD

WHAT TO DO

• Teach and integrate into your discussion of literature the following literary terms (see the Appendix for a more complete list):

  ▸ *Plot:* what happens

  ▸ *Form:* the aspect of a story that can be represented by a diagram or other graphic means

  ▸ *Design:* modular, episodic, linear

  ▸ *Time management:* how stories unfold across time

  ▸ *Tone:* how the text sounds

  ▸ *Character:* the person to whom everything is happening or who is making things happen

  ▸ *Imagery:* the pictures within a piece of writing that help the reader to see what they are reading, and elements of the text that have symbolic meaning

  ▸ *Theme:* the ideas that run throughout the story

• So that they better understand the narrative design, consider having your students:

  ▸ Draw the text (Reminder 74)

  ▸ Perform the text (Reminder 73)

  ▸ Use the following graphic organizers (Reminder 17)

    ▸ Story structures

    ▸ Time line

> ▶ Story board
> ▶ Idea cards (to allow students to manipulate the elements of the story)

• When introducing the elements of a story, use an elementary, universally familiar story (e.g., Cinderella, Jack and the Beanstalk) so that students can concentrate on mastering and applying the principles of narrative design instead of worrying about what the story is about.

• Have students write their own short story or narrative poem to better understand the principles of narrative design (through emulation and manipulation).

• Teach the different types of narrative design: linear, with the classical triangle shape; and episodic (aka modular), which can be organized in alternating, different time sequences.

• Decide ahead of time whether you should directly teach these design elements and then use the actual story to illustrate the principles of design, or should have them find and describe the different elements that make the story work. The latter allows for deeper engagement by training them to find for themselves such moments of heat, structural or thematic change as make a difference in the story.

• Examine and discuss the essential role conflict and suspense play in any story: what is the source of each in a story and how does the writer create these feelings in the reader?

• Discuss the following:

> ▶ Who is involved?
> ▶ What are they doing?
> ▶ Why are they doing it?
> ▶ What does the story line of the text look like if you draw it?
> ▶ How does time function in this text?
> ▶ How does the point of view affect the meaning and action in the text?
> ▶ How does the design of the story affect or mirror the action?
> ▶ What is the source of tension or conflict in the story?
> ▶ What does the writer do to draw you through the text (i.e., create suspense)?

SAMPLE ACTIVITY

Macbeth Prereading Activity: Build Your Own Story

Overview   In order to have some fun, think about how stories work, and prepare ourselves to read Shakespeare's *Macbeth*, we will use the attached story cards to create a story. We will do this by using the characters from *Macbeth* without referring to the actual text of the play. The point is not to "get it right" (i.e., as Shakespeare designed) but to create your own story from another's pieces. This activity is designed to:

• Prepare you to read *Macbeth*

• Enhance your knowledge about story grammar (i.e., how stories work)

• Create an opportunity for you to collaborate with others in the creation of the story

What to Do   Follow these steps to complete your story by the end of the period:

1. Cut up the page of character names.

2. Familiarize yourself with them.

3. Discuss them and brainstorm possible relationships, plots, and themes in the story.

4. Map out your story by arranging the character cards into a formation that represents the plot.

5. Write a summary of your plot as represented in your arrangement.

6. Give your story a title.

7. List the character traits of your main characters, using these questions to help you do so:
   ◗ What does this character want most?
   ◗ Why does the character want it?
   ◗ What are they willing to do to get it?
   ◗ How does this desire shape their behavior, values, and relationships?
   ◗ What is the consequence or their desire?

8. Use the story grammar organizer to write down your ideas and direct your discussion.

9. Present your story to the class.

10. Turn in your story organizer.

STUDENT EXAMPLES

FIGURE 88-1 These students used idea cards (see Appendix 9) to help them prepare to read *Macbeth*. They wrote the names of all the characters on the cards. After cutting them up, and without any prior knowledge about the play, they had to construct their own story by using the cards. The story one group came up with is shown in Figure 88-2.

Main Characters

- Three witches
- Lady Macbeth
- Duncan
- The Gentlewoman
- Donaldbain

Setting (time, place, atmosphere)

They were in Salem, Mass. In the 1600s. It was stressful. People were crazy, fearful.

Primary Conflict

Lady Macbeth was possessed by three witches.

List the main events in the story

Lady Macbeth hired a murderer to kill King Duncan's son, Malcolm. The murderer and Malcolm had a fight, and they both died. The king got really mad. Duncan sent a message with the letter to Macbeth saying "You will pay for my son's death!" Three witches hired another murderer to kill Duncan. Then Duncan died. Donalbain, the king's youngest son, was taken by Macbeth, but the witch didn't hurt him. After the climax, the doctors were reading a book about witchcraft. And the doctor and Seyton were looking for the witches. The doctor found the witches in the wood in a cave. Then the witches disappeared. They made Macbeth hire a murderer to kill Seyton. Then the murderer of Seyton died also. The doctor walked into the fight. Right before the murderer died, the doctor asked "Wo told you to kill Seyton?" Seyton replied, "Lady Macbeth." So the doctor read the spell that witched used to possess Macbeth. After the resolution, they never found the three witches that had possessed Lady Macbeth. She cared for Donalbain until he was well enough to be the king.

Climax

A gentlewoman overheard what the witches were doing to Macbeth and she went to Seyton, Macbeth's attendant, and sent him to tell the doctor the whole truth.

Resolution

The doctor found the antidote to the potion and had Macbeth drink it. He drugged her and made her drink it. She woke up and couldn't believe what she had done.

FIGURE 88-2   After manipulating the idea cards, students used the story structure graphic organizer (Appendix 20) to help them think about what a story must have and how their ideas might fit within that structure.

WHAT IT SHOULD HAVE	WHY IT SHOULD HAVE IT	EXAMPLE

• setting
• plot
• character quality
• main characters
• introduction
• climax
• conflict types
   • man vs. man
   • man vs. himself
   • man vs. nature
   • man vs. everything
• suspense
	• helps reader get involved in the story
	• because without it there is nothing
	• makes each character an individual
	• gives the story a base
	• gets the reader interested
	• the point of the story
	• a strong thing needed in the plot, creates action
	• makes the story interesting
	• creates interest and keeps it entertaining
		• In *Of Mice and Men* they were in different places
		• Romeo and Juliet fell in love
		• Lennie was big and dumb; George was smart
		• Romeo and Juliet were main characters
		• In *Catcher in the Rye* Holden talked a lot
		• In *Romeo and Juliet* they died
		• Romeo and Juliet vs. Family

FIGURE 88-3   I try to always have students develop the criteria of good stories first so they can revise their own understanding as we go. This also provides me useful information about what they already know and need to learn. This example is from Steve Gomez, Alex Dove, and Chris Dannels.

Discuss the Role of Character

89

RATIONALE

Don Graves's book *Bring Life into Learning* (1999) is grounded on the premise that everything—people, organisms, groups—can be understood by asking what they want most. This is a highly useful question to ask when it comes to reading in any subject area; it also provides a powerful cross-curricular connection for all teachers to use.

I don't drink a lot. That's perhaps one of the reasons why my characters are always drinking and taking drugs, because I am not.

ROBERT STONE

WHAT TO DO

- Ask your students these questions when discussing character:

  ▶ What does _____ want more than anything else?

  ▶ Why does he or she want that?

  ▶ What factors directly and indirectly influence the behavior of (e.g., Hamlet) in this situation?

  ▶ How does the subject's behavior reveal its character?

  ▶ What choices are available to the subject?

  ▶ Which factors most directly influence the subject's decision?

  ▶ What decision did it make—and why?

- Ask such questions in all subject areas. Consider the following examples:

  ▶ Science: What does the Ebola virus want most?

  ▶ Health: What do teenagers want most?

  ▶ English: What does Ophelia want most?

  ▶ Business: What does the client want most?

  ▶ History: What did Abraham Lincoln want most?

- Have students generate a list of adjectives that describe the person, group, or organism. Ask them to provide subsequent explanations about how these words relate to the subject.

- Have them compare a person with someone from a different situation, text, or era, and examine how each responded to the same event, idea, or situation.

• Have them look for any inconsistencies in <u>e.g., Lincoln's</u> behavior and consider whether these might reveal information about his or her character.

• Teach them about character by having them create their own character, then manipulate their character's circumstances to see how they might react to such changes. For example, would they act differently in this situation if they were a different gender? Race? Age? In a different era or place?

• Have them examine and discuss the relationship between name and character, looking at the name/word's origins.

• As a class, ask the essential questions:

  ‣ What is it?

  ‣ What does it do?

  ‣ What makes it move or act?

  ‣ How does it behave?

  ‣ What does it want most?

  ‣ Why does it want that?

  ‣ How does it try to obtain that end?

SAMPLE ASSIGNMENT

Character Study

Overview

The study of character is essential not only to reading literature but to understanding people. This assignment is designed to help you better understand (by asking you to read more closely) *Macbeth* and improve your general understanding of the role and meaning of character in life and literature.

Character (defined)

• a conventionalized graphic device placed on an object as an indication of ownership, origin, or relationship

• a graphic symbol (as a hieroglyph or alphabet letter) used in writing or printing

• one of the attributes or features that make up and distinguish an individual : a feature used to separate distinguishable things into categories

• moral excellence and firmness : a man of sound character

• **Word Origins:** Middle English *caracter*, from Middle French *caractére*, from Latin character mark, distinctive quality, from Greek *charakter*, from *charassein* to scratch, engrave; perhaps.

Part One

Please complete the following steps by Monday. Do not do this in your journal; all pages for this assignment will eventually need to be collected. If, for some reason, you are not comfortable writing in this way about yourself, you may choose to do the assignment about someone else.

• Write down five adjectives that describe your character.

• Include the definitions for each word.

• Write down an antonym and synonym for each word on that list.

• Include an example of each character trait from your own life.

• Identify the origins, causes, or consequences of each trait

SAMPLE: *DILIGENT*

Definition: Characterized by steady, earnest, and energetic application and effort.

Synonyms: *persistent, industrious, assiduous.*

Antonyms: *lazy, laggard, slow, leisurely.*

Example: Shown by how I always strive my hardest on my work and get it done without procrastination.

Origins: Originated from the good example my sister set by going all out on her work (and showing me how stressed out you can be when you procrastinate!).

Part Two

Repeat Part One but instead of doing this for yourself, come up with five words (and the required synonyms and antonyms) for Macbeth or Lady Macbeth. Complete all the steps outlined in Part One. Here is an example written by Ryan Marks from *Huck Finn*.

INDOMITABLE

Definition: incapable of being overcome, subdued, or vanquished.

Synonyms: *invincible, invulnerable, impregnable, unassailable, unbeatable.*

Antonyms: *weak, vulnerable, susceptible.*

Example: Example from Text: Huck refuses to give the money to his father so he gives it to the judge.

Origins: Huck's childhood experiences and his hopes provoke courage; he knows his father's history and wants nothing to do with him.

Part Three

We reveal our character in different ways—through speech, actions, gestures, dress, beliefs. However, the question that helps us to best understand someone's (as well as our own) character is a simple one: what does this person want very badly? All sorts of questions begin to emerge from this question: *why* do they want this? *What* are they willing to do to get it? *How* will they get it? What problems does this desire create for them and how will they solve them? What is the consequence of this desire? What does this desire tell us about them? Why do we think that? At this point in your reading you have met the main character(s) and should know them well enough to answer these questions. Please write a one-pager about the assigned character(s) using these questions (and any you come up with yourself) to guide you.

Part Four

Expression of Your Character. After doing Part Three about a character in the book, please do the same one-pager about yourself, using the same questions to guide your writing.

Part Five

Poem: "Aspects of (Character's Name)" or "Aspects of Myself." Using Weldon Kees's poem "Aspects of Robinson" as a model, write your own poem about the character or yourself. See Neal Cameron's example below:

> Huck aboard a raft observes the world as it passes by him.
> Warm houses with lit windows along the shore and on hillsides.
> Silhouettes of craft navigate the murky water.
> Their figures black on the blue night sky
> Ripples on the river's surface guide them. This is Mississippi Huck.
>
> Huck in a canoe alone, surrounded by the river's fog
> Separated from the raft, both drifting aimlessly.
> Whoops give their direction yet vision is useless and sound filtered
>   by fog
> Spun around by the river and pushed into the shore they find each
>   other.
> Excitement and disorientation, a door to mischief for Huck.

Huck laying in the woods talking with Jim, retelling his adventure,
Kings are discussed, and what they do, King Solomon in particular.
Discussion turns to debate. An argument erupts,
"Is Solomon the wisest man?" Neither see it the same.
He gives up arguing yet an impression has been made on Huck.

Huck up a tree, watching a feud end.
Two boys, rifle in hand, back to back behind a wood pile.
A burst of gunfire and smoke below him.
The wounded jumped for it into the river.
On the shore wash their bodies filling Huck with loss.

Huck swimming naked in the flowing river, then
Eating breakfast of fish caught fresh the past night
Day breaks with dawn from the east as Huck reflects on
The river traveled, the fish caught, the events of the past night
How he got to be here and the adventures along the way
What adventures lay ahead tomorrow, Huck?

STUDENT EXAMPLES

ASPECTS OF MARKS

Marks driving on Friday night. The music's on.
Friends are laughing. Everyone's happy.
We see other drivers. Some we know so we honk or wave.
Others not. Red lights last eternity, waiting to go. Buildings reflect.

Marks at the edge of the world. What does he do?
Turn back? Jump off?—ease down. All kinds of people.
A new environment. Interest. a new way of info. change.
People watch the emerging rookie.

Marks at night on Haight street. 3 friends.
Marks talking, observing, wondering.
Marks curious, Looking for something, yet unknown.
"Can ya spare a quarter?" "Yeah." Marks respecting.

Marks at home. Sleeping, watching, Reading and eating.
Marks peaceful in state of mind. Marks ready to go.
Start the car. Turn on the radio. Speed off to the city.
Marks coming home at midnight tired.

Marks in T-shirt and jeans. Adidas shoes. NY Yankees cap. Pro-fitted.
Blue and red stripes, athletic shoes. Flannel in mind. Buttoned up.
Old Navy, burgundy, black, Cold with no jacket. Happy with life.

—Ryan Marks

JASMINE Response

Jasmine wants very badly to escape her fate. This whole urge shapes her life and feelings because she will go to any lengths to achieve this. The book in short is her journey to find out who she really is. At the end we find this out as Jasse. This journey to escape her fate tests and develops her selves that surface along the way. Through the book the question that crops up is "To what lengths will she take this dream of being an individual?" These lengths extend across the Atlantic Ocean, into the heart of New York, setting in the isolation of Iowa, and finally finish in California. You wonder after this race is won if she ever turns around to see her footprints along the track of Johti, Jasmine, Jane, Death, and rebirth. As the starting gun popped under the banyan tree in Hasnapur, this dream, this race, transformed her as she gained character, experience, and knowledge. Jasmine ran in circles until she realized that the finish lay where she finally knew her true identity. In my ideas, this is Jase, confident, educated, happy Jase.

—Hannah Tucker

Know the Organizational Structures of Information

90

RATIONALE

Research consistently finds that reading comprehension is improved by a knowledge of the physical presentation of text and its structures. "Physical presentation of text" means such visual textual clues as headings, subheadings, signal words, and location of the main idea in a sentence or paragraph. "Text structures" refers to more abstact ideas such as those organizational patterns used to convey the writer's purpose (to persuade, describe, compare/contrast, or entertain within a story). Dickson, Simmons, and Kameenui (1995) identify three "areas of convergence" in the research on text organization:

- Well-presented text facilitates comprehension
- Text structure and student awareness of text structure are highly related to comprehension
- Explicitness in text presentation and structures facilitates comprehension

Read, read, read. Read everything— trash, classics, good and bad, and see how they do it. Just like a carpenter who works as an apprentice and studies the master. Read! You'll absorb it. Then write. If it is good, you'll find out. If it's not, throw it out the window.

WILLIAM FAULKNER

WHAT TO DO

Teach students the following about text organization:

- Physical presentation includes:
  - Headings and subheadings
  - Location of main ideas
  - Signal words
- Text structure
  - Narrative
  - Story grammars
  - Plot line
- Expository techniques include
  - Sequence (information/events arranged in order of occurrence)
  - Continuation (uses words to indicate continuation of same idea)

> Summation (signals effort to reiterate or conclude with main idea)

> Example (indicates to reader that an example is to follow)

> Descriptive (use of sensory details to help reader visualize)

> Enumeration (listing, usually in order of importance, ideas, steps, stages)

> Compare/contrast (how things are similar and different); usually organized side by side (e.g., A is this way, but B is that way) within a sentence or paragraph so readers can see the point of comparison immediately

> Persuasive (use of words to signal emphasis or concession)

> Problem/solution/effect (uses words like *as a result* to signal relationship)

Strategies to Use

• Teach students to use semantic and syntactic clues such as topic sentences which, if well-structured, signal the organizational structures to follow. Example: "A cell goes through many phases during the process of division" signals a sequential organization for the remainder of the paragraph. Syntactic clues are those words that signal sequence, such as *first, second,* or *finally;* they also include words like *but, in contrast,* or *similarly,* which are commonly used to indicate a compare/contrast text structure.

• "Chunk" the text into meaningful units of thought (e.g., noun or verb phrases) if the sentences are long or difficult.

• Develop students' story grammar by examining—through analysis, manipulation, and comparison/contrast—different examples (e.g., linear, collage, flashback, narrative leaps or what filmmakers call "cutaways") and how they affect meaning, how they work.

• Use different graphic organizers, depending on the type of text and purpose of the assignment, to help students organize the information. Example: Use the blank outline provided in the appendix to teach students how to identify the main ideas and their supporting details/examples, a technique appropriate when reading expository text. Other tools might include a time line or the Big Idea; a story map would work equally well with narrative or expository text.

• Spend adequate time developing and activating their schema as to the content and general structure of the text so students know how to read it. This might include reading a portion and modeling how you make sense of textual features or organizational patterns within the text.

• Whenever possible, choose expository texts based on the quality of their content and the books' organizational structures since these make a tremendous difference in performance.

• Use various visualizing strategies—maps, flowcharts, outlines—to help students see the different components and organize these in a useful way to improve comprehension.

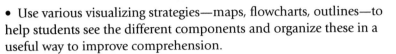

TRANSITIONS

Transitions are those words that make for smooth prose. They make one idea or sentence flow into the next. Such words signal how information is organized within the sentence and the entire text. Without them you have choppy, fragmented prose that distracts the reader from the ideas you are trying to convey. Also, the absence of these words undermines the coherence of your essay since the relationship between ideas cannot be clearly expressed. Learning how transitions work will help you read *and* write with greater control.

TRANSITIONAL WORDS

These words do not join sentences but link ideas; thus they should be preceded by a semicolon or even a period if the transitional word or phrase falls between two clauses.

Example: More and more high school students are working full-time; *however*, this does not mean that schools should compromise their standards.

TRANSITIONAL WORDS & PHRASES

• again	• along
• also	• although
• among	• and
• and so	• another
• as	• as a result
• as for me	• because
• besides	• but
• consequently	• despite
• equally important	• even more important
• even though	• finally
• first	• furthermore
• hence	• however
• in addition	• in fact
• in order	• in the end
• indeed	• moreover
• nevertheless	• next
• on the other hand	• since
• sometimes	• still
• such	• then
• therefore	• thus
• whereas	• while
• yet	

DIRECTIONS

Identify and explain the effect of each transitional word or phrase in the following paragraph. Do you see other words that could be used?

A new poll suggests that today's teenagers are less prejudiced than their parents. Moreover, the poll also found that the shift in attitudes was caused by some of the very same things that most concern parents. For instance, rap music, movies, and television shows accounted for dramatic changes in perception of other races; however, films released by Hollywood remain consistently divisive in their racial content. For instance, most films reduce blacks to stereotypes or elevate them to heroic status. Yet so few kids can pay the high prices for theaters these days, that teens rarely see these films and are thus left with the free entertainment provided by MTV and other programs whose audience reflects the diversity of our culture. Finally, there seems to be some truth to the argument that this generation is too comfortable to be angry and active; while they may have some frustrations, everyone also has a television and a VCR and a stereo, all of which keep most people entertained and distracted from the problems that once upon a time drove such writers as James Baldwin to leave this country for another where he hoped he might be able to live as a man whose color neither defined nor limited him.

FIGURE 90-1   I use this handout to explain transitional words and improve students' knowledge about how texts work and are organized.

Improve Speed, Fluency, and Stamina

91

RATIONALE

Successful readers are able to read a variety of texts with reasonable fluency and speed. Fluency involves their ability to make sense of different aspects and keep moving at a productive pace. Stamina further distinguishes strong from developing readers. Stamina, an essential capacity, ensures that readers are able to maintain attention over a long period of time. Such capacities can be of vital importance when it comes to reading such texts as tests that require sustained attention over a period of time, all of which has the added stress of what will happen if they fail.

Reading is to the mind what exercise is to the body.

SIR RICHARD STEELE

WHAT TO DO

• Read aloud so students hear how the text should sound, thereby improving their fluency with different textual structures.

• Use repeated reading to have students increase their speed, comprehension, and fluency (if the text is adequately short and within their reading level).

• Use sustained silent reading (SSR) in predictable ways using self-selected books. (I do it twice a week for twenty minutes each time.)

• Develop their awareness of aspects of performance: when they finish with SSR have them evaluate their performance by responding to the following statements and questions:

> ▶ I read _____ pages in _____ minutes, which averages out to _____ minutes per page.

> ▶ This is (circle one):   slow   typical   fast

> ▶ How many pages did I read last time?

> ▶ How do I explain the difference (if there is one) between the two scores?

• Using the same journal, have them use these prompts to further develop their awareness of what they do while reading:

> ▶ I got confused when . . .
> ▶ I was distracted by . . .
> ▶ I started to think about . . .
> ▶ I got stuck when . . .
> ▶ The time went quickly because . . .
> ▶ A word/some words I didn't know were . . .
> ▶ I stopped because . . .
> ▶ I lost track of everything except . . .
> ▶ I figured out that . . .
> ▶ I first thought . . . but then I realized . . .

- Improve students' fluency by using the strategies in this book to:

  - ▶ Improve students' word-recognition skills
  - ▶ Recognize words and sentence structures
  - ▶ Identify troublesome words and information

STUDENT EXAMPLES

ALLI BORNSTEIN'S SSR LEARNING LOG

February 8: While reading my book during SSR today I found myself getting very confused when the author wrote long and dawn out quotes and sentences. I lost interest when those types of long sentences occurred. I found myself distracted by low whispering and talking, and also noises and voices outside the room. This book is going very quickly for me because of how good the story is so far. SSR went surprisingly fast because of how interested I was in the story. This book [*Girl, Interrupted*] has made me think about the real experiences the author Susanna Kayson had to go through during her stay at McLean, which was an institution. The only reason I stopped reading was because of the time limit, but I am really enjoying this book and hope to read more tonight.

February 10: While reading a little bit more of my book today I found the reading a bit more difficult. I was frustrated and confused when trying to sort through all of the different clips and phrases she was jotting down about her experiences. The author kept skipping from one topic to another, and it got me very mixed up. I got stuck when the author started to talk about something interesting, and then totally skipped to some topic extremely different. I started to lose my train of thought when reading this story. I found myself getting off track, but I'm starting to warm up a little bit to this author's style of writing.

February 29: Today while reading I found myself not being as distracted as I have been recently. I found the couple chapters I was reading today unusually interesting, since in the past I have mentioned that I do not really enjoy this author. I blocked out every distraction around me and tried really concentrating on my book. Blocking out everything around me really helped and I will try using this method when we read during class again.

March 7: I am very excited about finishing my book, and very proud of myself that I finished so much of it in class. I found that once I started to really concentrate on the book the distractions around me quickly disappeared. I'm trying to understand the book a little bit more. I'm finding myself understanding the concept of this story a lot better, since I'm almost finished with the story. I know that this story meant a lot to the author when she was writing about it because this whole story is about her, and her life story when she was in the hospital.

FIGURE 91-1   Rebecca Farac uses the bookmark (see Appendixes 30 and 31) to help her reflect on her reading at the end of an SSR session.

92 Determine What Is Important

RATIONALE

We are always wanting to know what is important. We are a practical people who, at least in expository writing, want the author to "get to the point." Yet most authors, whether writing fiction or nonfiction, convey many ideas they think are important. Strong readers can sift through stacks of ideas contained in an article or chapter and identify those that are most important, and explain why. This ability precedes most other reading skills we hope students develop. In life they will read contracts, work-related documents, and other writings of consequence; their success as consumers, parents, and employees will depend on their ability to discern what is important and to explain why it is, citing examples to support their explanation.

WHAT TO DO

Ensure that students know why they are reading a document, so they know what information to look for. The information will depend on the type of document they are reading. In a textbook, for example, readers can look at textual clues like bold or italic type, headings, and topic sentences at the beginning of each paragraph to determine the most important facts. Additional clues can be gleaned by consulting the questions that inevitably appear at the end of the chapter and that signal what the publisher thinks is important to know.

Communicate to students the criteria for importance. What will be on the test? What the student thinks is important? What is important to the character in the story? Perhaps what is important to know about each stage in a scientific process? Providing an example to anchor students' reading will help immensely. When teaching *The Odyssey*, for example, I ask students to identify the one most important event in each chapter and to explain why they think it is so important. Before turning them lose, however, I show them three student exemplars from previous years, one of which is excellent, one of which is mediocre, and the third of which is weak. I ask them to develop criteria for what is important after looking at these three examples. Then we discuss their criteria and, as a class, establish guidelines for what is an important event and what an insightful explanation looks like.

Help readers identify what is important by directing their attention to certain words, phrases, sections, or aspects of the text that you think merit scrutiny. Remember that they not only need to learn to recognize what is important but to know where to find it. You can thus help them develop this capacity by doing the following:

- Asking them to look for specific information (words, ideas, structures)
- Modeling for them how you read the same text and find the important information, narrating what you are doing and thinking as you read
- Giving students photocopied passages from the text which you then ask them to annotate, saying each underlined word or phrase should be "important" by the criteria discussed
- Asking them to explain why certain events or information is *not* important so they develop a comparative sense of importance
- Requiring that they always anchor their rationale in the text as students too often think something is important because of what they believe according to their culture or experience, neither of which is likely to help them in this situation, though it does provide a useful entry point for subsequent discussion of the text

STUDENT EXAMPLE

Nitya Bandla's World War I Time Line

Nitya created the time line shown in Figure 92-1 as a means of preparing herself to read *All Quiet on the Western Front*. Realizing my students lacked the necessary background information, I had them cull the most important moments from several different time lines prior to reading the book.

Timeline: As you read look for those moments that indicate a new and crucial stage in a process or journey. On each bar of the timeline write the word(s) that will clearly delineate that stage from the others. Under the bar you should note the specific details such as date and what happened so you can use these notes later for writing or discussions. The important point is to identify the essential events and the order in which they occur.

1. 6/28/14   ARCHDUKE ASSINATED
   This event led to WWI

2. 8/26-30/14 BATTLE OF TANNENBURG
   Germany army achieves its greatest victory on Eastern front against Russia

3. 9/5/14   BATTLE OF MARNE
   German invasion in France. Led to the World War I.

4. 2/4/15 GERMANY DECLARES A SUBMARINE BLOCKADE to any boat approaching England is considered a legitimate target.

5. 5/7/15 SINKING OF THE PASSENGER SHIP in Luisitania. Led to many people's death.

6. 8/30/15
   Germany responds to U.S anger by ceasing to sink ships without warning.

7. 2/21/16 - 22/8/16
   The longest battle of the war, the Battle of Verdun, is fought to draw in one million.

8. 2/1/17 Unrestricted submarine warfare. Germany declared they're going to attack any ships without warning.

9. 11/7/1917 RUSSIAN REVOLUTION
   Bolshevik socialists, led by Lenini overthrew Kerensky's government.

10. 1/8/18 14 points
    President Woodrow Wilson declares 14 points as the path to world peace.

11. 11/10/18 GERMAN REPUBLIC
    After Kaiser Wilhelm II abdicated a german republic was founded.

12. 1919 DEMOBILIZATION OF THE ARMIES
    Germany had to pay a huge preparation, this won the war.

13. 6/28/19 TREATY OF VERSAILES
    Peace treaty was signed by German and Allies in Versailes.

14. 3/19/20
    The Senate fails to ratify the Treaty

15. 1924-1925
    Adolf Hitler imprisoned for sedition; writes Mein Kampf.

16. 9/2/1939 SECOND WAR BEGINS
    Extension of World War I in someways.

FIGURE 92-1   Nitya's time line allows her to organize the information from different sources; it also allows me to evaluate her ability to determine what the most important information is and how well she understood what she read.

Explain Their Thinking: Elaboration Strategies

RATIONALE

Students often understand and have thoughts they'd like to share about what they read, but sometimes they lack the capacity to develop those fledgling ideas. They may, when called on, make a simple or brief statement that contains an obvious gem in it, but they don't know how to flesh it out. The following examples and ideas are designed to help teachers develop these elaboration strategies in students so they can discuss what they read better and thereby understand what they read—and think—more fully. One final rationale for this idea is its obvious connection to writing and its subsequent contribution to improving their ability in that area, too, as they learn to ask themselves the same questions their reader will pose.

WHAT TO DO

• Keep in mind that the most important learning device is the well-phrased, timely question. The students in the scenario just described may or may not know they have a good idea on their hands. Part of the process of learning to elaborate on ideas is recognizing that they are in fact powerful ideas that merit development.

• Use the following strategies to help students internalize the ability to recognize and elaborate upon their ideas' potential value:

> ▸ Recognize when their response to a reading is insightful, singling out some specific detail that revealed the quality of their thinking: "I never thought of that connection, Jason, but I can definitely see it because of the example you used to explain it!"

> ▸ Pose questions to help them clarify and evaluate their ideas prior to elaborating on them: "I think I understand what you're saying, Jane, and it sounds like a potentially incredible insight. Can you think of another way of saying that or find an example in the text to help us better see what you mean?" or "Why do you think that's such an important aspect of the text?"

The value of great fiction, we begin to suspect, is not that it entertains us or distracts us from our troubles, not just that it broadens our kowledge of people and places, but also that it helps us to know what we believe, reinforces the qualities that are noblest in us, leads us to feel uneasy about our failures and limitations.

JOHN GARDNER

▶ Use think-alouds (written or spoken) to reinforce the habit of thinking through a response (see Reminder 64).

• Keep in mind that students develop these strategies and intellectual habits to the extent that they reflect on their own reading and thinking process, have time to practice these strategies, and learn which questions to ask, and when and how to ask them.

• Encourage them to elaborate on their own reading/ideas, using these prompts:

▶ I think _____ because . . .

▶ A good example of _____ is . . .

▶ This reminded me of _____ because . . .

▶ This was important because it . . .

▶ One thing that surprised me was . . . since I had always thought . . .

▶ I'm not sure about this, but it seemed to me that the author was trying to say . . . This idea is consistent with his other statements on this subject. For example, . . .

• Have them elaborate on others' reading/ideas, using these prompts:

▶ I understand why _____ thinks that, but there are other reasons why _____ could have happened.

▶ I never thought of it that way before, probably because I usually think . . .

▶ Jesse helped me see the main idea in a different way; I think she missed several other important ideas which I'd like to discuss . . .

▶ I thought what John meant when he was talking about that poem was . . . I thought this because he said . . .

▶ My understanding of _____'s interpretation is . . . If this is what she means then I would like to add . . .

• Use these questions, and help students learn to use them, when writing and discussing their reading. Such questions develop the habits of clarifying, questioning, supporting, and evaluating their ideas while they read and after, when they are discussing or writing about the passage.

• Model regularly how to elaborate your thoughts about what you read. When appropriate remind them that this strategy is not designed to make their papers or sentences longer but their thinking more forceful, their writing more precise, and their reading more insightful.

STUDENT EXAMPLES

While reading my story today [Sophie's World] *I realized* that philosophy is quite interesting to me and I have a lot of fun relating what I know about philosophy to what the book tells me about philosophy. *I now see* that all people think of things in all different ways of who is God or what is God and how the world came to what it is today and where do we get our knowledge to back everything up with.
—Holly Penland, sophomore

In *On a Pale Horse, at first I thought* it was just going to be about a guy who has to become on of Satan's henchmen. It says he had to take over for the man who killed the incarnation of Death, so he would just take over. *Also, I thought he was* just going to kill his girlfriend *but then I realized* it was much more than that. They got around by flying on a magic carpet and magic is just as evolved as science. Ghosts are real in this book.
—Taralyn Lewis, sophomore

FIGURE 93-1   Henry Ortiz, who began the semester as a resistant reader, made good progress by reading books he chose and reflecting on *how* he read after each SSR session.

94 Discuss Their Reading: Reporting Strategies

RATIONALE

I read on, I skip, I look up, I dip in again.

ROLAND BARTHES

Students sometimes lack the langauge or skills needed to participate fully or successfully in discussions during or after reading a passage. The absence of such language and intellectual tools undermines their performance in other areas, most notably writing and, in a more global sense, thinking. The absence of such reporting strategies, which often depend on language or structures specific to a discipline, can often impede the development of struggling readers who feel unprepared both to read and to discuss what they read. Teachers need to help students develop these vocabularies and strategies through direct teaching, opportunity to practice them, and, most importantly, modeling. Over time, through such modeling and practice, the students will not need the artificial structures provided here as they learn to use their own language to convey the same ideas.

WHAT TO DO

Allow students to occupy the role of a practioner of a certain field; by "playing scientist," the student understands and uses this reporting language in a more appropriate context, one in which they understand why such terms or phrases are useful.

In reporting their ideas, have them use these prompts:

- When I began reading this passage I assumed that . . . but by the end I realized . . .
- I agree/disagree with what the author says because . . .
- The text/writer mentions _____ throughout; therefore I would emphasize the importance of . . .

In reporting their ideas as a group, have them use prompts such as:

- Tara's idea about the text was the most interesting: She thought it meant . . . because . . .
- Our group concluded . . .

- We saw several new connections as we discussed this passage . . .
- Our group ended up with an entirely different result/ interpretation than the others but we think we know why . . .
- Jake brought together everything we were saying in his learning log entry; he should read that because it sums it all up.

Teach them the forms of reporting:

WRITING

- Journals
- Poems
- Written conversations
- Notes

PRESENTING

- Panels of readers presenting a specific chapter or segment of the text
- A group's interpretation of the text that relies on the board, the overhead, or butcher paper to report their thinking to the class

DISCUSSING

- In small groups where they report their reading to each other
- In rotating or "jigsaw" groups so that each person must report to the entire group they join
- As a full class to which the group or individual reports what it read and concluded about the reading

REPRESENTING

- Using images
- Using others' words, songs, or images to report their understanding of the text at hand (e.g., using various antiwar songs played on a stereo to report ideas about what *All Quiet on the Western Front* says about war)
- Using multimedia to incorporate images, sounds, words, and actions into a dynamic presentation through which they report their interpretation.

Teach them to clarify their thinking or ask for clarification of others' reported thinking by using these prompts:

- Let me summarize the main ideas in this passage . . .
- At first _____ can confuse you, but if you think about _____ it will help you better understand the relationship between . . .
- I was unsure about a few things in your report. Could you review the three main ideas you mentioned?
- It sounds like you are saying that . . . Is that correct?

Make the Abstract Concrete

95

RATIONALE

As expert readers we forget how complicated texts can be for developing readers. Novice readers consistently struggle to make sense of abstractions encountered in texts. Abstract material challenges them in every subject area whether it is the abstraction of "health" or other abstractions such as freedom, power, or love. Students need help learning to identify and understand these abstractions as they move into more sophisticated texts in all subject areas.

Abstract words such as glory, honor, courage, or hollow were obscene.

ERNEST HEMINGWAY, FROM *A FAREWELL TO ARMS*

WHAT TO DO

• Sequence readings from easiest to most difficult so that each step develops the reader's capacity to meet the demands of the next step. One aspect of such a move toward more difficult texts is the degree of abstraction; typically the more difficult the text the more abstract is the content found there. Students should always be challenged to read what challenges but does not frustrate them.

• Have students use the following techniques as readers to make the abstract more concrete:

  ▶ Draw the text (as an image, cartoon, diagram, plot, time line, map), using whatever clues (colors, patterns, shapes) the text offers to guide your hand.

  ▶ Model, by demonstration and think-aloud, how you go about making sense of abstract ideas.

  ▶ Use the following graphic organizers (see the appendices for reproducible versions) to help you build a conceptual bridge between the abstract and the concrete:

    ▶ Analogical Thinking
    ▶ Venn Diagram
    ▶ KWL
    ▶ Is/Means/Represents
    ▶ Conversational Roundtable

> ▸ Clarifying What Confuses
> ▸ What's the Big Idea?
> ▸ Feature Analysis
> ▸ Think in Threes

> ▸ Enact the text (as a performance, speech, reading) to help yourself hear and better understand it.

• Activate students' prior knowledge about this and related subjects to help them to link the abstraction with what is more familiar, more concrete. This includes linking the new idea to not only their own experiences and ideas but those texts you have read before and to which the current text is related thematically, conceptually.

• Use video (if available and appropriate) to help them see the subject better; they can move into the deeper, more abstract material of *Macbeth* on the page once they have seen the witches and what the abstract notion of greed for power looks like on the screen.

• Have them ask these questions about abstractions they need to understand:

> ▸ What does it look like?
> ▸ What does it do?
> ▸ What is it made of?
> ▸ How does it work?
> ▸ What are its characteristics?
> ▸ In what context is it offered?
> ▸ How does it behave?
> ▸ What does it want?
> ▸ What category best describes it?
> ▸ Vocabulary square

• Use semantic mapping, clustering, or rapid-fire brainstorming to answer many of the previous questions and help you generate useful connections to the subject. You might, for example, generate adjectives to describe the concept or examples that seem to relate to it somehow, pushing yourself to explain (at least in your own head) how they relate.

• Keep in mind that, as words are themselves abstractions, many of the techniques described here can help students make better sense of the words they encounter while they read; it is often such words, after all, that make a text abstract. Beginning with those words can often be the logical first step toward the pleasure we call understanding.

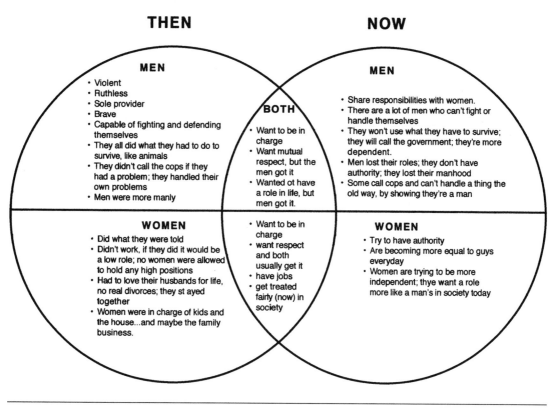

THEN　　　　　　　　　　　　　　　　**NOW**

MEN
- Violent
- Ruthless
- Sole provider
- Brave
- Capable of fighting and defending themselves
- They all did what they had to do to survive, like animals
- They didn't call the cops if they had a problem; they handled their own problems
- Men were more manly

BOTH
- Want to be in charge
- Want mutual respect, but the men got it
- Wanted ot have a role in life, but men got it.

MEN
- Share responsibilities with women.
- There are a lot of men who can't fight or handle themselves
- They won't use what they have to survive; they will call the government; they're more dependent.
- Men lost their roles; they don't have authority; they lost their manhood
- Some call cops and can't handle a thing the old way, by showing they're a man

WOMEN
- Did what they were told
- Didn't work, if they did it would be a low role; no women were allowed to hold any high positions
- Had to love their husbands for life, no real divorces; they st ayed together
- Women were in charge of kids and the house...and maybe the family business.

- Want to be in charge
- want respect and both usually get it
- have jobs
- get treated fairly (now) in society

WOMEN
- Try to have authority
- Are becoming more equal to guys everyday
- Women are trying to be more independent; thye want a role more like a man's in society today

FIGURE 95-1　Gino Donati used the Venn diagram graphic organizer (Appendix 24) to synthesize a range of information from different texts about men and women in the past and present.

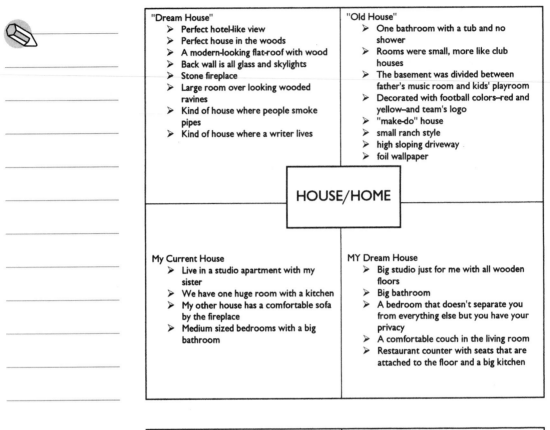

"Dream House"
- Perfect hotel-like view
- Perfect house in the woods
- A modern-looking flat-roof with wood
- Back wall is all glass and skylights
- Stone fireplace
- Large room over looking wooded ravines
- Kind of house where people smoke pipes
- Kind of house where a writer lives

"Old House"
- One bathroom with a tub and no shower
- Rooms were small, more like club houses
- The basement was divided between father's music room and kids' playroom
- Decorated with football colors–red and yellow–and team's logo
- "make-do" house
- small ranch style
- high sloping driveway
- foil wallpaper

HOUSE/HOME

My Current House
- Live in a studio apartment with my sister
- We have one huge room with a kitchen
- My other house has a comfortable sofa by the fireplace
- Medium sized bedrooms with a big bathroom

MY Dream House
- Big studio just for me with all wooden floors
- Big bathroom
- A bedroom that doesn't separate you from everything else but you have your privacy
- A comfortable couch in the living room
- Restaurant counter with seats that are attached to the floor and a big kitchen

HOME (characteristics of)
- A place where you feel comfortable
- It is unique
- It has your own personal style
- It has memories in it

HOUSE (characteristics of)
- You feel uneasy
- They all look the same
- Not fun
- Boring

FIGURE 95-2 Holly Penland used the Conversational Roundtable (Appendix 4) to make connections between her own life and the people in the essay she read. Moreover, the organizer helped her read at different and increasingly sophisticated levels.

Develop
Confidence

96

RATIONALE

Nothing distinguishes good readers more than their capacity and willingness to persevere in the face of failure. They know if they work at it the text will yield to them, though they may need to employ a number of strategies until they find the right one. Confidence in this case applies not only to ability but perception since inexperienced readers tend not to trust their interpretation of a text even if they read it successfully. Experienced readers learn to recognize when, where, or why a text might not make sense and they can adjust their reading to accommodate these demands.

WHAT TO DO

• Develop readers' textual intelligence (see Reminder 77) so they know how to read a given text. Inexperienced readers tend to read all texts the same, ignoring their structural and semantic differences.

• Remind students of the continuum of complexity along which texts are arrayed. Mastery of a particular text does not mean mastery of, for example, the domain of poetry as there are always more complex poems to read that make new and different demands on the reader's abilities.

• Have students write about and discuss their reading performance—habits, strategies, reactions—so as to make them more cognizant of what they do well and what they must improve.

• Help students achieve and see rapid results in their reading by providing quick but meaningful feedback that shows them how and how much they are improving.

• Build on confidence in other domains: e.g., tell athletes that the same use of repetition and practice they use in basketball will help them succeed in reading. Remind them of their slow but actual progress in that sport or some other domain by way of encouraging them to be patient and persistent when it comes to reading.

The most seasoned reader . . . does not bother about understanding; not, at least, at first. I know that some of the poetry to which I am most devoted is poetry which I did not understand at first reading; some is poetry which I am not sure I understand yet. . . .

T. S. ELIOT

• Sequence reading assignments so students can move from their level of comfort and competence toward mastery in small, manageable increments that provide useful feedback about their performance. This means not only arranging different assignments from easiest to most difficult, but organizing the tasks for a specific text from easiest (e.g., literal interpretation, summary of what happens) to more complex (e.g., explain how a character contributed to the outcome).

• Use basic texts (e.g., Jack and the Beanstalk or other fairy tales they all know) so they can concentrate not on understanding the text but on applying the strategies to the text before moving on to more sophisticated texts.

• Ask yourself whether you are allowing students adequate time, whether the amount of reading is reasonable, and whether the readings are challenging but not frustrating.

• Mentor struggling readers by modeling for them, giving them tools to support their reading, and suggesting books you think they will enjoy.

• Have students reflect on their reading performance in order to identify their weaknesses and strengths, and to assess the effectiveness of different strategies they use while reading. You might go so far as to have them develop a problem-solution table to which they can refer: If I get confused . . . Then try these strategies . . .

• Have students set reasonable but challenging goals about the amount of reading and the specific ways in which they will improve.

• Have them periodically revisit the reading scale and evaluate their performance, noting ways in which they have improved and reasons for that improvement. In addition, use other means to assess and communicate to students their improvement in the area of reading.

*   *   *

Take a moment to reflect on your reading and teaching. You may find the following discussion points useful, or you can come up with your own:

• Write a summary of the last section. Include in this summary three main ideas—techniques, strategies, tools—that relate to your own classes.

• Which reminders from the preceding section might help you the most?

• Looking ahead to the next section, consider its title and, before you begin reading, create your own list of reminders for this topic. After checking yours with mine, discuss which of these reminders—from your list and mine—will help you and your students the most.

Evaluate and Monitor

Their Understanding,

Performance, and Progress

Declare if thou hast
understanding.

—THE BOOK OF JOB

Jenna reads one of the many books she credited with making her into a more
mature reader by semester's end.

I do not have much to add to what I wrote in the introduction to "Evaluate Your Students," since these two sections complement each other. One point, however, bears repeating and emphasis: students must eventually take over these functions as they move toward mastery and independence as readers. The habit of reflecting on their performance, the capacity to articulate those insights to themselves or others—these are what they must accomplish if they are to be ready for the wide world of texts they will encounter as adults.

A reader like Kay, one of the sophomores in my class, exemplifies these different capacities as her learning log shows in the following entry: "I'm a pretty slow reader because if I want to learn and remember everything I read, I have to read very slowly, but for school books that I don't like I read faster cause I don't care about it." As her entry reminds us—and I have pointed out elsewhere—such evaluations give us as much information as they do the student. When I read Craig's following entry, it allows me to monitor what he is doing as well as how well he is doing it:

> I never really just read. I usually only read small things like signs and such. And when I haven't preread something I have trouble with a good flow of reading. When I am reading an assignment I have trouble describing the information and understanding what I read unless helped. And I nearly never read on my own. The only time that I do things like that is when I see something that I want to know about. For example like car magazines or street signs, store names, clothes brands, advertisements on TV. Things of that nature. When I am reading a book it is usually because I am doing it for a class or something.

Such evaluations and reflections as Craig's help him and us to know where to begin, which in his case is by helping him to realize how aware he is of all that he *does* read and how able he is do it. Craig is keeping the conversation with himself and me open through his learning log entry. He is not closing the door in my face or his own but showing me there is a door, one on which I will continue to knock throughout the semester in hopes of getting him to walk through it and count himself a member of the club.

Review, Reflect, and Reinforce

97

RATIONALE

As readers finish a text, they can do several things to improve their reading and ensure the gains they've made this time around last. Only by reviewing all the parts and reflecting on their relationship to the whole of the text can the reader gain any sense of the bigger picture. Providing opportunities to reflect on what they read, how they read it, and what the text was about helps to reinforce both their understanding and the skills they developed or used while reading. These "three R's" are the essential habits that will ensure that all students become adept at the most important R: Reading. Jerome Bruner (1977) said it long ago: "At its best a learning episode reflects what has gone before it and permits one to generalize beyond it."

To doubt everything or to believe everything are two equally convenient solutions; both dispense with the necessity of reflection.

JULES-HENRI POINCARÉ, AS QUOTED BY BERTRAND RUSSELL

WHAT TO DO

Keep in mind that students moving toward independence make choices while reading—about how to read the text and its meaning—they must now evaluate as they finish a text. The following questions or activities will help them in this process:

- Now that you are finished or finishing, what is the Big Idea (see Figure 39-1 and Appendix 27) in this text?
- How has your understanding of or response to the text changed from the beginning to the end? Explain that change using examples from the text.
- What strategies did you use to help you read this text? Did they prove effective? Explain how they did or did not help.
- Reviewing the habits of effective readers, how would you evaluate your own performance? If possible, provide specific examples to illustrate your remarks about decisions you made or actions you took while reading.
- Write a précis (aka paraphrase, synopsis, or abstract—see Reminder 84).

Remember that these culminating activities can be done using any or all of the following: talking, speaking, writing, drawing.

Have students return to the beginning of the text to see how the end relates to the beginning; writers sometimes embed many of the text's guiding ideas in the opening. Returning to review and even reread this segment can help readers see how and why writers do this.

If they have been taking notes or making an outline while reading the text, now is a perfect time to have them review it and, in the margins, jot down connections they see and realizations they have. For example, a certain pattern or theme of family might appear to them upon further reflection. Now is the time to supplement their notes with these observations.

Ask your students the following questions:

- What remains confusing to you at this point?
- What do you know now that you did not know before you read this?
- What more would you like to know about this subject?
- Using your learning log for individual reflection or as preparation for subsequent writing or discussions, how would you respond to the following prompts [developed by Kate Kinsella]?

  ▶ I learned . . .
  ▶ I discovered . . .
  ▶ I observed . . .
  ▶ I was surprised . . .
  ▶ I am beginning to wonder . . .
  ▶ I now realize . . .
  ▶ I would like to find out more about . . .
  ▶ I am still confused by . . .

- How does what you now know compare with what you predicted or thought you knew prior to reading this text? Provide, if possible, examples to illustrate your thinking.
- What conclusions can your draw about this subject or these characters after reading? Be sure to provide examples from the text to support your conclusions.
- What connections can you make to what you read before this text?
- What structures, textual features, devices, or techniques did you encounter in this text that were new to you or particularly difficult? How did you make sense of them?

- How will this relate to what you read next?
- What is the best way to assess and evaluate your reading of this text?

STUDENT EXAMPLES

These two examples come from students' learning logs in which they reflect on what they read and *how* they read.

> While I read for 20 minutes I got kind of distracted because it's really hard for me to get into a book when people are whispering around me. I felt that while I was reading that I understood my book but I had to look over paragraphs again and again so I started off pretty slow. I also felt that the time was good but a little bit short because I wasn't able to get into the story quick enough. I got stuck in a few places when the philosopher talked about philosophy but it was okay once I continued to read. I realized that if I read slow that I'm really reading faster because I don't have to read over and over again.
> —Holly Penland, sophomore

> I am really happy with my book because Andrea is finally realizing what she is doing is wrong. She is now suffering from the consequences by feeling disgusted with herself. A really good line that I read was, " . . . it just seemed like the older you got the more corrupt you became and really, if you thought about it, in terms of your morals and stuff: you were dying from the day you were born." My reading was a 4 today. I read ten pages in twenty minutes.
> —Amy Hirsch, sophomore

Develop Reading Goals

RATIONALE

Without goals we have nothing to challenge us or guide our efforts to improve. Athletes constantly develop new goals, measuring their progress toward them by various methods. Developing reading goals—as well as goals in other areas of the curriculum—is just as important for the teacher and the student since both should be continually trying to improve their performance. Students should make goals to individualize their learning and measure their progress in those areas most crucial to them; teachers should make goals for the class as a whole to help them achieve at those levels they and society at large expect. Goals and the conversations through which we create them invite us to reflect on what we should be able to do and how we can accomplish it. Even as we read we should have that most obvious of goals in mind: understanding.

WHAT TO DO

• Develop the class goals collaboratively, beginning with a serious brainstorming session during which you write all suggested goals on the board. An alternative is to have students begin this discussion in groups, then identify their top three suggestions. Write all these top suggestions on the board and then evaluate them as a class.

• Complete the initial reading survey and, at term's end, the follow-up survey.

• Develop class and personal reading goals so that students have to reflect on their own strengths and needs as readers. Consider using the profile of effective and ineffective readers to help them get thinking. They should develop no more than three goals since we can only concentrate on so many things at a time.

• After they develop their goals, students should explain (through discussion or in writing) the following:

⯈ Why they chose these goals
⯈ What steps they will follow to achieve them
⯈ What obstacles they anticipate—and what they can do to avoid or overcome them
⯈ How they will know they achieved these goals

- Create a reminder for these goals—both class and personal—that keeps them within sight at all times when in class. Class goals, for example, could be made into a poster to which the class can refer when discussing their reading. This board could also include ongoing brainstorms of possible strategies and activities to help achieve these goals. The criteria for meeting the goals must be clearly posted in their binder and/or on the class wall so they can measure their progress toward this goal and know when they need to create a new set of goals.

- Goals should be of two kinds: short term and long term. All learners need "rapid results" (Schmocker 1996) to create a sense of momentum, to prove that their efforts make a difference. Other, more ambitious goals might take as long as a semester or school year to achieve. All goals should have measurable, clearly articulated criteria so the student (or teacher) will know when the goals have been reached.

- Make sure the goals are meaningful to the teacher, the community, and most importantly to the students themselves.

- Feature the goals in their reading portfolio (Reminder 35).

- Model goal-setting behavior as often as possible. Talk about what you are doing in class in terms of what you are trying to achieve and how you are trying to achieve it. Remind them periodically to revisit their journals by doing the same yourself: "I'm really pleased with the amount of time we've been able to spend on poetry lately since that's one of my goals. And it's clear that it is paying off. Yesterday's discussion of the poems was one of the best yet. Everyone was showing incredible progress toward our class goal of supporting what we discuss by finding examples in the text they read. What are your goals—and what kind of progress are you making toward them?"

- Measure progress toward the goals using a variety of measures: observation, conferences, objective scores, and self-evaluation.

- Be sure to have students evaluate goals before and after the prescribed period of time (e.g., what they can do when they develop the goals at the beginning of the semester and what they can do at the end of the semester), reflecting on how they made that progress and what evidence of this progress they can provide (and include in their reading portfolio).

- Evaluate your own progress and work by asking these questions: What was I trying to accomplish today? How did I try to accomplish that? Why did I think it was the best approach? What happened? Why did that happen? What could I do better if I did it again?

99 Recast the Text

RATIONALE

We learn best by doing, by taking things apart or otherwise manipulating them to better understand how they are made, how they work. Recasting a text into a different form or perspective allows you to compare the two or more versions of the same idea/subject and thereby understand why the one the author chose is (perhaps) the best approach. This approach also bolsters students' textual intelligence as they learn through such manipulations how different types of texts and elements function to shape meaning and affect the reader.

WHAT TO DO

• Note that recasting here means changing the shape, form, or perspective of a text. Consider how it would affect the meaning of a text or your experience of it as a reader if you changed it:

▶ Into a poem, short story, essay, article, recipe, set of directions, advertisement, diagram, drawing, hypertext, multimedia text, or dramatic performance

▶ From one perspective (that of a man, a child, one ethnic or cultural group) to another to better understand the original perspective and how that point of view relates to their character

▶ From one era or culture to another

▶ From one domain (e.g., science) to another (e.g., literature)

▶ Out of one mode (e.g., reading) into another (e.g., dramatic interpretation)

▶ From one medium (e.g., written story) into another (e.g., interactive multimedia simulation)

▶ From one side of an argument (e.g., evolution) into another (e.g., creationism)

▶ Out of one style or voice into another

▶ From one form (e.g., novel) into another (e.g., series of diary entries from the main or a peripheral character)

- From the perspective of the main character (e.g., Hamlet) to another (e.g., Rosencrantz and Gildenstern)
- From one time frame (e.g., present) into a new tense (e.g., past)

• Consider the value—aesthetic, rhetorical, grammatical—of recasting Major Sullivan Ballou's letter to his wife into a "found poem" (i.e., in which you keep all the original words but arrange the words into poetic lines, breaking to emphasize or allow room for multiple meanings), just a sense of which I will give you here:

> Sarah, my love for you is deathless,
> it seems to bind me with mighty cables
> that nothing but Omnipotence can break,
> and yet my love of country comes over me
> like a strong wind and bears me irresistibly
> with all those chains to the battlefield.
>
> The memory of all the blissful moments
> I have enjoyed with you come crowding
> over me, and I feel most deeply grateful
> to God and you that I have enjoyed
> them so long. And how hard it is for me
> to give them up and burn to ashes
> the hopes of future years when God
> willing we might still have lived
> and loved together and seen our boys
> grown up to honorable manhood
> around us . . . If I do not return,
> my dear Sarah, never forget
> how much I loved you, nor
> that when my last breath escapes
> me on the battlefield it will whisper
> your name.
>
> Forgive my many faults
> and the many pains I have caused you,
> how thoughtless, how foolish
> I have sometimes been.
> But, Oh Sarah, if the dead can come
> back to earth and flit unseen
> around those they love,
> I shall always be with you
> in the brightest day
> and the darkest night
> always, always, and when the soft

breeze fans your cheek,
it shall be my breath,
or the cool air your throbbing
temple, it shall be my spirit
passing by. Sarah,
do not mourn me dead. Think
I am gone and wait for me
for we shall meet again.
—Donald Graves, *Bring Life into Learning: Creating a Lasting Literacy*,
1999

STUDENT EXAMPLE

Macbeth Scene as Newscast

To mix things up and help the students get deeper inside the text they were struggling to understand, we performed various adaptations of the scenes in Act Two. Here is a newscast a group of boys came up with (and which they prepared for and performed with genuine enthusiasm).

Indy: Hi we interrupt this program to bring you this special news bulletin. The king has just been murdered. Well now let's go to Michael Loftus to the crime scene.

Mike: Well the killer has not been found but we have Macbeth to interview. Macbeth who do you think the killer is?

Henry: I was in the court of my castle and Banquo and his son Fleance were talking for a while then I interrupted them and I started to talk to Banquo and he looked very nervous. I think he knew I was listening to what his son and him were talking about. Then he mentioned that he remembered the king saying "This diamond he greets your wife with all." Banquo and his son were acting weird. I think that they murdered the king.

Mike: Thank you.

Wait: Look over there—it's Banquo and his son. Let's go over there. Hello Banquo can I ask you some questions?

Steve: Yes.

Mike: I just talked to Macbeth and he told me that your son Fleance and you killed the king. Is this true?

Steve:	Nonsense. I never saw the king last night. I was out with my son Fleance. I think it might be Macbeth, because if he is trying to blame it on me it has to be him just trying to cover himself up.
Lee:	Yes my dad was telling the truth, nothing but the truth. Macbeth was talking about some weird stuff last night.
Steve:	He was saying that he was running out of time to do something. He didn't tell why he was in a hurry.
Mike:	Thank you both.
Steve and Lee:	You're welcome.
Mike:	Let's go back to the studio with Indy Johal.
Indy:	This is a tragedy—let's go to the political analyst, Ben.
Ben:	(Looks confused; says nothing.)
Indy:	Thank you, Ben. If we get any more information we will inform you. Thanks.

Keep a
Learning Log

RATIONALE

Given that reading is a skill we expect to improve the more we do it, it helps to have a process to document that growth. While there are various formal and other informal methods for assessing reading performance, the portfolio provides the reader (and the teacher) with a tangible record of what the student has read over the course of the year. It also allows readers to revisit their goals and, by adding new evidence of their progress, monitor their progress toward those goals. Finally, portfolios always provide the teacher with a powerful means of evaluating their own work since the portfolio invites them to reflect on what their students read, how they read it, and how much they improved their attitude and ability as a reader during their tenure in your class.

WHAT TO DO

- Have students reflect on their reading using the following prompts:
  - ▶ I wonder . . .
  - ▶ I began to think of . . .
  - ▶ I suppose . . .
  - ▶ I don't see . . .
  - ▶ I like the idea of . . .
  - ▶ I know the feeling of . . .
  - ▶ I noticed . . .
  - ▶ I was surprised . . .
  - ▶ I thought . . .
  - ▶ If I had been . . .
  - ▶ Why did . . .
  - ▶ Maybe . . .
  - ▶ What if . . . ?
  - ▶ This book was . . . (please explain with examples from the text)

- Have them reflect on their learning using the following prompts:

  ▶ I found _____ difficult to overcome while I read this.

  ▶ I used the following strategies throughout the reading for the following reasons and in the following ways . . .

  ▶ _____ was confusing so I . . .

  ▶ I didn't read the whole text because . . .

  ▶ I picked this book to read because . . .

  ▶ A good word to describe this book or my experience in reading it would be . . .

- Use exemplars to show them what a good performance looks like and to establish the standard against which they will be measured. Here are samples to use in class:

  While I read for 20 minutes I got kind of distracted because it's really hard for me to get into a book when people are whispering around me. I felt that while I was reading that I understood my book but I had to look over paragraphs again and again so I started off pretty slow. I also felt that the time was good but a little bit short because I wasn't able to get into the story quick enough. I got stuck in a few places when the philosopher talked about philosophy but it was okay once I continued to read. I realized that if I read slow that I'm really reading faster because I don't have to read over and over again.
  —Holly Penland

  I am really happy with my book because Andrea is finally realizing what she is doing is wrong. She is now suffering from the consequences by feeling disgusted with herself. A really good line that I read was, "it just seemed like the older you got the more corrupt you became and really, if you thought about it, in terms of your morals and stuff: you were dying from the day you were born." My reading was a 4 today. I read ten pages in twenty minutes.
  —Amy Hirsch

- Have them use learning logs at different times for different purposes:

  ▶ Before reading (to activate prior knowledge, develop necessary questions, or paraphrase what they read before).

  ▶ After a discussion (to help them understand the ideas and information at deeper levels by reflecting on, responding to, or rephrasing in their own words the discussion about what they read).

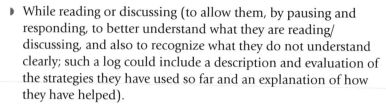

- ▶ While reading or discussing (to allow them, by pausing and responding, to better understand what they are reading/ discussing, and also to recognize what they do not understand clearly; such a log could include a description and evaluation of the strategies they have used so far and an explanation of how they have helped).
- ▶ After reading the passage (to identify the strategies they used, how they used them, how they helped; to make connections between this and other texts, discussions, ideas, or experiences; to paraphrase).

SAMPLE ASSIGNMENT

WHAT IT SHOULD HAVE	WHY SHOULD IT HAVE IT
❏ How much you read in the 20 minutes.	❏ So you can show if you are improving in your reading ability.
❏ The difficulty of the reading.	❏ To show what you thought were interesting in the book and what's going on.
❏ Quotes from your reading.	
❏ Questions on what was read.	❏ So when you go on you may get your answer in the book. You can go back and answer it.
❏ Things you figured out through your reading.	❏ To answer your questions that you may have had in the past.
❏ Things that confused you.	❏ To try to understand later on when you refer back to.
❏ Are you easily distracted.	❏ So you can see if you're still getting distracted as easily and what distracts you.
❏ Comprehension check.	❏ To see if you're understanding it and to compare.

FIGURE 100-1 Cortney Laugesen and Paige Bocci's criteria for a good learning log response. We discussed this in the class so as to establish and begin the process of internalizing such standards.

MACBETH Response Log Guidelines/Example with Analysis

Burke/Sophomore English

Overview   While we read the play I will provide quotes that merit further consideration. They might be important to the play or just relate to ideas that we should make time to discuss. Please dedicate a specific area in your journal to write about these. See the example below to get an idea of how you might write about each quote, and the subsequent analysis of this response so you can understand what makes it good.

QUOTE	RESPONSE
"Go pronounce his present death and with his formal title greet Macbeth." (I, ii, 65)	It seems like a great advance for a loyal soldier like Macbeth to receive such recognition. Back then the world was ruled by titles and so this is a big step up for Macbeth. But it seems a bit eerie to be given the title of a man whose head was lopped off and put on a stake as an example to all who would betray the king. Would you want to live in Benedict Arnold's house after he was known as a traitor by all? Some cultures believe it is bad luck to move into the house of someone who died in that house. Can it be good luck for Macbeth to be given such a prize as the title and rank of one who will always be known as a traitor? I think "what Macbeth hath won" is trouble though he may not know it yet. Still, most people would be happy to get the title as we tend to want the prize no matter what the cost.

Discussion   The above response is a good one because it:

• Speculates about the benefits or meaning of the event (e.g., "it seems like a great advance . . .")

• Comments on the event in light of its historical context (e.g., "back then the world was ruled by titles . . .") in order to better understand its importance.

• Makes various connections: personal, historical (Benedict Arnold), cultural, and political (e.g., the implications of such a high office). These connections help you better understand the foreign by making it more familiar.

• Predicts what will happen and speculates about the outcome (e.g., "I think [Macbeth is in] trouble though he may not know it yet.")

• Wonders what it would be like to be in such a position (e.g., What would it be like to be Benedict Arnold? Would you want to be?)

• Philosophizes about human nature (e.g., "we tend to want the prize no matter what the cost. . . .") and character (e.g., "most people would be happy to get the title. . . .")

FIGURE 100-2   Sample learning log response and analysis.

Appendices

Allen, Janet. 1995. *It's Never Too Late: Leading Adolescents to Lifelong Literacy*. Portsmouth, N.H.: Heinemann.

———. 1999. *Words Words Words: Teaching Vocabulary in Grades 4–12*. York, Maine: Stenhouse.

Allen, Janet, and Kyle Gonzales. 1998. *There's Room for Me Here: Literacy Workshop in the Middle Schools*. York, Maine: Stenhouse.

Allington, Richard. 1999. "Ten Principles for Looking at Reading/Language Arts Lessons in Your Classroom." Available online at the National Council of Teachers of English Web site (http://www.ncte.org/chronicle/allingMay1999.html).

Applebee, Arthur. 1996. *Curriculum as Conversation: Transforming Traditions of Teaching and Learning*. Chicago: University of Chicago Press.

Barnes, Douglas. 1992. *From Communication to Curriculum*. 2d ed. Portsmouth, N.H.: Boynton/Cook.

Barr, Mary, and Margaret Syverson. 1999. *Assessing Literacy with the Learning Record: A Handbook for Teachers, Grades 6–12*. Portsmouth, N.H.: Heinemann.

Beck, Isabel L., Margaret G. McKeown, and Rebecca L. Hamilton. 1997. *Questioning the Author: An Approach for Enhancing Student Engagement with Text*. Newark, Del.: International Reading Association.

Bell, Madison Smart. 1997. *Narrative Design: A Writer's Guide to Structure*. New York: Norton.

Briggs, Sandy. 1991. "The Multi-Lingual/Multicultural Classroom." (Early draft of article that appeared in *Phi Delta Kappan Record* [May].)

Bruner, Jerome. 1977. *The Process of Education*. Cambridge, Mass.: Harvard University Press.

Burke, Jim. 1999. *I Hear America Reading: Why We Read • What We Read*, Portsmouth, N.H.: Heinemann.

———. 1999. *The English Teacher's Companion: A Complete Guide to Classroom, Curriculum, and the Profession*. Portsmouth, N.H.: Boynton/Cook.

California Academic Standards Commission. 1998. *The California Language Arts Content Standards*. Sacramento: California Department of Education.

Christenbury, Leila. 1994. *Making the Journey: Being and Becoming a Teacher of English Language Arts*. Portsmouth, N.H.: Boynton/Cook.

Christenbury, Leila, and Patricia P. Kelly. 1983. *Questioning: A Path to Critical Thinking*. Urbana, Ill.: ERIC and National Council of Teachers of English.

Daniels, Harvey. 1994. *Literature Circles: Voice and Choice in the Student-Centered Classroom*. York, Maine: Stenhouse.

Dickson, Shirley V., Deborah C. Simmons, and Edward J. Kameenui. 1995. "Text Organization and Its Relation to Reading Comprehension: A Synthesis of the Research." Available online at http://idea.uoregon.edu/~ncite/documents/techrep/tech17.html. Accessed May 15, 2000.

Graves, Donald H. 1999. *Bring Life into Learning: Creating a Lasting Literacy*. Portsmouth, N.H.: Heinemann.

Harris, Douglass E., and Judy F. Carr, with Tim Flynn, Marge Petit, and Susan Rigney. 1996. *How to Use Standards in the Classroom*. Alexandria, Va.: Association of Supervision and Curriculum Development.

Keene, Ellin, and Susan Zimmerman. 1997. *Mosaic of Thought: Teaching Comprehension in a Reader's Workshop*. Portsmouth, N.H.: Heinemann.

Krashen, Stephen. 1993. *The Power of Reading: Insights from the Research*. Englewood, Colo.: Libraries Unlimited.

Langer, Judith. 2000. "Six Features of Effective English Instruction: How Do They Play Out in Middle and High School Classrooms?" *English Update*. Spring.

McQuillan, Jeff. 1998. *The Literacy Crisis: False Claims, Real Solutions*. Portsmouth, N.H.: Heinemann.

National Archives and Records Administration and National Council for the Social Studies. 1989. *Teaching with Documents: Using Primary Sources from the National Archives*. Vols. 1 and 2. Washington, D.C.

Northwest Regional Educational Laboratory. nd. "Traits of an Effective Reader: Reading a Literary Text Scoring Guide." Available online at http://www.nwrel.org/eval/reading/scoring.html. Accessed May 15, 2000. Used by permission of the Northwest Regional Educational Laboratory.

Nystrand, Martin, with Adam Gamoran, Robert Kachur, and Catherine Prendergast. 1997. *Opening Dialogue: Understanding the Dynamics of Language and Learning in the English Classroom*. New York: Teachers College Press.

Padgett, Ron. 1997. *Creative Reading: What It Is, How to Do It, and Why*. Urbana, Ill.: National Council of Teachers of English.

Pilgreen, Janice. 2000. *How to Organize and Manage a Sustained Silent Reading Program*. Portsmouth, N.H.: Boynton/Cook.

Robinson, Linda. 1998. "Understanding Middle School Students." In *Into Focus: Understanding and Creating Middle School Readers*, ed. Kylene Beers and Barbara G. Samuels. Norwood, Mass.: Christopher-Gordon.

Schmoker, Michael. 1996. *Results: The Key to Continuous School Improvement*. Alexandria, Va.: Association for Supervision and Curriculum Development.

Schoenbach, Ruth, Cynthia Greenleaf, Christine Cziko, and Lori Hurwitz. 1999. *Reading for Understanding: A Guide to Improving Reading in Middle and High School Classrooms*. San Francisco: Jossey-Bass.

Scholes, Robert. 1986. *Textual Power: Literary Theory and the Teaching of English*. New Haven, Conn: Yale University Press.

Smith, Frank. 1995. *Between Hope and Havoc: Essays into Human Learning and Education*. Portsmouth, N.H.: Heinemann.

Suzuki, Shunryu. 1988. *Zen Mind, Beginner's Mind*. New York: Weatherhill.

Tierney, Robert J., and John. E Readence. 2000. *Reading Strategies and Practices: A Compendium*. 5th ed. Boston: Allyn and Bacon.

Welker, William. 1999. "Critical Reading Instruction That Improves Comprehension Skills (CRITICS)." *Journal of Adolescent and Adult Literacy*. International Reading Association. Fall, page 188.

Wiggins, Grant, and Jay McTighe. 1998. *Understanding by Design*. Alexandria, Va.: Association for Supervision and Curriculum Development.

Wood, Karen D., Diane Lapp, and James Flood. 1992. *Guiding Readers Through Text: A Review of Study Guides*. Newark, Del.: International Reading Association.

Zemelman, Steve, Harvey Daniels, and Arthur Hyde. 1998. *Best Practice: New Standards for Teaching and Learning in America's Schools*. Portsmouth, N.H.: Heinemann.

RATIONALE

I found many books useful during my research for this book. While *Reading Reminders* offers classroom teachers the quick reference support they need, many teachers will want to investigate certain strategies and ideas in greater depth. The books included in the following list will help you learn more about the ideas in this book.

WHAT TO DO

Reading for Style

Toolan, Michael. 1998. *Language in Literature: An Introduction to Stylistics*. London: Edward Arnold.

Literacy

Myers, Miles. 1996. *Changing Our Minds: Negotiating English and Literacy*. Urbana, Ill.: National Council of Teachers of English.

Student Engagement

Wilhelm, Jeffrey D. 1995. *"You Gotta BE the Book": Teaching Engaged and Reflective Reading with Adolescents*. New York: Teachers College Press and National Council of Teachers of English.

Reading Across the Curriculum/Academic Literacy

Schoenbach, Ruth, Cynthia Greenleaf, Christine Cziko, and Lori Hurwitz. 1999. *Reading for Understanding: A Guide to Improving Reading in Middle and High School Classrooms*. San Francisco: Jossey-Bass.

Recast the Text

Claggett, Fran, Louann Reid, and Ruth Vinz. 1996. *Recasting the Text*. Portsmouth, N.H.: Heinemann.

Reading the Web

Alexander, Janet E. and Marsha Ann Tate. 1999. *Web Wisdom: How to Evaluate and Create Information Quality on the Web*. Mahwah, N.J.: Erlbaum Associates.

English-Language Learners

Richard-Amato, Patricia A. 1996. *Making It Happen: Interaction in the Second Language Classroom: From Theory to Practice*. 2d ed. White Plains, N.Y.: Longman.

Peitzman, Faye, and George Gadda, eds. 1994. *With Different Eyes: Insights into Teaching Language Minority Students Across the Disciplines*. White Plains, N.Y.: Longman.

Standards

Tucker, Marc S., and Judy B. Codding. 1998. *Standards for Our Schools: How to Set Them, Measure Them, and Reach Them*. San Francisco: Jossey-Bass.

Reading Literature

Scholes, Robert. *Protocols of Reading*. 1989. New Haven, Conn.: Yale University Press.

Narrative Design

Bell, Madison Smartt. 1997. *Narrative Design: A Writer's Guide to Structure*. New York: Norton.

Reading Films

Teaseley, Alan, and Ann Wilder. 1997. *Reel Conversations: Reading Films with Young Adults*. Portsmouth, N.H.: Boynton/Cook.

Talking About Reading

Barnes, Douglas. 1992. *From Communication to Curriculum*. Portsmouth, N.H.: Boynton/Cook.

Using and Developing Questions

Beck, Isabel L., Margaret G. McKeown, and Rebecca L. Hamilton. 1997. *Questioning the Author: An Approach for Enhancing Student Engagement with Text*. Newark, Del.: International Reading Association.

Study Guides

Wood, Karen D., Diane Lapp, and James Flood. 1992. *Guiding Readers Through Text: A Review of Study Guides*. Newark, Del.: International Reading Association.

General Reading About Reading

Bloom, Harold. *How to Read and Why*. 2000. New York: Scribners.

Burke, Jim. 1999. *I Hear America Reading: Why Why We Read • What We Read*. Portsmouth, N.H.: Heinemann.

Reading to Change Your Life

Denby, David. 1996. *Great Books: My Adventures with Homer, Rousseau, Woolf, and Other Indestructible Writers of the Western World*. New York: Simon and Schuster.

Reading for Character

Graves, Donald. 1998. *Bring Life into Learning: Creating a Lasting Literacy*. Portsmouth, N.H.: Heinemann.

Assessment

Wiggins, Grant. 1998. *Educative Assessment: Designing Assessments to Inform and Improve Student Performance*. San Francisco: Jossey-Bass.

Strickland, Kathleen, and James Strickland. 1998. *Reflections on Assessment: Its Purposes, Methods, and Effects on Learning*. Portsmouth, N.H.: Boynton/Cook.

History of Reading

Manguel, Alberto. 1996. *A History of Reading*. New York: Penguin.

Shannon, Patrick. *The Struggle to Continue: Progressive Reading Instruction in the United States*. 1990. Portsmouth, N.H.: Heinemann.

Teaching the Classics

Jago, Carol. 2000. *With Rigor for All: Teaching the Classics to Contemporary Students*. Portland, Maine: Calendar Islands Publishers.

Language in the Classroom

McWhorter, John. 2000. *Spreading the Word: Language and Dialect in America*. Portsmouth, N.H.: Heinemann.

Curriculum Planning: Teaching by Design

Wiggins, Grant, and Jay McTighe. 1998. *Understanding by Design*. Alexandria, Va.: Association for Supervision and Curriculum Development.

Reading Poetry

Hirsch, Edward. 1999. *How to Read a Poem and Fall in Love with Poetry*. New York: Harcourt Brace.

Reading Images

Kress, Gunther R., and Theo Van Leeuwen. 1995. *Reading Images: The Grammar of Visual Design*. New York: Routledge.

Trachtenberg, Alan. 1989. *Reading American Photographs: Images As History, Mathew Brady to Walker Evans*. New York: Hill and Wang.

Reading Information

Feathers, Karen M. 1993. *Infotext: Reading and Learning*. Markham, Ontario: Pippin.

Tufte, Edward R. 1990. *Envisioning Information*. Cheshire, Conn.: Graphics Press.

———. 1997. *Visual Explanations: Images and Quantities, Evidence and Narrative*. Cheshire, Conn.: Graphics Press.

Reading Media

Stephenson, Mitch. 1998. *The Rise of the Image, the Fall of the Word*. New York: Oxford University Press.

Monaco, James. 2000. *How to Read a Film: The World of Movies, Media, and Multimedia: Language, History, and Theory*. New York: Oxford University Press.

Drawing the Action

Claggett, Fran, with Joan Brown. 1992. *Drawing Your Own Conclusions*. Portsmouth, N.H.: Boynton/Cook.

Sustained Silent Reading (SSR)

Pilgreen, Janice. 2000. *The SSR Handbook: How to Organize and Manage a Sustained Silent Reading Program.* Portsmouth, N.H.: Boynton/Cook.

Vocabulary

Allen, Janet. 1999. *Words, Words, Words: Teaching Vocabulary in Grades 4–12.* York, Maine: Stenhouse.

Blachowicz, Camille, and Peter Fisher. 1996. *Teaching Vocabulary in All Classrooms.* Englewood Cliffs, N.J.: Merrill.

Reading Tests

Calkins, Lucy, Kate Montgomery, and Donna Santman. 1998. *A Teacher's Guide to Standardized Reading Tests.* Portsmouth, N.H.: Heinemann.

Reading Strategies

Tierney, Robert J., and John E. Readence. 2000. *Reading Strategies and Practices: A Compendium.* Boston: Allyn and Bacon.

Schoenbach, Ruth, Cynthia Greenleaf, Christine Cziko, and Lori Hurwitz. 1999. *Reading for Understanding: A Guide to Improving Reading in Middle and High School Classrooms.* San Francisco: Jossey-Bass.

Beers, Kylene, and Barbara Samuels. 1998. *Into Focus: Understanding and Creating Middle School Readers,* Norwood, Mass.: Christopher-Gordon.

Literary Form and Function

Scholes, Robert, Nancy R. Comley, and Gregory L. Ulmer. 1995. *Text Book: An Introduction to Literary Language.* 2d ed. New York: St. Martin's.

Langer, Judith. 1995. *Envisioning Literature: Literary Understanding and Literature Instruction.* New York: Teachers College Press.

Teaching, Learning, and Assessing

Smith, Frank. 1992. *Joining the Literacy Club: Further Essays into Education.* Portsmouth, N.H.: Heinemann.

Wiggins, Grant, and Jay McTighe. 1998. *Understanding by Design.* Alexandria, Va.: Association for Supervision and Curriculum Development.

CATEGORICAL THINKING

Student _____ Period _____ Date _____

BRANCHING CATEGORIES

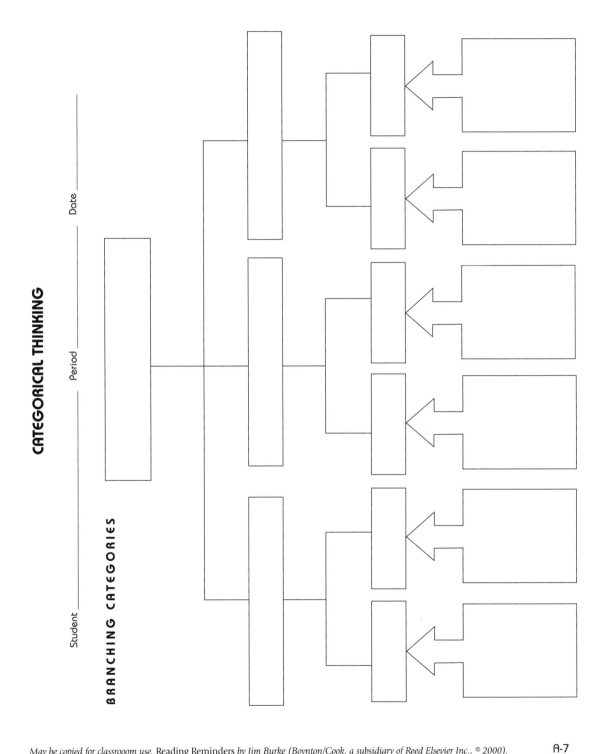

Appendix 4

THE CONVERSATIONAL ROUNDTABLE

Student _____ Period _____ Date _____

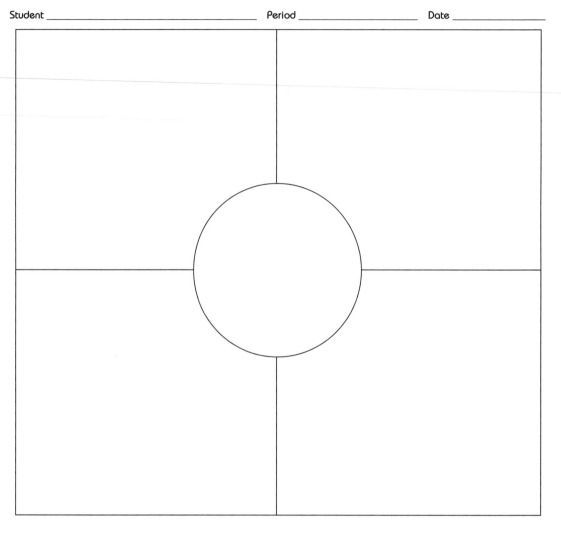

May be copied for classrooom use. Reading Reminders by Jim Burke (Boynton/Cook, a subsidiary of Reed Elsevier Inc., © 2000).

CORNELL NOTES I

Student _____ Period _____ Date _____

Project _____ Idea _____ Page _____

Appendix 6

CORNELL NOTE-TAKING FORM

Student _____ Period _____ Date _____

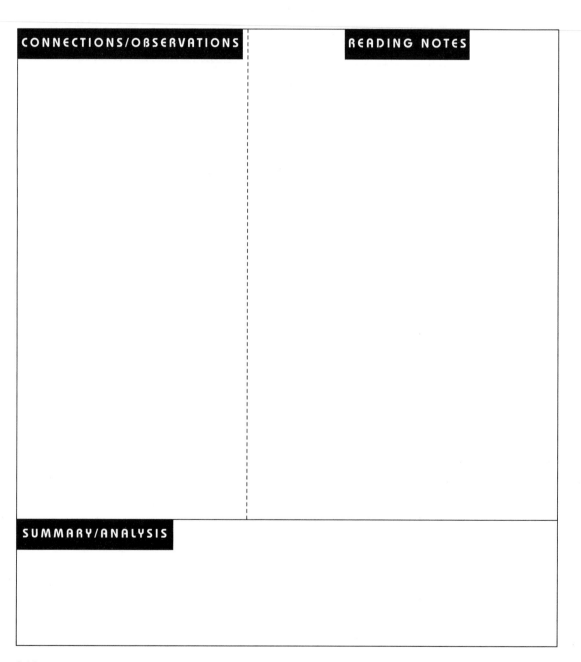

CONNECTIONS/OBSERVATIONS

READING NOTES

SUMMARY/ANALYSIS

May be copied for classroooom use. Reading Reminders by Jim Burke (Boynton/Cook, a subsidiary of Reed Elsevier Inc., © 2000).

CORNELL NOTE-TAKING FORM

Student _____ Period _____ Date _____

READING NOTES	CLASS/LECTURE NOTES	CONNECTIONS/OBSERVATIONS

SUMMARY/ANALYSIS

Appendix 8

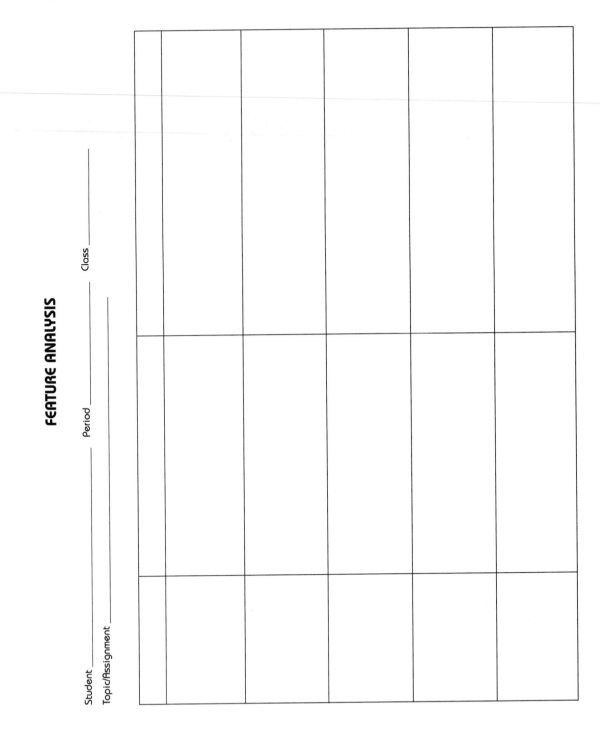

FEATURE ANALYSIS

Student _____ Period _____ Class _____

Topic/Assignment _____

May be copied for classrooom use. Reading Reminders *by Jim Burke (Boynton/Cook, a subsidiary of Reed Elsevier Inc., © 2000).*

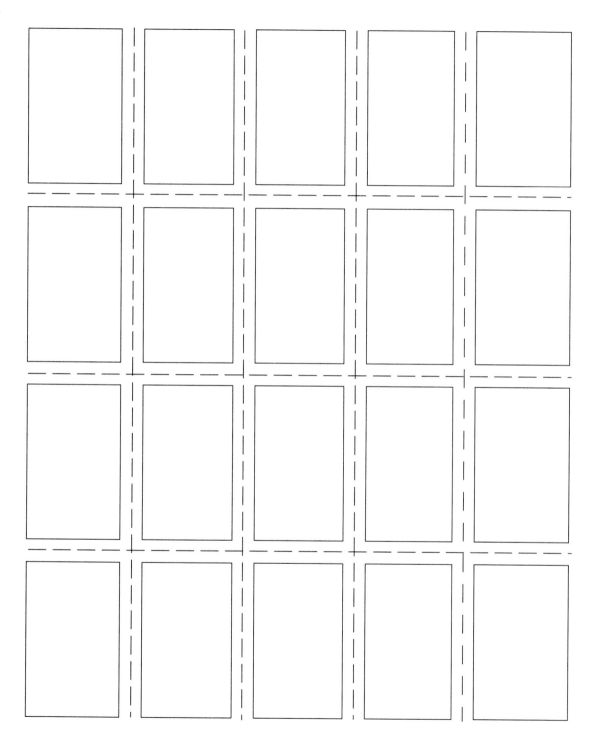

INTERACTIVE READING (CRITICS PROCEDURE)

Student _____ Period _____ Class _____

1. WHAT I KNOW FOR SURE	2. WHAT I THINK I KNOW	3. READ/VERIFY (WITH POSSIBLE DISCUSSION TIME)*	4. WHAT I KNOW NOW	5. QUESTIONS ABOUT READING	WHERE TO FIND ANSWERS TO REMAINING OR NEW QUESTIONS

*Identify items in column 3 with a + (info is accurate), a – (item is not accurate), a ? (not enough info).

KWL ORGANIZER

Student _____ Period _____ Date _____

WHAT I KNOW	WHAT I WANT TO KNOW	WHAT I LEARNED

Possible Categories for Information

SUMMARY/RESPONSE/STILL NEED TO KNOW

A-15

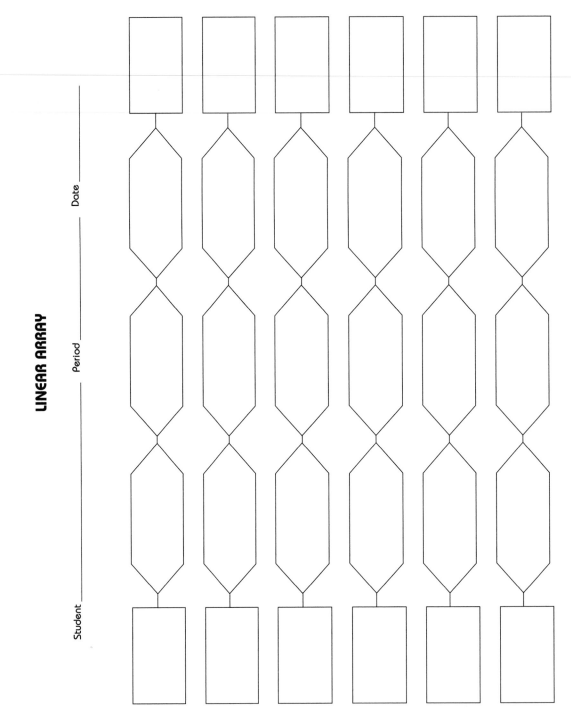

LINEAR ARRAY

Student _____ Period _____ Date _____

May be copied for classrooom use. Reading Reminders by Jim Burke (Boynton/Cook, a subsidiary of Reed Elsevier Inc., © 2000).

ON TARGET

Student _____ Period _____ Date _____

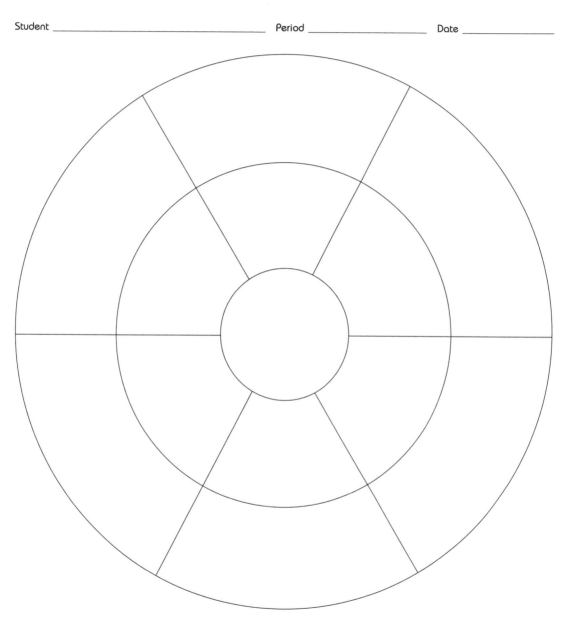

Appendix 14

OUTLINE TEMPLATE

Student _____   Period _____   Date _____

Main Idea/Subject I. _____

    Support/Idea A. _____

    Details/Examples 1. _____

                     2. _____

                     3. _____

                     4. _____

                     5. _____

    Support/Idea B. _____

    Details/Examples 1. _____

                     2. _____

                     3. _____

                     4. _____

                     5. _____

    Support/Idea C. _____

    Details/Examples 1. _____

                     2. _____

                     3. _____

                     4. _____

                     5. _____

    Support/Idea D. _____

    Details/Examples 1. _____

                     2. _____

                     3. _____

                     4. _____

                     5. _____

Summary/Observations

May be copied for classrooom use. Reading Reminders by Jim Burke (Boynton/Cook, a subsidiary of Reed Elsevier Inc., © 2000).

PLOT THE ACTION

Student _____ Period _____ Class _____

Directions: Transferring what we read into a visual form often helps us see what is happening. By revealing the patterns and relationships within a story, process, or historical period we can get a better sense of what is happening and why since we need to be able to explain the different changes on the graph. Using the simple system described below, represent the text you are reading on the graph. Be sure to label each event and, if there is room, identify the cause for the change. Also, clearly indicate what the axes along the continuum represent (e.g., a year, a chapter, a phase). Finally, connect your dots to show the pattern more clearly.

    0 = Neutral or nothing

−5 = Very negative value (e.g., in mood, action, condition, life)

+5 = Very positive value (e.g., change for the better, important event, realization)

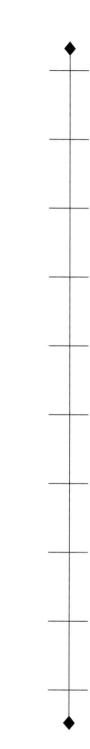

READING AN ARGUMENT

Student _____ Period _____ Date _____

Position Statement

Position: Support	**Position: Oppose**
Argument 1:	**Argument 1:**
Evidence	Evidence
Argument 2:	**Argument 2:**
Evidence	Evidence
Argument 3:	**Argument 3:**
Evidence	Evidence

For •	**Position: Third Perspective** •	**Against**

Summarize their reasons for support	**Explain why they would oppose this**

READING TO COMPARE

Student _____ Period _____ Date _____

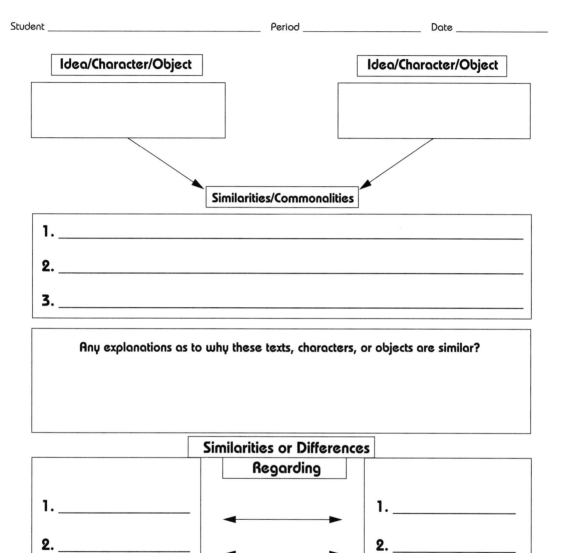

Idea/Character/Object

Idea/Character/Object

Similarities/Commonalities

1. _____
2. _____
3. _____

Any explanations as to why these texts, characters, or objects are similar?

Similarities or Differences
Regarding

1. _____
2. _____
3. _____
4. _____
5. _____

1. _____
2. _____
3. _____
4. _____
5. _____

Appendix 18

SEMANTIC MAP

Student _____   Period _____   Date _____

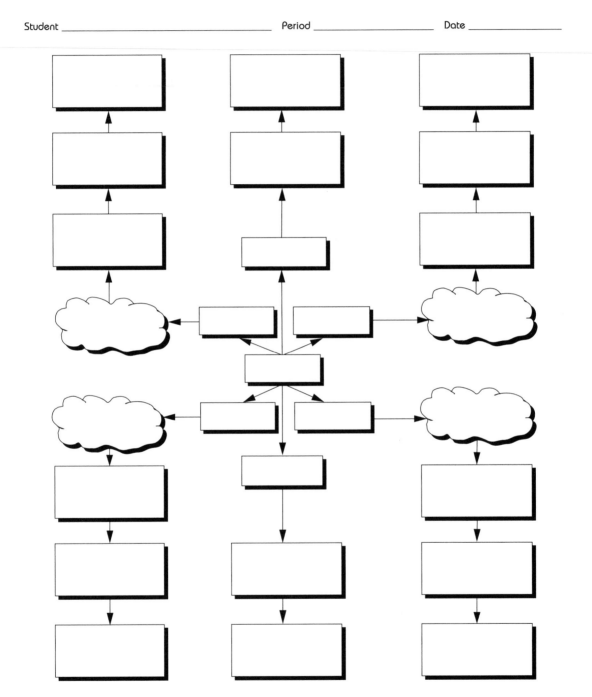

May be copied for classrooom use. Reading Reminders *by Jim Burke (Boynton/Cook, a subsidiary of Reed Elsevier Inc., © 2000).*

STORY BOARD

Student _____ Period _____ Date _____

Appendix 20

STORY STRUCTURE

Main Characters

↓

Setting (time, place, atmosphere)

↓

Primary Conflict

↓

List the main events in the story

Climax	Resolution

May be copied for classrooom use. Reading Reminders *by Jim Burke (Boynton/Cook, a subsidiary of Reed Elsevier Inc., © 2000).*

THINK IN THREES

Student _____ Period _____ Date _____

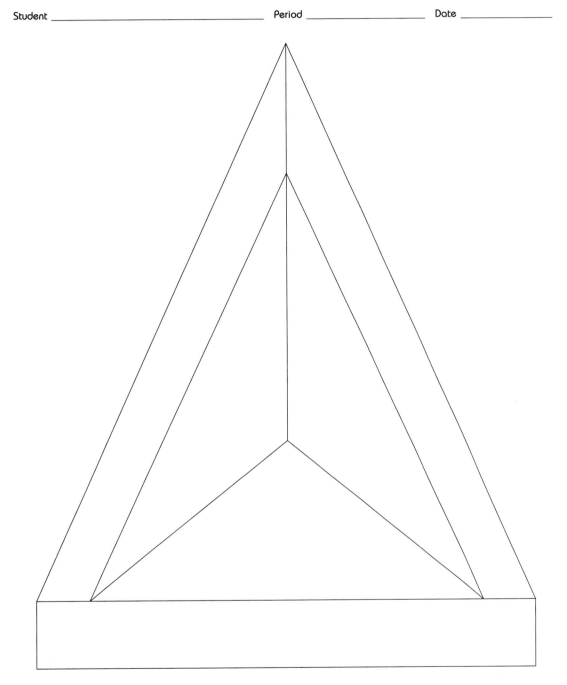

A-25

THREE-COLUMN ORGANIZER

Student _____ Period _____ Date _____

May be copied for classrooom use. Reading Reminders by Jim Burke (Boynton/Cook, a subsidiary of Reed Elsevier Inc., © 2000).

TIME LINE ORGANIZER

Student _____ Period _____ Date _____

Time line: As you read, look for those moments that indicate a new and crucial stage in a process or journey. On each bar of the time line write the word(s) that will clearly delineate that stage from the others. Under the bar you should note the specific details such as date and what happened so you can use these notes later for writing or discussions. The important point is to identify the essential events and the order in which they occur.

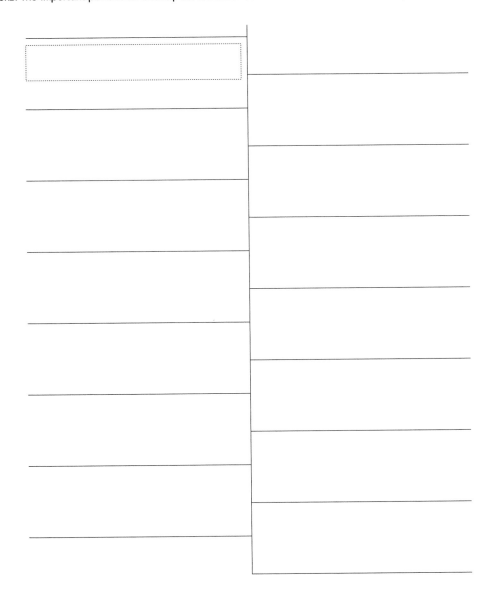

VENN DIAGRAM

Student _____ Period _____ Date _____

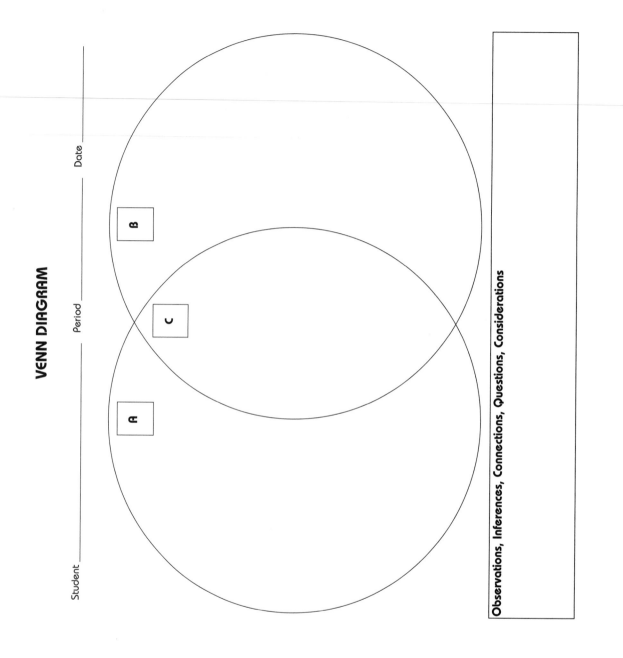

A

B

C

Observations, Inferences, Connections, Questions, Considerations

VOCABULARY SQUARE

Student _____ Period _____ Date _____

Root/Part of Speech/ Sentence	Variations on the Word
Picture/Logo	Definition

Root/Part of Speech/ Sentence	Variations on the Word
Picture/Logo	Definition

Root/Part of Speech/ Sentence	Variations on the Word
Picture/Logo	Definition

Root/Part of Speech/ Sentence	Variations on the Word
Picture/Logo	Definition

Root/Part of Speech/ Sentence	Variations on the Word
Picture/Logo	Definition

Root/Part of Speech/ Sentence	Variations on the Word
Picture/Logo	Definition

Appendix 26

What confuses me the most is . . .

Summarize it as you understand it.

Ask the author 2–3 questions about it.

What makes it hard to understand?

Review my
notes here

Seek help

Decide: If you are ready, turn the page over
and explain it to someone else, then move
ahead in your reading. If you are not ready,
decide what to do next.

Return to text

Read ahead

Student _____ Period _____ Date _____

What's the Big Idea?

Narrow It Down: What's the Most Important Point?

How do you know that's the most important idea? Write three examples or comments that support your assertion that this is the most important idea. If they are quotes, include the page numbers so you can refer to them later when writing about or discussing this idea.

1. _____

2. _____

3. _____

SSR READING ESSAY GUIDELINES

Exemplar written by freshman Chris Ferren-Cirino

Directions   Every book you read has at its heart some idea; it might be about how complicated people are, the desire for power, or growing up. When you finish each SSR book you must write a one-page essay about an *idea* in your book, then use examples and details from your book throughout the essay. *Your essay should not be a summary of what happens in the book.* It should *not* begin, "This book is about three friends . . . ," or "I didn't like this book," or "You would like this book because . . ." I have included an exemplar below to show you one way of writing such an essay.

GROWING UP

At every point in a young person's life, they must learn right from wrong through many different struggles and new experiences. It is something that cannot be prevented, no matter what is done to stop it. Growing up is a natural behavior that we all must participate in as a young child. Some of our experiences may be bad or good, but we all must live through them. Later, many years down the road, we all have the chance to look back and relive the joys and sorrows that we once had earlier in our life. The memories from the past will always live on in our hearts.

Growing up for everyone is hard to do, but for Russell Baker, it seemed especially hard. Russell grew up during a time when the depression was at its peak. His mother and father seemed to want the best for Russell, but they were a small, poor farm family. Later, his father died and his mother, sister, and he, were left alone to survive in a world that was cruel and unforgiving. Even though she was poor, and not too bright, his mother wanted only the best for her young boy. In the end, he was able to rise from the bottom of the society, to the top, because of his hard work and dedication.

This story of a young man becoming something more than anyone ever thought possible makes me realize how hard some people have to work to survive. He came from a family that was always fighting to survive on a day-to-day basis, but rose higher than that. For many people in the United States, the world seems to be cruel, and full of the worst of luck. These people look at others who seem to be living high on the hog, and they can only wonder what it must feel like to be so rich and have no financial problems. This seems to be so unfair. How is it possible, that some people work so hard, and have hardly enough money to feed and cloth their kids, while others are so rich they don't even need to work? It doesn't seem fair to me.

It's hard enough for parents to feed their kids and give them what they need from day to day, but how are they supposed to also put their children through college? This was the dilemma Russell's mother had. With hardly any money saved up in the bank, this sad problem seems to be real for many Americans, also. Even though parents have much love and hope for their children, they need more than that to put them through college. It seems that the rich will continue to remain rich, while the poor continue to be poor.

Parents who struggle to provide for their children are such strong individuals. Russell's story showed me that you don't have to be rich in order to have happiness among your family members. Though the rich have a better chance of what America calls "succeeding in life," they are not always the ones that are successful individuals. As you can see, Russell started out very poor, but with much help from his mother and sister, he was able to succeed in an unfair world. People like this are the real heroes of the world.

READING

4. Show a deep understanding of what you read through your remarks about it in the essay.

3. Show a sound understanding of what you read but lack insight.

2. Show a limited understanding of what you read but have a basic understanding.

1. Didn't read it.

WRITING

4. Thoroughly address prompt and include strong, appropriate examples; no intrusive mechanical errors.

3. Competently address prompt; include some examples; minor interference from mechanical errors.

2. Do not address the topic; have no examples or they are inappropriate; intrusive mechanical errors.

1. Writing suggests you did not read the book.

ASSIGNMENT REQUIREMENTS

4. You satisfied all requirements of the assignment.

3. You satisfied half of the requirement—i.e., you read one book.

2. You satisfied part of the assignment—i.e., you read part of a book.

1. You did not read as assigned.

CALIFORNIA ASSESSMENT PROGRAM CATEGORIES

AUTOBIOGRAPHIC
❏ Focus on a single incident—a moment, a few hours, no more than a day; also give reader a sense of what this meant to you personally.
❏ Recreate the experience by using vivid sensory details, scene description, dialogue, action, internal thoughts, personal commentary, explanations.
❏ Use essay format—beginning, middle, end.

OBSERVATION
❏ Focus on the topic: a specific place to describe.
❏ Imagine that you are a reporter and a camera person all in one.
❏ Recreate the scene by using vivid sensory details, names of people and places, action, dialogue, personal observations.
❏ Give the reader a sense of movement and perspective—in and out of the scene, move around, a sense of the writer's attitude toward the observation as expressed through the choice of language and detail.
❏ Have an organization—beginning, middle, end.

INTERPRETATION
❏ Take a stand (i.e., have a clear thesis) and support it.
❏ Give good reasons, examples, "for instance," factual information, experiences that support.
❏ Organize into clear paragraphs; topic sentences.
❏ Provide logical supports—don't stray from the topic.
❏ Conclude with both summary and an extension of your ideas.

EVALUATION
❏ Take a clear stand—for or against the issue to evaluate.
❏ Establish criteria for evaluating—these are the points by which you judge something to be good or bad, right or wrong, pleasant or unpleasant. They may be stated directly at the beginning and then used throughout, or they may be scattered throughout the essay as you argue your points.
❏ Use specific examples and details to support your arguments. These may be taken from your own or others' experiences or from what you have read or seen or heard.

TRADITIONAL COLLEGE RHETORICAL MODES

NARRATIVE
❏ Answers the question "What happened and when?"
❏ Emphasis on chronological order of events; use of transitional words helps such events to flow smoothly from one to the next.
❏ Point of view is important as it shapes the voice, tone, and purpose of the story.
❏ Mood is of fundamental importance as it directs the reader's response: is this a fond memory of a loved one or an angry account of an event that left a lasting scar?

DEFINITION
❏ Answers the question "What is it?"
❏ Attempts to explain an important word or concept to the reader.
❏ Uses negation to also clarify what the word does *not* mean.
❏ Might focus on the origins of the word as a means of establishing its meaning.

DIVISION/CLASSIFICATION
❏ Answers the question "What kind is it?" or "What are its parts?"
❏ Arranges information into categories in order to establish and articulate the relationships between items in each category.
❏ Categories should be distinct to avoid confusion.
❏ Exemplary essay, "Friends, Good Friends—and Such Good Friends," by Judith Viorst.

PROCESS ANALYSIS
❏ Answers the question "How did it happen?"
❏ Two choices: how *to do* something or how something *was done*.
❏ Establish who your audience is so you know what must be carefully explained.
❏ Uses other modes such as narration to explain the process.

CAUSE AND EFFECT
❏ Answers the question "Why did it happen?
❏ Carefully examines what happened and why.
❏ Clear, logical writing is crucial in order to be effective.
❏ Descriptive writing helps illustrate the relationship between the cause and the effect.

CALIFORNIA ASSESSMENT PROGRAM CATEGORIES (continued)

❏ Begin essay with your position—**thesis**—statement in the introduction. Organize all subsequent paragraphs logically into main points to develop your thesis.
❏ Conclude with summary and a good recommendation that fits your thesis.

REFLECTION

❏ See the instructions for the Autobiographical essay. This essay is similar but more sophisticated.
❏ Use the technique of recreating an incident but raise your commentary and observation to a philosophical, universal level. How does this incident reflect a truth about life in general or about something universal to human experience? As you develop your paragraphs, you will want to include commentary that is more reflective about the meaning of events.

CONTROVERSIAL ISSUE

❏ Take a side on the issue given. Argue either for or against.
❏ Write an introduction that does what you have been taught: hook the reader, give background material, present a clear, arguable thesis.
❏ Organize your main arguments into logical paragraphs with clear topic sentences.
❏ Support your arguments with specific examples and details drawn from your own or friends' or family's experiences. Don't worry about having to use precise statistics, but do not use logical well known facts.
❏ Use counter arguments: these are points that someone on the other side would use and that you "demolish" with your own arguments.
❏ Write a conclusion that pulls together your main ideas and provides perspective and a recommendation.

TRADITIONAL COLLEGE RHETORICAL MODES (continued)

ARGUMENTATION/PERSUASION

❏ Answers the question "Why should I want to do or think that?"
❏ The thesis is especially important as this is what your essay will convince the reader to think or do.
❏ Logic is crucial so as to make argument effective.
❏ You must anticipate the counterarguments and address them in your essay.
❏ *Argument* focuses on the logical appeal.
❏ *Persuasion* focuses on the emotional appeal.

COMPARISON/CONTRAST

❏ Answers the question "What is it (not) like?"
❏ In *comparison* the similarities are carefully established and developed.
❏ In *contrast*, the differences between the two elements or sides are emphasized.
❏ You must clearly establish early on the basis of the comparison so as to provide a context for all that follows it.

EXAMPLE/ILLUSTRATION

❏ Answers the question "For example?"
❏ Clarity depends on concrete, vivid examples that reveal the concept being discussed or the position advocated.
❏ Active verbs will help the reader by showing them exactly what this subject does.
❏ Exemplary essay: Nikki Giovanni's "My Own Style," in which she illustrates her way of living by describing specific objects and explaining how they exemplify her lifestyle.

**READING:
THINK ABOUT IT! 2.0**

Thinking about *how you read*

- ❑ I was distracted by . . .
- ❑ I started to think about . . .
- ❑ I got stuck when . . .
- ❑ I was confused/focused today because . . .
- ❑ One strategy I used to help me read this better was . . .
- ❑ When I got distracted I tried to refocus myself by . . .
- ❑ These word(s) or phrases were new/interesting to me . . . I think they mean . . .
- ❑ When reading I should . . .
- ❑ When I read today I realized that . . .
- ❑ I had a hard time understanding . . .
- ❑ I'll read better next time if I . . .

Thinking about *what you read*

- ❑ Why does the character/author . . .
- ❑ Why doesn't the character/author . . .
- ❑ What surprised me most was . . .
- ❑ I predict that . . .
- ❑ This author's writing style is . . .
- ❑ I noticed that the author uses . . .
- ❑ The main character wants/is . . .
- ❑ If I could, I'd ask the author/ character . . .
- ❑ The most interesting event/idea in this book is . . .
- ❑ I realized . . .
- ❑ The main conflict/idea in this book is . . .
- ❑ I wonder why . . .
- ❑ One theme that keeps coming up is . . .
- ❑ I found the following quote interesting . . .
- ❑ I _____ this book because . . .

Elaborating on *what you think*

- ❑ I think _____ because . . .
- ❑ A good example of _____ is . . .
- ❑ This reminded me of _____ because . . .
- ❑ This was important because . . .
- ❑ One thing that surprised me was because I always thought . . .
- ❑ The author is saying that . . .

**READING:
THINK ABOUT IT! 2.0**

Thinking about *how you read*

- ❑ I was distracted by . . .
- ❑ I started to think about . . .
- ❑ I got stuck when . . .
- ❑ I was confused/focused today because . . .
- ❑ One strategy I used to help me read this better was . . .
- ❑ When I got distracted I tried to refocus myself by . . .
- ❑ These word(s) or phrases were new/interesting to me . . . I think they mean . . .
- ❑ When reading I should . . .
- ❑ When I read today I realized that . . .
- ❑ I had a hard time understanding . . .
- ❑ I'll read better next time if I . . .

Thinking about *what you read*

- ❑ Why does the character/author . . .
- ❑ Why doesn't the character/author . . .
- ❑ What surprised me most was . . .
- ❑ I predict that . . .
- ❑ This author's writing style is . . .
- ❑ I noticed that the author uses . . .
- ❑ The main character wants/is . . .
- ❑ If I could, I'd ask the author/ character . . .
- ❑ The most interesting event/idea in this book is . . .
- ❑ I realized . . .
- ❑ The main conflict/idea in this book is . . .
- ❑ I wonder why . . .
- ❑ One theme that keeps coming up is . . .
- ❑ I found the following quote interesting . . .
- ❑ I _____ this book because . . .

Elaborating on *what you think*

- ❑ I think _____ because . . .
- ❑ A good example of _____ is . . .
- ❑ This reminded me of _____ because . . .
- ❑ This was important because . . .
- ❑ One thing that surprised me was because I always thought . . .
- ❑ The author is saying that . . .

**READING:
THINK ABOUT IT! 2.0**

Thinking about *how you read*

- ❑ I was distracted by . . .
- ❑ I started to think about . . .
- ❑ I got stuck when . . .
- ❑ I was confused/focused today because . . .
- ❑ One strategy I used to help me read this better was . . .
- ❑ When I got distracted I tried to refocus myself by . . .
- ❑ These word(s) or phrases were new/interesting to me . . . I think they mean . . .
- ❑ When reading I should . . .
- ❑ When I read today I realized that . . .
- ❑ I had a hard time understanding . . .
- ❑ I'll read better next time if I . . .

Thinking about *what you read*

- ❑ Why does the character/author . . .
- ❑ Why doesn't the character/author . . .
- ❑ What surprised me most was . . .
- ❑ I predict that . . .
- ❑ This author's writing style is . . .
- ❑ I noticed that the author uses . . .
- ❑ The main character wants/is . . .
- ❑ If I could, I'd ask the author/ character . . .
- ❑ The most interesting event/idea in this book is . . .
- ❑ I realized . . .
- ❑ The main conflict/idea in this book is . . .
- ❑ I wonder why . . .
- ❑ One theme that keeps coming up is . . .
- ❑ I found the following quote interesting . . .
- ❑ I _____ this book because . . .

Elaborating on *what you think*

- ❑ I think _____ because . . .
- ❑ A good example of _____ is . . .
- ❑ This reminded me of _____ because . . .
- ❑ This was important because . . .
- ❑ One thing that surprised me was because I always thought . . .
- ❑ The author is saying that . . .

**READING:
THINK ABOUT IT! 2.0**

Thinking about *how you read*

- ❑ I was distracted by . . .
- ❑ I started to think about . . .
- ❑ I got stuck when . . .
- ❑ I was confused/focused today because . . .
- ❑ One strategy I used to help me read this better was . . .
- ❑ When I got distracted I tried to refocus myself by . . .
- ❑ These word(s) or phrases were new/interesting to me . . . I think they mean . . .
- ❑ When reading I should . . .
- ❑ When I read today I realized that . . .
- ❑ I had a hard time understanding . . .
- ❑ I'll read better next time if I . . .

Thinking about *what you read*

- ❑ Why does the character/author . . .
- ❑ Why doesn't the character/author . . .
- ❑ What surprised me most was . . .
- ❑ I predict that . . .
- ❑ This author's writing style is . . .
- ❑ I noticed that the author uses . . .
- ❑ The main character wants/is . . .
- ❑ If I could, I'd ask the author/ character . . .
- ❑ The most interesting event/idea in this book is . . .
- ❑ I realized . . .
- ❑ The main conflict/idea in this book is . . .
- ❑ I wonder why . . .
- ❑ One theme that keeps coming up is . . .
- ❑ I found the following quote interesting . . .
- ❑ I _____ this book because . . .

Elaborating on *what you think*

- ❑ I think _____ because . . .
- ❑ A good example of _____ is . . .
- ❑ This reminded me of _____ because . . .
- ❑ This was important because . . .
- ❑ One thing that surprised me was because I always thought . . .
- ❑ The author is saying that . . .

READING REMINDERS

When reading remember to:

- ❑ Ask questions of the text, yourself, and the author.
- ❑ Make connections to yourself, other texts, the world.
- ❑ Use different strategies to achieve and maintain focus while reading.
- ❑ Determine ahead of time why you are reading this text and how it should be read.
- ❑ Adjust your strategies as you read to help you understand and enjoy what you read.

Evaluate how well you read

Evaluate and decide which of the following best describes your reading performance today. Explain why you gave yourself the score, also. My reading was:

1. Excellent because I
   - ❑ read the full 20 minutes
   - ❑ read actively (e.g., used different strategies and techniques)
   - ❑ understood what I read
2. Successful because I
   - ❑ read almost the entire 20 minutes
   - ❑ tried to use some strategies that mostly helped me read better
   - ❑ understood most of what I read
3. Inconsistent because I
   - ❑ read only about half the time
   - ❑ used some strategies but they didn't help me much
   - ❑ understood some of what I read
4. Unsuccessful because I
   - ❑ read little or nothing
   - ❑ did not read actively
   - ❑ did not understand what I read
   - ❑ I didn't understand because . . .

Develop your own questions

Develop your own question(s) or prompt(s) that you find helpful when thinking about how or what you read:

READING REMINDERS

When reading remember to:

- ❑ Ask questions of the text, yourself, and the author.
- ❑ Make connections to yourself, other texts, the world.
- ❑ Use different strategies to achieve and maintain focus while reading.
- ❑ Determine ahead of time why you are reading this text and how it should be read.
- ❑ Adjust your strategies as you read to help you understand and enjoy what you read.

Evaluate how well you read

Evaluate and decide which of the following best describes your reading performance today. Explain why you gave yourself the score, also. My reading was:

1. Excellent because I
   - ❑ read the full 20 minutes
   - ❑ read actively (e.g., used different strategies and techniques)
   - ❑ understood what I read
2. Successful because I
   - ❑ read almost the entire 20 minutes
   - ❑ tried to use some strategies that mostly helped me read better
   - ❑ understood most of what I read
3. Inconsistent because I
   - ❑ read only about half the time
   - ❑ used some strategies but they didn't help me much
   - ❑ understood some of what I read
4. Unsuccessful because I
   - ❑ read little or nothing
   - ❑ did not read actively
   - ❑ did not understand what I read
   - ❑ I didn't understand because . . .

Develop your own questions

Develop your own question(s) or prompt(s) that you find helpful when thinking about how or what you read:

READING REMINDERS

When reading remember to:

- ❑ Ask questions of the text, yourself, and the author.
- ❑ Make connections to yourself, other texts, the world.
- ❑ Use different strategies to achieve and maintain focus while reading.
- ❑ Determine ahead of time why you are reading this text and how it should be read.
- ❑ Adjust your strategies as you read to help you understand and enjoy what you read.

Evaluate how well you read

Evaluate and decide which of the following best describes your reading performance today. Explain why you gave yourself the score, also. My reading was:

1. Excellent because I
   - ❑ read the full 20 minutes
   - ❑ read actively (e.g., used different strategies and techniques)
   - ❑ understood what I read
2. Successful because I
   - ❑ read almost the entire 20 minutes
   - ❑ tried to use some strategies that mostly helped me read better
   - ❑ understood most of what I read
3. Inconsistent because I
   - ❑ read only about half the time
   - ❑ used some strategies but they didn't help me much
   - ❑ understood some of what I read
4. Unsuccessful because I
   - ❑ read little or nothing
   - ❑ did not read actively
   - ❑ did not understand what I read
   - ❑ I didn't understand because . . .

Develop your own questions

Develop your own question(s) or prompt(s) that you find helpful when thinking about how or what you read:

READING REMINDERS

When reading remember to:

- ❑ Ask questions of the text, yourself, and the author.
- ❑ Make connections to yourself, other texts, the world.
- ❑ Use different strategies to achieve and maintain focus while reading.
- ❑ Determine ahead of time why you are reading this text and how it should be read.
- ❑ Adjust your strategies as you read to help you understand and enjoy what you read.

Evaluate how well you read

Evaluate and decide which of the following best describes your reading performance today. Explain why you gave yourself the score, also. My reading was:

1. Excellent because I
   - ❑ read the full 20 minutes
   - ❑ read actively (e.g., used different strategies and techniques)
   - ❑ understood what I read
2. Successful because I
   - ❑ read almost the entire 20 minutes
   - ❑ tried to use some strategies that mostly helped me read better
   - ❑ understood most of what I read
3. Inconsistent because I
   - ❑ read only about half the time
   - ❑ used some strategies but they didn't help me much
   - ❑ understood some of what I read
4. Unsuccessful because I
   - ❑ read little or nothing
   - ❑ did not read actively
   - ❑ did not understand what I read
   - ❑ I didn't understand because . . .

Develop your own questions

Develop your own question(s) or prompt(s) that you find helpful when thinking about how or what you read:

ENGLISH LANGUAGE ARTS

1. Students develop and use a range of strategies to identify and explain how authors employ the following to convey meaning and achieve certain effects on the reader:
   - The elements of language: grammar, semantics, syntax, diction
   - The elements of story: plot, character, setting, theme, point of view
   - The senses: color, sound, texture, taste, smell
   - The different devices available to them in each genre

2. Students improve their capacity by expanding their study of literary and expository texts to include the study of:
   - The elements of a writer's style
   - The characteristics and constraints of each genre
   - The author's philosophies, culture, and biases as they relate to the text
   - The text in its original historical context versus its current context

3. Students identify and analyze the forms and functions that characterize literary, expository, media, procedural, and functional texts, which include but are not limited to:
   - Elements of design
   - Rhetorical devices

4. Students develop and use a range of strategies to help them read a range of literary, expository, media, procedural, and functional texts, which include but are not limited to:
   - Visualizing abstract ideas
   - Asking (the author, text, teacher, and peers) questions as they read
   - Using those note-taking, organizing, and reflective techniques they find helpful
   - Making predictions
   - Skimming for essential information

5. Students search for and choose texts appropriate to their purpose and ability from all genres.

6. Students determine why they are reading a particular text and decide how they should read it, adjusting their approach as needed. During the course of the school year they read:
   - to understand
   - to enjoy
   - to answer a question
   - to learn
   - to reflect
   - to know

May be copied for classrooom use. Reading Reminders by Jim Burke (Boynton/Cook, a subsidiary of Reed Elsevier Inc., © 2000).

7. Students develop and learn when to use different strategies to define and extend understanding of new and specialized vocabulary encountered while reading. These strategies include but are not limited to:
   - applying knowledge of word origins and derivations
   - learning to use the dictionary
   - semantic mapping
   - word study

8. Students reflect on what has been learned after reading, and formulate ideas, opinions, and personal responses to texts.

9. Students draw conclusions and make inferences based on explicit and implicit information in texts, which they use to support their claims.

10. Students differentiate between fact and opinion when reading a text.

11. Students distinguish between essential and superficial information when reading a text.

12. Students scan a passage to determine whether it contains relevant information and thus should be read.

HOME ECONOMICS

1. Students determine the quality and appropriate use of products and information based on:
   - Consumer reviews
   - Labels
   - Observation of performance
   - Product information (print and online editions)
   - Product package information
   - Warranties

2. Students successfully complete a procedure or answer questions in order to demonstrate their ability to read:
   - Directions
   - Diagrams
   - Recipes

3. Students learn the crucial terms necessary to reading in this domain.

HEALTH

1. Students read the following and, based on observations and inferences, make appropriate decisions:
   - Informational and procedural documents
   - Persuasive texts in different media

- Contextual cues in various social situations
- Observable patterns of behavior in people, products, or processes
- Statistical and factual information found in informational documents, including labels, directions, and warnings
- Visual explanations such as tables, symbols, charts, graphs, and images
- Nonverbal signs such as facial and bodily gestures

2. Students explain their decisions using evidence from the texts to support their reasoning and interpretation.

3. Students evaluate the effectiveness of different media and the message they communicate.

4. Students develop and learn to apply appropriate strategies to help them determine the credibility of an idea or a text they read.

5. Students know how to determine the credibility of a particular idea or text before acting on or passing on health-related information.

VISUAL AND PERFORMING ARTS

1. Students read, critique, analyze, and interpret the following:
   - Instrumental or vocal scores
   - Informal and formal theatre, film, television, and electronic media productions
   - Dramatic performances of plays from different cultures, eras, and authors
   - Critical reviews and analyses of visual and performing arts productions

2. Students explain how the elements of a text—i.e., musical score, painting, or play—function and relate to each other in order to affect the audience for that production

3. Students know the meaning and function of symbols, terms, and conventions common to each of the visual and performing arts.

4. Students identify and explain the political, cultural, and historical influences of/on a particular work of art.

5. Students develop and use a range of strategies to identify and explain how visual and performing artists employ the following to convey meaning and achieve certain effects within the reader:
   - Language
   - Sound
   - Images
   - Color
   - Form

6. Students develop and apply aesthetic criteria to different works of art in order to evaluate the quality and success of a given work, using specific examples from that artwork and their rubric to support their interpretation.

May be copied for classrooom use. Reading Reminders by Jim Burke (Boynton/Cook, a subsidiary of Reed Elsevier Inc., © 2000).

7. Students infer the possible meanings of an artwork by analyzing the form, function, and relationship between different aesthetic components.

8. Students interpret a work by examining the artist's intentions, the context in which the work was created, and the work's relationship to past and subsequent works on the same subject by this and other artists.

BUSINESS

1. Students develop and use a range of strategies to identify and explain how the following types of text convey meaning and affect the reader:
   - Laws
   - Reports
   - Contracts
   - Commercial advertisements
   - Product packaging
   - Functional documents (maps, directions, etc.)
   - Graphic texts (diagrams, charts, graphs)
   - Web sites

2. Students identify and make predictions based on important information in different texts, supporting their predictions and interpretations with evidence from these texts.

3. Students learn the appropriate concepts and terminology of the discipline.

4. Students develop and use a range of appropriate strategies to interpret the message conveyed by different media.

5. Students identify and synthesize the ethical, ideological, and psychological positions advanced in the text, drawing examples from the text to support their analysis.

6. Students read, identify, and draw meaningful conclusions about different types of information and raw data to help them make informed decisions.

7. Students identify and analyze the form and functions that characterize financial, commercial, legal, media, procedural, and functional texts, which include but are not limited to:
   - Brochures
   - Newsletters
   - Product packaging
   - Statements
   - Résumés
   - Commercial advertisements (print, online, and television)
   - Letters
   - Product support materials

8. Students evaluate and make decisions about the validity and credibility of information contained in different texts in different media.

9. Students develop and use appropriate strategies to read the contextual and behavioral clues that will help them successfully complete a business transaction.

10. Students know and ask the appropriate questions needed to make sense of different texts in different media.

SCIENCE

1. Students evaluate and make decisions about the validity and credibility of information contained in different texts in different media.

2. Students know and ask the appropriate questions to help them make sense of different texts in different media.

3. Students identify and analyze the form and functions that characterize scientific, expository, media, procedural, and functional texts, which include but are not limited to:
   - Elements of design
   - Pattern formations
   - Observable behaviors and features
   - Experiments
   - Systems
   - Equations
   - Directions

4. Students know and use the appropriate concepts, symbols, and terminology for this subject.

5. Students develop and use different strategies to help them read and interpret such devices as computer-linked probes, spreadsheets, and graphing calculators, maps, or computerized simulations while performing tests, collecting data, analyzing relationships, and displaying information.

6. Students call upon and use strategies from different branches of science to analyze situations and solve problems encountered while interpreting incoming data in different (i.e., visual, statistical, behavioral) forms.

7. Students develop and apply logic and skepticism in order to determine what is important and what is insignificant, what is fact and what is opinion.

8. Students identify and analyze the relationship between the individual elements that make up an experiment, an observable formation, or other phenomena they are studying, using inferences to support their interpretations.

9. Students read data and other texts to determine what is known as well as what is not known.

10. Students read expository essays about the field as a supplement to their more formal scientific or procedural texts in order to expand their scientific thinking.

May be copied for classroooom use. Reading Reminders by Jim Burke (Boynton/Cook, a subsidiary of Reed Elsevier Inc., © 2000).

MATHEMATICS

1. Students develop and use a range of strategies to analyze and make sense of the following:
   - Word problems
   - Equations
   - Symbolic expressions
   - Arguments
   - Probabilities
   - Theorems
   - Geometrical shapes
   - Statements
   - Graphs
   - Tables
   - Charts
   - Diagrams
   - Patterns

2. Students develop and use the concepts, terminology, and symbolic language of mathematics and the sciences so they can read in this discipline.

3. Students develop and use appropriate strategies to help them make sense of mathematical texts including:
   - Inductive and deductive reasoning
   - Spatial and algebraic reasoning
   - Speculation
   - Prediction
   - Testing hypotheses
   - Trial and error

4. Students use these strategies in order to:
   - solve a range of problems
   - perceive logical subtleties
   - develop sound arguments
   - determine mathematical hypotheses
   - determine the validity of arguments and data

5. Students learn to perceive logical subtleties and develop sound mathematical arguments before making conclusions.

6. Students lean to identify and explain the flaws in an argument and any errors in reasoning by analyzing the components of the argument.

7. Students know how to judge the validity of an argument by analyzing its components and testing it against various reliable sources.

Appendix 32 *Continued*

8. Students demonstrate understanding by identifying and giving examples of undefined terms, axioms, theorems, and inductive and deductive reasoning.
9. Students develop an appreciation for the beauty and power of mathematics.
10. Students read and apply their mathematical thinking to real-world problems.
11. Students develop and ask appropriate questions to help them make sense of various mathematical texts they read.

HISTORY/SOCIAL SCIENCES

1. Students develop and use a range of strategies to analyze and make sense of the following texts common to the history/social sciences curriculum:
   - Maps
   - Textbooks
   - Historical documents
   - Visual explanations (charts, graphs, time lines, etc.)
   - Expository texts
   - Primary source documents (letters, diaries, etc.)
   - Demographic and statistical information
   - Documents concerning historical patterns and trends
   - Stock market reports
2. Students develop and use a variety of strategies to help them read and analyze different texts, which include but are not limited to:
   - Speculating
   - Predicting
   - Questioning
   - Comparing and contrasting
   - Evaluating
3. Students know and use the concepts and terminology appropriate to the discipline to read various texts in different media.
4. Students evaluate the validity of information, probability of events, and rhetorical content of different arguments throughout history, taking into consideration such contextual factors as culture and the era.
5. Students analyze and explain historical trends and other observable patterns using such tools as maps, graphs, and charts to organize their information and convey their understanding.
6. Students identify and explain the flaws in arguments, interpretations, and documents, taking into consideration such factors as bias and the original context.
7. Students analyze historical texts for examples of bias, motivation, validity, philosophical influences, and alternative explanations.

May be copied for classrooom use. Reading Reminders by Jim Burke (Boynton/Cook, a subsidiary of Reed Elsevier Inc., © 2000).

8. Students compare and contrast different explanations of historical events in light of their original context and their current explanation.

9. Students read analytically in order to determine the influences on, and cause and effect of, different historical events and trends.

10. Students develop and apply different strategies to analyze financial, economic, philosophical, and historical trends and patterns throughout history.

11. Students read and critique those primary source documents by which the world was organized and governed, focusing on their influence, structure, argument, philosophical principles, cultural values, and historical effect on the world and its people.

12. Students identify the structural design and elements of different documents, and are able to explain their effect on the reader and the text.

13. Students recognize the difference between and can identify rumor, opinion, truth, and fact in a variety of texts in different media.

MEDIA LITERACY

1. Students develop and use a range of strategies to analyze and make sense of the following types of text:
   - Visual images
   - Video
   - Film
   - Television
   - Commercial advertisements (print, online, and broadcast)
   - Multimedia presentations
   - Multimedia productions
   - Newspapers
   - Magazines
   - Music
   - Web sites

2. Students know and use the concepts and terminology appropriate to the medium when reading it.

3. Students identify and explain the function of different elements in media productions, including:
   - Symbols
   - Special effects
   - Point of view
   - Multiple media

- Stories
- Arguments
- Color
- Texture
- Shape
- Images
- Stereotypes
- Sound

4. Students identify and explain the consequences of the author's choices.

5. Students distinguish between superficial and significant information in a media production, supporting their analysis with examples and data from credible sources.

6. Students interpret and evaluate how visual image makers such as illustrators, documentary filmmakers, and political cartoonists represent meanings.

7. Students compare and contrast the same story or idea and its treatment in different media, explaining how effectively each one conveys the central ideas.

8. Students assess how language, medium, and presentation contribute to the message.

9. Students explain how meanings are communicated through elements of design, including shape, line, color, and texture.

10. Students identify and explain the purpose of various media forms such as informative texts, entertaining texts, and advertisements.

11. Students recognize and explain those strategies used by media groups to inform, persuade, entertain, and transmit culture through advertising, perpetuation of stereotypes, use of visual representations, special effects, and language.

12. Students learn the basic techniques used to create different media texts so that they can deconstruct the products of such techniques and be informed readers of such texts.

13. Students develop and ask the right questions of texts and their authors in order to determine bias, credibility, and validity.

Your Name _____   Period _____

Course _____   Fall or Spring

READING SURVEY: WHAT, WHY, HOW, AND WHEN DO YOU READ?

Directions   Write all responses to questions on a separate sheet of paper. The more honest your answers, the better I can teach you. This is the first step in a series of assignments that will use the information from this survey; to do well on them all you must first do well on this—that is, take it seriously. Unless otherwise indicated, feel free to mark as many as you like in response to any question.

1. I read the following: (F = Frequently; O = Occasionally; and N = Never)

   ❏ Newspapers   (F   O   N)
   ❏ Magazines   (F   O   N)
   ❏ Novels   (F   O   N)
   ❏ Web sites   (F   O   N)
   ❏ Reference books   (F   O   N)
   ❏ Inspirational books   (F   O   N)
   ❏ Poems (includes song lyrics)   (F   O   N)
   ❏ Essays   (F   O   N)
   ❏ Plays   (F   O   N)
   ❏ History   (F   O   N)
   ❏ Auto/biographies   (F   O   N)
   ❏ Comics/graphic novels   (F   O   N)
   ❏ Manuals   (F   O   N)
   ❏ Self-help books   (F   O   N)
   ❏ E-mail/instant messages   (F   O   N)
   ❏ Chatrooms   (F   O   N)
   ❏ Textbooks/assignments   (F   O   N)
   ❏ Work-related documents   (F   O   N)

2. I would rate myself as a _____ on a scale of 1–10 as a reader. Why?

3. Circle the types of reading you enjoy most (using the list from #1).

4. Which types of reading listed in #1 are most difficult for you? (Pick one and explain.)

Appendix 33 *Continued*

5. I would describe myself as a _____ reader. Explain.

6. My favorite book of all time is _____. Explain.

7. The best reader I know is _____. Explain.

8. Reading is something you either can or cannot do well: Agree   Disagree   (Circle one.)

9. Check any of the following that help you understand what you read better:

❏ Reading it aloud to yourself

❏ Having someone else read it aloud to you

❏ Talking about what you read with others

❏ Taking notes

❏ Drawing or doing art in response to or inspired by what you read

❏ Reading silently to yourself during class time

❏ Talking in groups about what you read

❏ Talking as a class about what you read

10. Which class (that you are currently taking) asks you to read the most?

11. Which class (that you are currently taking) has the most difficult reading?

12. What was the last book you read—and when was that?

13. Check the following response that best describes you as a reader:

❏ I will do what I need to in order to read anything. With enough effort I can understand anything I am asked to read. I am confident in my abilities as a reader.

❏ I try but eventually give up if it is too hard. I understand most of what I read but not as well as I would like to. I am somewhat confident in my abilities as a reader but recognize there are certain texts I just don't know how to read yet.

❏ Reading is hard for me. I rarely feel like I understand what the writer is saying. This is why I give up easily. Even when I feel like I understand it I don't trust myself and assume I am probably wrong.

14. Describe your biggest achievement as a reader (on the separate sheet).

15. How do you choose what you read? Explain.

16. I read when: (Check all that apply.)

❏ I'm bored.

❏ I need to escape.

❏ I am sad.

❏ I want to learn about something.

May be copied for classroooom use. Reading Reminders *by Jim Burke (Boynton/Cook, a subsidiary of Reed Elsevier Inc., © 2000).*

❏ My friends are reading the same book.

❏ I feel alone and need company.

❏ I want to think about something.

❏ I do not ever choose to read.

❏ I read all the time, anything, for a million different reasons: I *have* to read.

17. Check the statement that most matches your own belief:

❏ Reading is not important. By the sixth grade you know everything you need to know about reading.

❏ Reading is crucial to your success in the adult world.

❏ Reading is more important now than ever before.

❏ Reading is less important than it used to be.

18. Mark those with which you most agree:

❏ I like it when a book challenges my beliefs, ideas, or assumptions.

❏ I prefer to read books that do not make me think about unfamiliar things.

❏ I like to read in order to do things; this makes reading seem useful and valuable to me.

19. I expect the reading I do for school to be:

❏ Boring

❏ Interesting

❏ Difficult

❏ Useful

20. If I could improve up to three things about myself as a reader, I would choose:

1. _____

2. _____

3. _____

21. Circle the one (of the three listed in #20) most important goal you have as a reader.

22. The following consistently interfere with my ability to read as well as I would like:

❏ Distractions

❏ Lack of time

❏ Lack of knowledge

❏ Lack of interest

❏ None of the above: this is not a problem for me

23. Check all that describe what you do when you read your school assignments:

❏ Eat and drink while I read.

❏ Listen to music or have television on while I read.

❏ Read at my desk with the computer on and connected to the Internet or a computer game.

❏ Lay on my bed while I read.

❏ Sit in a comfortable chair while I read.

❏ I read in a room where the rest of my family is assembled while I read.

❏ I reread the directions for the assignment prior to doing the required reading.

❏ I have a phone or pager on and in my study environment while I read.

❏ I make sure I have the necessary tools—paper, dictionary, other support materials—handy before I begin reading.

24. When I am reading something and I get stuck I try the following strategies: (Check any that apply.)

❏ I skip the difficult part.

❏ I skip the difficult part and come back to it later.

❏ I reread it.

❏ I read it aloud.

❏ I try to put it into my own words to help me understand it.

❏ I look at other information on the pages (pictures, words in bold or italic, captions).

❏ I explain it to someone else.

❏ I ask others (friends, parents, teacher) for help.

❏ I try to draw it (or somehow see it—e.g., time line, cluster, decision tree).

❏ I ask someone else to read it out loud so I can hear it.

May be copied for classrooom use. Reading Reminders *by Jim Burke (Boynton/Cook, a subsidiary of Reed Elsevier Inc., © 2000).*

THE ELEMENTS OF A TEXT

Author/World

- assumptions
- bias
- culture
- era
- expectations
- ideology
- influences
- intent
- situation

Elements

EXPOSITORY

- argument
- body text
- caption
- citations
- conclusion
- introduction
- thesis

GENERAL

- directions
- genre
- idea
- numbers
- theme
- time
- title (of text)
- URL

NARRATIVE

- action
- character
- climax
- conflict
- ending
- exposition
- names
- narrator
- place
- plot
- point of view
- setting
- story

VISUAL

- charts
- diagrams
- graphics
- graphs
- illustrations
- maps
- photographs
- tables
- time lines

Credibility

- affiliation
- awards
- byline
- categories
- context (original)
- domain name
- endorsements
- evidence
- means of production
- production quality
- publisher
- signature
- sources
- title (position)

Devices

- abbreviations
- acronyms
- analogies
- animation
- buttons
- color
- date
- embedded media
- footnotes
- hyperlinks
- icons
- intertextual links
- jumplines
- kicker
- lead
- lists
- omissions
- parallelism
- patterns
- pop-up menus
- pullout quotes
- puns
- rhyme
- sequencing
- sidebars
- silence
- sinks
- sound
- special effects
- symbols
- teaser
- transition
- typography
- Web site counter
- white space

Components

- acknowledgments
- afterword
- appendix
- borders
- boxes
- breaks
- columns
- cover
- dedication
- epigraphs
- epilogue
- fonts
- footer
- foreword
- front matter
- glossary
- header
- headings
- index
- introduction
- layout
- margins
- material
- medium
- notes
- page numbering
- preface
- prologue
- section dividers
- shape
- table of contents
- title page

Stylistics

ARRANGEMENT

- composition
- indentation
- line breaks
- placement

CONVENTIONS

- gestures
- paragraphs
- punctuation
- sentences
- violations

GENERAL

- allusions
- ambiguity
- characterization
- homage
- imagery
- intonation
- metaphors
- motifs
- repetition
- sensory details
- tone

LANGUAGE

- diction
- foreign words
- grammar
- semantics
- special terms
- syntax

Qualities

EXPERIENTIAL

- clarity
- consistency
- emphasis
- movement
- pace
- seduction
- significance
- surprise
- tension
- unity

STRUCTURAL

- complexity
- condition
- integrity
- length
- multimedia
- shape
- size

Appendix 35

CALIFORNIA LANGUAGE ARTS CONTENT STANDARDS CHECKLIST (GRADES 9–10)*

Student Name: _____   Spring/Fall of _____

Course Title: _____   Freshman or Sophomore

1.0 WORD ANALYSIS, FLUENCY, AND SYSTEMATIC VOCABULARY DEVELOPMENT

❑　　Apply their knowledge of word origins to determine the meaning of new words.

Vocabulary and Concept Development

❑ ❑　Identify and use the literal and figurative meanings of words.

❑ ❑　Distinguish between the denotative and connotative meanings of words.

❑ ❑　Identify and use origins of Greek, Roman, and Norse mythology to understand new words.

2.0 READING COMPREHENSION (FOCUS ON INFORMATIONAL MATERIALS)

❑ ❑　Analyze the organizational patterns, arguments, and positions advanced.

❑ ❑　Students read two million words in different genres annually on their own.

Structural Features of Informational Materials

❑ ❑　Analyze the structure, format, and textual features of workplace documents.

❑ ❑　Analyze how authors use these features to achieve their purposes.

❑ ❑　Prepare a bibliography using a variety of consumer, workplace, and public documents.

Comprehension and Analysis of Grade-Level-Appropriate Text

❑ ❑　Generate relevant questions about readings that can be researched.

❑ ❑　Synthesize the content and ideas from multiple sources/documents.

❑ ❑　Paraphrase and connect ideas to other sources or ideas to demonstrate understanding.

❑ ❑　Extend ideas through analysis, evaluation, and elaboration.

❑ ❑　Demonstrate ability to use sophisticated learning tools by following technical directions.

Expository Critique

❑ ❑　Analyze the organizational structure of documents by evaluating sequence and possible misreadings.

❑ ❑　Evaluate the credibility of an author's argument.

❑ ❑　Critique the relationship between generalizations and evidence.

❑ ❑　Evaluate an author's intent and how that affects the text's structure, tone, and meaning.

3.0 LITERARY RESPONSE AND ANALYSIS

❑ ❑　Analyze recurring patterns and themes in historically or culturally significant works of literature.

❑ ❑　Analyze the form, function, and characteristics of different forms of dramatic literature.

❑ ❑　Compare and contrast a theme or topic across genres to show how genre shapes the text and ideas.

Narrative Analysis of Grade-Level-Appropriate Text

❑ ❑　Analyze how internal and external conflicts, motivations, relationships, and influences affect the plot.

❑ ❑　Examine how characters reveal themselves through what they say and how they say it.

❑ ❑　Compare and contrast literary works' universal themes using examples and ideas found in the text.

❑ ❑　Analyze and trace an author's development of time and sequence in a story.

❑ ❑　Examine literary devices, techniques, and elements and how they function within different texts.

❑ ❑　Explain how voice, persona, and narrator affect tone, characterization, plot, and credibility.

Literary Criticism

❑ ❑　Evaluate the impact of diction and figurative language on tone, mood, and theme using literary terms.

❑ ❑　Analyze how a work of literature reflects and is influenced by its historical period.

*Note: These are not the actual standards—This is a checklist I made based on the standards.

May be copied for classrooom use. Reading Reminders by Jim Burke (Boynton/Cook, a subsidiary of Reed Elsevier Inc., © 2000).

1.0 WRITING STRATEGIES
❑ ❑ Demonstrate an awareness of audience and purpose, and use of the stages of the writing process.

Organization and Focus
❑ ❑ Establish and maintain a controlling idea or coherent thesis through a piece of writing.

❑ ❑ Use precise language, action verbs, sensory details, and appropriate modifiers instead of a passive voice.

Research and Technology
❑ ❑ Formulate and guide their writing using clear research questions and effective research methods.

❑ ❑ Synthesize ideas from multiple sources, examining how the different perspectives affect meaning.

❑ ❑ Integrate quotations and citations into written text, while maintaining the flow of ideas.

❑ ❑ Use appropriate conventions to document sources when writing in any medium or genre.

❑ ❑ Design and publish multi-page documents in different media for a range of audiences.

Revising and Evaluating Strategies
❑ ❑ Use the writing process to evaluate the needs and improve the logic and coherence of the text.

❑ ❑ Evaluate use of word choice and tone as they relate to the writer's audience, purpose, and context.

WRITING APPLICATIONS (GENRES AND THEIR CHARACTERISTICS)
❑ ❑ Know when/how to use the rhetorical strategies of narration, exposition, persuasion, and description.

❑ ❑ Write biographical and autobiographical narratives or short stories.

❑ ❑ Use sensory details to evoke or describe the people or events in a scene.

❑ ❑ Use appropriate devices and techniques to develop character, plot, and setting in a scene.

❑ ❑ Recognize the decisions that writers face and understand how those decisions affect the story.

Writing Responses to Literature
❑ ❑ Use examples from the text to support and illustrate the ideas their writing tries to convey.

❑ ❑ Write expository compositions, including analytical essays and research reports.

❑ ❑ Convey the significance of ideas by using various rhetorical and grammatical devices.

❑ ❑ Use visual aids to organize and record information on charts, maps, and graphs.

❑ ❑ Anticipate and address readers' potential misunderstandings, biases, and expectations.

❑ ❑ Structure ideas and arguments in a sustained and logical fashion using examples to support.

❑ ❑ Write a business letter and various other types of functional documents.

❑ ❑ Write a technical document that follows the criteria appropriate for that audience.

WRITTEN AND ORAL ENGLISH LANGUAGE CONVENTIONS: GRAMMAR AND MECHANICS
❑ ❑ Identify and use clauses, phrases, and punctuation for effect and clarity.

❑ ❑ Identify and use different types of sentence structures.

❑ ❑ Know how words, sentences, and paragraphs are used to convey different effects and meanings.

LISTENING AND SPEAKING STRATEGIES
❑ ❑ Deliver speeches and presentations in various contexts for different purposes.

❑ ❑ Compare and contrast how the media cover the same event.

❑ ❑ Structure and provide emphasis within their speeches to achieve the desired effect.

❑ ❑ Analyze historically significant speeches (e.g., Lincoln's "Gettysburg" or King's "Dream").

❑ ❑ Analyze and employ the different types of arguments including causation, analogy, authority, and logic.

❑ ❑ Evaluate the aesthetic effects used in speeches (in films, campaigns, and other contexts).

SPEAKING APPLICATIONS (GENRES AND THEIR CHARACTERISTICS)
❑ ❑ Deliver extemporaneous presentations that combine different rhetorical strategies.

❑ ❑ Interview a range of people for different purposes.

❑ ❑ Participate in class discussions about literature using appropriate vocabulary and examples for support.

❑ ❑ Deliver informational and procedural speeches using appropriate aids to convey your ideas.

❑ ❑ Use multimedia tools to support your presentation of information.

CALIFORNIA LANGUAGE ARTS CONTENT STANDARDS CHECKLIST (GRADES 11–12)*

Student Name: _____   Spring/Fall of _____

Course Title: _____   Junior or Senior

1.0 WORD ANALYSIS, FLUENCY, AND SYSTEMATIC VOCABULARY DEVELOPMENT

❏ ❏ Apply their knowledge of word origins to determine meaning of words.

❏ ❏ Know etymology of terms from political science and history.

❏ ❏ Know Greek, Latin, and Anglo-Saxon roots/affixes for scientific and mathematical terms.

❏ ❏ Know how to make sense of metaphorical/figurative language.

2.0 READING COMPREHENSION (INFORMATIONAL MATERIALS)

❏ ❏ Recognize and comprehend use of different types of public documents.

Comprehension and Analysis of Grade-Level-Appropriate Text

❏ ❏ Identify and analyze different types of rhetorical devices in public documents.

❏ ❏ Explain how various techniques affect meaning.

❏ ❏ Examine and clarify facts used in a variety of public documents.

❏ ❏ Recognize and demonstrate the difference between fact and opinion.

❏ ❏ Make reasonable assertions about the author's arguments.

❏ ❏ Support assertions using effective examples, quotes, and conclusions.

Expository Critique

❏ ❏ Critique the power, validity, and truthfulness of arguments set forth in public documents.

3.0 LITERARY RESPONSE AND ANALYSIS

❏ ❏ Read significant works of literature that complement studies in history.

❏ ❏ Identify and analyze recurring themes.

Structural Features of Literature

❏ ❏ Read and know characteristics of subgenres (e.g., satire, parody, allegory) used in various genre.

❏ ❏ Read and understand the structure of novels.

❏ ❏ Read and understand the devices used in short fiction.

❏ ❏ Read and understand the devices used in drama.

❏ ❏ Read and understand the devices used in poetry.

❏ ❏ Read and understand the devices used in literary essays.

Narrative Analysis of Grade-Level-Appropriate Text

❏ ❏ Use textual evidence to support claims.

❏ ❏ Know and use literary terms when responding to literary texts.

❏ ❏ Explain use of various literary techniques and how they affect the text.

❏ ❏ Trace the development of American literature across time.

❏ ❏ Compare works—i.e., themes and styles—from one period to another.

❏ ❏ Explain the historical/philosophical influences of a historical period on a text and its writer.

❏ ❏ Understand and use archetypes from myth and literary tradition to examine literature.

Literary Criticism

❏ ❏ Examine literary texts using philosophical arguments (e.g., feminism, existentialism).

*Note: These are not the actual standards—This is a checklist I made based on the standards.

May be copied for classrooom use. Reading Reminders by Jim Burke (Boynton/Cook, a subsidiary of Reed Elsevier Inc., © 2000).

1.0 WRITING STRATEGIES (ORGANIZATION AND FOCUS)

❑ ❑ Know and use different elements of discourse when writing.
❑ ❑ Use variety of stylistic and rhetorical devices when writing.
❑ ❑ Support ideas and arguments with precise and relevant examples.

Research and Technology

❑ ❑ Develop and use surveys and interviews to generate data.
❑ ❑ Use a variety of sources from different media for research.
❑ ❑ Organize information during research using appropriate strategies (e.g., outlining).
❑ ❑ Integrate databases, graphics, and spreadsheets into word-processed documents.
❑ ❑ Revise documents to improve voice, style, and meaning.

Writing Applications (Genre and Their Characteristics)

❑ ❑ Write documents of at least 1500 words each.
❑ ❑ Demonstrate a command of Standard American English.
❑ ❑ Write a variety of narratives.
❑ ❑ Write a literary response essay.
❑ ❑ Write a reflective essay.
❑ ❑ Write an historical investigation report (research project).
❑ ❑ Write a job application and resume.
❑ ❑ Deliver multimedia presentations.
❑ ❑ Demonstrate mastery of business letter by writing one.
❑ ❑ Write letters of complaint, inquiry, and intent.
❑ ❑ Write a proposal.
❑ ❑ Write a précis.

1.0 WRITTEN AND ORAL ENGLISH LANGUAGE CONVENTIONS

❑ ❑ Know and use proper formatting in all documents.
❑ ❑ Produce work that is legible.
❑ ❑ Write a paragraph that is focused, organized, and developed.
❑ ❑ Write a variety of types of sentence patterns.
❑ ❑ Use a variety of grammatical structures and modifiers in sentences.

1.0 LISTENING AND SPEAKING STRATEGIES

❑ ❑ Identify and evaluate strategies used by media to inform, persuade, and entertain.
❑ ❑ Explain the impact of media on the political process.
❑ ❑ Compare and interpret various ways in which events are presented by visual media.

Organization and Delivery of Oral Communication

❑ ❑ Use different rhetorical devices to achieve clarity, force, and effect.
❑ ❑ Identify and evaluate use of logical, ethical, and emotional appeals in presentations.
❑ ❑ Use language, imagery, metaphor to create effective presentations.

Analysis and Evaluation of Oral and Media Communications

❑ ❑ Analyze techniques used by media to convey meaning.
❑ ❑ Analyze four basic types of persuasive speech.

2.0 SPEAKING APPLICATIONS (GENRES AND THEIR CHARACTERISTICS)

❑ ❑ Deliver effective presentations.
❑ ❑ Deliver reports on historical investigations.
❑ ❑ Deliver oral responses to literature.
❑ ❑ Deliver multimedia presentations.
❑ ❑ Perform a variety of literary texts (e.g., from plays, poems, speeches).

To: Concerned Parent
From: Jim Burke
Re: *Jasmine*, by Bharati Mukherjee

Dear Concerned Parent,

Thank you for taking the time to have this conversation about a book I respect a great deal for the conversation it allows us to have in my classroom. As a parent myself, I appreciate your concern for and participation in your child's education.

Briefly, let me give you some background on why we chose this book in particular. *Jasmine* (Mukherjee, 1989) provides a dramatic contrast to *Nectar in the Sieve* (Markandaya, 1961), the book we previously used in our interdisciplinary course. *Nectar* is a polite, rural story of a family's struggles in the wake of a failed crop that results in their almost immediate destitution. After subsequent discussions with a few parents who read *Jasmine* with their children during the summer, I decided it offered more contemporary, thematic links between the American and Indian cultures.

Several aspects of Mukherjee's book further recommended it:

- A portion of the book appeared on one of the practice Advanced Placement tests last year, thus signaling an "institutional recognition" of the book's merit.

- Literary merit: it remains consistently read and discussed; Mukherjee herself has since won several major American writing awards.

- It allows us to examine, in the course of our discussions, such themes and questions as: Who are we? How does where we are affect who we are or how we act? What does it mean to be an "American"? What role do women play in our two cultures and how has that changed over the years?

I recognize that the novel contains several mature scenes, both involving sex. Though these scenes might make some readers uncomfortable with their intimacy and violence, they are important elements of the story. The scene between Jane and her husband establishes the depth of her love for a man she will ultimately refuse to marry; the rape scene emphasizes the plight of the young woman's entry into a terrifying, carnivorous world of illegal immigrants who are at the mercy of such pirates. Furthermore, this second incident provides powerful thematic links to both the *Odyssey* and their study of India's culture as Jasmine chooses to let her former (Indian) self die and gives birth to a new, stronger (American) self in the wake of a terrible event that she refuses to let defeat her.

I respect your inquiry into the book and its role in our curriculum. I am grateful for the opportunity to reflect here on why I think the book is a sound choice. I stand by the decision, though realize that in the future I should provide more specific information to parents so they feel better informed about the book we ask them to buy and their children to read. I would also be happy, should you wish, to offer your daughter a suitable alternative to *Jasmine* to read in its place. Please contact me if you have any further concerns about this or any other books we teach in our course.

Sincerely,

Jim Burke
Freshman 1H Teacher/English Department Chair

THE TRAITS OF AN EFFECTIVE READER READING AN INFORMATIONAL TEXT SCORING GUIDE

DEVELOPING INTERPRETATIONS

- Identify problems, gaps, ambiguities, conflicts, and/or disparate points of view in the text.
- Analyze the text to pose explanations that bridge gaps, clarify ambiguity, and resolve textual problems.
- Use the context to connect analytical explanations to a "bigger picture."

5   The advanced response interprets to analyze and think critically about informational texts.
- ❑ Directly answers the question by employing problem-solving techniques—using specific evidence, clues, and "on target" information.
- ❑ Examples, quotes, and events are cited from the text and connected strongly to the analysis.
- ❑ Responds beyond the question to engage the bigger picture by creating framework of historical significance, cultural importance, or universal theme.

3   The developing response interprets to expand the text, but is still developing connections to a larger worldview.
- ❑ Uses some language that indicates an initial layer of interpretation understanding.
- ❑ Gives a safe response citing very obvious examples. Connections between the examples and the analysis are not always evident.
- ❑ Does not yet move beyond the question—engaging the "bigger picture" is still a developing skill.

1   The emerging response sees interpretation as "talking about a book." Reading and interpreting are still separate processes. Little evidence exists that the student understands the concept of interpretation.
- ❑ Does not adequately address the question.
- ❑ Does not cite examples, quotes, or evidence from the text to use as a basis of interpretation.
- ❑ Sometimes restates the question words.

INTEGRATING FOR SYNTHESIS

- Put information in order to explain the text's progress or chronology.
- Compare and contrast examples, facts, or events in order to make defensible judgments or interpretations.
- Recognize and describe cause and effect relations.
- Integrate personal experience, background knowledge, and/or content knowledge with the text to create a "synthesis" of text plus knowledge.

5   The advanced response integrates textual material and other types of knowledge to create a synthesis of ideas.
- ❑ Directly, specifically, and concretely performs the synthesis application directed by the question by using synthesis language.
- ❑ Uses well-chosen examples that have a strong parallel development if the question demands it.
- ❑ Responds beyond the question, integrating several layers of knowledge into a harmonious whole.

3   The developing response integrates textual material with other types of knowledge to create a surface-level synthesis.
- ❑ Uses some synthesis language to reflect a basic understanding of the skills of integrating for synthesis.
- ❑ Uses general and "safe" examples.
- ❑ The layers and types of knowledge in the response are not always well integrated.

1   The emerging response employs some skills of synthesizing, but a fully developed integration is still emerging.
- ❑ Does not perform the synthesis application directed by the question.
- ❑ Does not accurately use synthesis language.
- ❑ Does not integrate sources, texts, and understandings to a measurable degree.

CRITIQUING FOR EVALUATION

- Experiment with ideas in the text.
- Express opinions about the text.
- Raise questions about the text.
- Make good judgments about the text by using a synthesis of material derived from multiple sources.
- Challenge the ideas of the author or source by noting bias, distortion, and/or lack of coherence.
- Contrast the accuracy of textual information with other sources and form solid, defensible critiques.

5   The advanced response evaluates to assert a strong voice in the text.
- ❑ Directly and thoughtfully answers the question, using evaluation terminology effectively and precisely to indicate the reader's critique of the text.
- ❑ The examples are well developed, placed in context, and connected well to other ideas.
- ❑ Responds beyond the parameters of the question to critically engage the text and its ideas in a solid, defensible judgment.

3   The developing response hesitates to evaluate thoroughly; it still plays it somewhat "safe."
- ❑ Generally answers the evaluation question, but hesitant to critically engage with the text.
- ❑ Selects safe and obvious examples that are connected to other ideas in fairly limited ways.
- ❑ Does not yet move beyond the question to venture into the larger world of critical discourse.

1   The emerging response is just beginning to explore a critical stance to the text.
- ❑ Uses evaluation terminology sporadically or not at all.
- ❑ The examples are incomplete or sketchily described, not connected to other ideas/issues.
- ❑ The response is incomplete or restates the question words.

THE TRAITS OF AN EFFECTIVE READER READING AN INFORMATIONAL TEXT SCORING GUIDE

DECODING CONVENTIONS

• Decode the writing *conventions* of grammar, punctuation, word recognition, and sentence structure.
• Recognize the organizational *conventions* of the author or organizational framework and features of the text.
• Identify the genre *conventions* (newspaper, magazine, textbooks, brochures, instructions) and the types of modes appropriate to each informational genre (cause and effect, comparison, sequential, etc.).

5 The advanced response uses conventions information to form a confident "thinking frame" of a text.
□ Directly answers the question using text structure language in specific and precise ways.
□ Selects well-chosen and well-supported examples to illustrate understanding of the conventions.
□ Responds "beyond" the question by enlarging the initial thinking frame.

3 The developing response uses conventions information to form an initial "thinking frame" of the text.
□ Uses some basic text structure language to indicate general understandings.
□ Selects "safe" and obvious examples to illustrate understanding of the conventions.
□ The response is fairly safe and stays definitely within the confines of the question.

1 The emerging response is beginning to decode conventions and the challenge of decoding gets in the way of a "thinking frame" for the text.
□ Does not adequately answer the question but may use some text structure language.
□ Focuses on more general information rather than providing examples from the text.
□ The response can be characterized as sketchy and incomplete.

ESTABLISHING COMPREHENSION

• Identify and explain the vocabulary key to the main thesis of the text.
• Identify the main idea, major and minor examples, facts, expert authority, and turning moments.
• Distinguish between significant and supporting details that elaborate the main idea.
• Summarize and paraphrase with purpose to move toward making inferences and interpretations.

5 The advanced response demonstrates a purposeful, expansive, and knowledgeable comprehension of the text.
□ Directly answers the question using comprehension terms to indicate precise understandings.
□ Selects well-chosen examples to illustrate in-depth comprehension. Examples are well developed using clear, specific language and terms.
□ Responds "beyond" the question by increasing comprehension of the text into inferential and interpretative levels.

3 The developing response demonstrates an adequate comprehension of the text. Purposeful comprehension is still evolving.
□ Uses some comprehension terms to indicate general understandings.
□ Selects "safe" and obvious examples to illustrate literal comprehension.
□ Does not venture information beyond the initial question.

1 The emerging response is searching to establish a basic comprehension of the text.
□ Does not provide examples for evidence but sometimes restates the question.
□ Shows little evidence that a basic comprehension of the text has been achieved.
□ The response can be characterized as sketchy and incomplete.

REALIZING CONTEXT

• Identify the time period and its accompanying social realities in the text.
• Recognize the perspective—point of view—of the text and its relationship to social factors.
• Identify the vocabulary reflective of the context.
• Recognize the writing mode, tone, and voice of the author or source selected with respect to the context.
• Recognize the subject matter's context and its applications to many aspects of the text.

5 The advanced response realizes context and sees inferential meanings and intended purposes, both implicit and explicit.
□ Directly and specifically answers the question to demonstrate understanding of inferential meaning.
□ Selects well-chosen examples to illustrate understandings of contextual issues.
□ Goes beyond the question's limits and extends into in-depth understandings of contextual relationships.

3 The developing response realizes the context of the text to some degree and recognizes obvious types of inference. The idea of contextual relationships between many factors and issues is still in development.
□ Uses some context terminology to show a basic level of understanding.
□ Selects "safe" and obvious examples that stay close to the surface of the text.
□ Stays within the safe confines of the question.

1 The emerging response guesses at context, but has difficulty accessing inferential knowledge.
□ Does not use examples from the text to illustrate inferential understandings.
□ Not enough evidence to demonstrate an understanding of contextual layers of the text.
□ Demonstrates little effectiveness at "reading between the lines."

THE TRAITS OF AN EFFECTIVE READER READING A LITERARY TEXT SCORING GUIDE

DEVELOPING INTERPRETATIONS

- Identify problems, gaps, ambiguities, conflicts, symbols, and/or metaphors in the text.
- Analyze the text to pose explanations that bridge gaps, clarify ambiguity, and resolve textual problems.
- Use the context to connect analytical explanations to a "bigger picture."

5 The advanced response interprets to analyze and think critically about informational texts.
- ❏ Directly answers the question by employing problem-solving techniques—using specific evidence, clues, and "on target" information.
- ❏ Examples, quotes, and events are cited from the text and connected strongly to the analysis.
- ❏ Responds beyond the question to engage the bigger picture by creating framework of historical significance, cultural importance, or universal theme.

3 The developing response interprets to expand the text, but is still developing connections to a larger worldview.
- ❏ Uses some language that indicates an initial layer of interpretation understanding.
- ❏ Gives a safe response citing very obvious examples. Connections between the examples and the analysis are not always evident.
- ❏ Does not move beyond the question—engaging the "bigger picture" is still a developing skill.

1 The emerging response sees interpretation as "talking about a book." Reading and interpreting are still separate processes. Little evidence exists that the student understands the concept of interpretation.
- ❏ Does not adequately address the question.
- ❏ Does not cite examples, quotes, or evidence from the text to use as a basis of interpretation.
- ❏ Sometimes restates the question words.

INTEGRATING FOR SYNTHESIS

- Put information in order to explain the text's process or chronology.
- Compare and contrast characters, story lines, events, and primary and secondary sources in order to make defensible judgments and interpretations.
- Recognize and describe cause-and-effect relations.
- Integrate personal experience, background knowledge, and/or content knowledge with the text to create a "synthesis" of text plus knowledge.

5 The advanced response integrates textual material and other types of knowledge to create a synthesis of ideas.
- ❏ Directly, specifically, and concretely performs the synthesis application directed by the question by using synthesis language.
- ❏ Uses well-chosen examples that have a strong parallel development if the question demands it.
- ❏ Responds beyond the question, integrating several layers of knowledge into a harmonious whole.

3 The developing response integrates textual material with other types of knowledge to create a surface-level synthesis.
- ❏ Uses some synthesis language to reflect a basic understanding of the skills of integrating for synthesis.
- ❏ Uses general and "safe" examples.
- ❏ The layers and types of knowledge in the response are not always well integrated.

1 The emerging response employs some skills of synthesizing, but a fully developed integration is still emerging.
- ❏ Does not perform the synthesis application directed by the question.
- ❏ Does not accurately use synthesis language.
- ❏ Does not integrate sources, text, and understandings to a measurable degree.

CRITIQUING FOR EVALUATION

- Experiment with ideas in the text.
- Express opinions about the text.
- Raise questions about the text.
- Make good judgments about the text by using a synthesis of material derived from multiple sources.
- Challenge the ideas of the author by noting bias, distortion, and/or lack of coherence.
- Contrast the accuracy of textual information with other sources and form solid, defensible critiques.

5 The advanced response evaluates to assert a strong voice in the text.
- ❏ Directly and thoughtfully answers the question, using evaluation terminology effectively and precisely to indicate the reader's critique of the text.
- ❏ The examples are well developed, placed in context, and connected well to other ideas.
- ❏ Responds beyond the parameters of the question to critically engage the text and its ideas in a solid, defensible judgment.

3 The developing response hesitates to evaluate thoroughly; it still plays it somewhat "safe."
- ❏ Generally answers the evaluation question, but hesitant to critically engage with the text.
- ❏ Selects safe and obvious examples that are connected to other ideas in fairly limited ways.
- ❏ Does not yet move beyond the question to venture into the larger world of critical discourse.

1 The emerging response is just beginning to explore a critical stance to the text.
- ❏ Uses evaluation terminology sporadically or not at all.
- ❏ The examples are incomplete or sketchily described, and not connected to other ideas or issues.
- ❏ The response is incomplete or restates the question words.

THE TRAITS OF AN EFFECTIVE READER READING A LITERARY TEXT SCORING GUIDE

DECODING CONVENTIONS

- Decode the writing *conventions* of grammar, punctuation, word recognition, and sentence structure.
- Recognize the organizational *conventions* of the author, the title, the characters, the theme, the conflict, and the resolution of stories and plays.
- Identify the genre *conventions* (poetry, drama, fiction) of the types of modes (narrative autobiographical, persuasive, ironic) appropriate to each literary genre, the distinctions between genres, the expectations the readers have for genres.

5 The advanced response uses conventions information to form a confident "thinking frame" of a text.

❑ Directly answers the question using text structure language in specific and precise ways.

❑ Selects well-chosen and well-supported examples to illustrate understanding of the conventions.

❑ The response is fairly safe and stays definitely within the confines of the question.

1 The emerging response is beginning to decode conventions and the challenge of decoding gets in the way of a "thinking frame" for the text.

❑ Does not adequately answer the question but may use some text structure language.

❑ Focuses on more general information rather than providing examples from the text.

❑ The response can be characterized as sketchy and incomplete.

ESTABLISHING COMPREHENSION

- Use strategies to "squeeze" meaning out of the text.
- Identify the plot, the major (round) characters and minor (flat) characters, the "turning moments," and main themes of the text.
- Distinguish between significant and supporting details and events for plot, characters, main ideas, and main themes.
- Summarize and paraphrase with purpose to move toward making inferences and interpretations.

5 The advanced response demonstrates a purposeful, expansive, and knowledgeable comprehension of the text.

❑ Directly answers the question using comprehension terms to indicate precise understandings.

❑ Selects well-chosen examples to illustrate in-depth comprehension. Examples are well developed using clear, specific language and terms.

❑ Responds "beyond" the question by increasing comprehension of the text into inferential and interpretative levels.

3 The developing response demonstrates an adequate comprehension of the text. Purposeful comprehension is still evolving.

❑ Uses some comprehension terms to indicate general understandings.

❑ Selects "safe" and obvious examples to illustrate literal comprehension.

❑ Does not venture information beyond the initial question.

1 The emerging response is searching to establish a basic comprehension of the text.

❑ Does not provide examples for evidence but sometimes restates the question.

❑ Shows little evidence that a basic comprehension of the text has been achieved.

❑ The response can be characterized as sketchy and incomplete.

REALIZING CONTEXT

- Identify the time period and its accompanying social realities in the text.
- Identify the setting of the text and its relationship to social factors.
- Identify the vocabulary reflective of the context.
- Recognize the writing mode, tone, and voice of the author or source selected with respect to the context.
- Recognize the cultural aspects of the text.

5 The advanced response realizes context and sees inferential meanings and intended purposes, both implicit and explicit.

❑ Directly and specifically answers the question to demonstrate understanding of inferential meaning.

❑ Selects well-chosen examples to illustrate understandings of contextual issues.

❑ Goes beyond the question's limits and extends into in-depth understandings of contextual relationships.

3 The developing response realizes the context of the text to some degree and recognizes obvious types of inference. The idea of contextual relationships between many factors and issues is still in development.

❑ Uses some context terminology to show a basic level of understanding.

❑ Selects "safe" and obvious examples that stay close to the surface of the text.

❑ Stays within the safe confines of the question.

1 The emerging response guesses at context, but has difficulty accessing inferential knowledge.

❑ Does not use examples from the text to illustrate inferential understandings.

❑ Not enough evidence to demonstrate an understanding of contextual layers of the text.

❑ Demonstrates little effectiveness at "reading between the lines."

A CONCISE GLOSSARY OF LITERARY TERMS

Note: After surveying a number of colleagues, I found the following terms and ideas to be the most consistently identified as important for students to know and teachers to teach.

Action: What happens in the story.

Allusion: Indirect reference to an event, person, place, or artistic work that the writer assumes the reader knows about; used effectively, the allusion economically links the text to the larger meaning of the other text. When J. D. Salinger alludes to David Copperfield in *Catcher in the Rye*, he is placing his novel in a historical, literary context he assumes the reader should understand.

Analogy: Illustrates the idea by linking the current idea to a more familiar idea to better communicate the idea at hand; typically involves the use of an extended simile—Blake's "Tyger, Tyger" in which the industrial plants are compared to a tiger's appearance and danger.

Antagonist: Most prominent of a story's characters who opposes the hero (see Protagonist) in the story; in *Lord of the Flies* the antagonist is Jack, who embodies evil and seeks to kill Ralph.

Autobiography: Personal remembrance in which the writer tells the story of his or her own life or a particular event during that life (see Memoir). *I Know Why the Caged Bird Sings* by Maya Angelou exemplifies this genre of writing.

Ballad: A song or orally performed poem that dramatically retells the story of a popular figure (e.g., Billy the Kid).

Biography: Book or story written about the life of someone else; one example would be Justin Kaplan's biography of Mark Twain, *Mr. Twain and Mr. Clemens*.

Blank Verse: Unrhymed form of poetry; each line composed of 10 syllables in which every other syllable, beginning with the second one, is stressed (iambic pentameter). It is often used in long poems. Tennyson's "Ulysses" (1842) effectively illustrates this form:

> One equal temper of heroic hearts,
>
> Made weak by time and fate, but strong in will
>
> To strive, to seek, to find, and not to yield.

Cadence: Occasionally used as a synonym for "rhythm" or "meter." Relates to the rising and falling, the rhythm of speech; often an important aspect of a poet's style.

Caesura (sometimes spelled "cesura"): A pause in a line of verse, often caused by either grammar, logic, or cadence, which is similar to the pause for breath.

Conflict: The primary source of tension within a story. Often divided into four categories: the individual vs. themselves (see J. D. Salinger's *Catcher in the Rye*); the individual vs. society (see Ken Kesey's *One Flew over the Cuckoo's Nest*); the individual vs. nature (see John Steinbeck's *The Grapes of Wrath*); the individual vs. fate/gods (see Homer's *Odyssey*).

Connotation: Range of further associations that a word or phrase suggests in addition to the primary dictionary meaning (i.e., its denotation).

Context: Those parts of the text that precede and follow a passage or event that help to give it meaning; helpful to readers who encounter information they cannot immediately understand.

Convention: Established practice used by authors of literary works. Involves technique, style, structure, or subject matter; particularly essential to poetry and literature, which depend on such conventions as rhyme or the genre conventions of short stories.

Couplet: Pair of lines in verse that form a unit; there are several types—e.g., the heroic, open, and end-stopped, and most notably those that appear at the end of Shakespearean sonnets that form the last two lines and rhyme with each other.

Denotation: Accepted meaning of a word (i.e., the one that appears in the dictionary).

Dénouement: Resolution or undoing of the central "problem" or complications of the story.

Dialect: Variation of pronunciation and usage within standard form of speech; typically based on regional, cultural, or social class differences. Good examples are the different dialects used by Mark Twain in *Huck Finn*. Another word for this is *vernacular*.

Dialogue: Conversation carried on between characters in a literary work.

Diction: Choice of words used in a literary work. The writing can be characterized by such features as archaisms, colloquialisms, profanity, slang, trite expressions, or vulgarity.

Digression: Temporary departure from the main subject to address a separate idea or event within the story.

Dramatic Monologue: Speech in which the poet or character speaks to a silent audience of one or more.

Empathy: Act of placing yourself "in the shoes" of another and forcing yourself to imagine how that person must feel. This is what fiction asks the reader to do.

Epic: Long narrative poem or story that tells of the deeds and adventures of a hero (e.g., *Beowulf*).

Epigram: Brief, witty poem or thought that often makes fun of the idea it examines. Oscar Wilde raised it to such an art form he became known as an "epigrammatist."

Epigraph: Short poem or verse placed at the beginning of a book that bears some relation to the book's themes or subject.

Epilogue: Concluding section of a literary work.

Episodic: Narrative constructed around a series of distinct but related incidents rather than a carefully woven plot.

Epitaph: Words or poem suited for inscription on a tomb or gravestone.

Essay: Short written composition in prose that examines a particular subject in depth. There are various "rhetorical modes" for the essay, e.g., analytical, reflective, cause-effect, personal narrative.

Existentialism: European philosophy that several authors, among them Albert Camus and Jean Paul Sartre, have adapted to fiction and drama to explore the themes of meaninglessness, individual freedom, and alienation that plague humanity at the close of the millennium. (For fun, search the Internet for the hilarious "Jean Paul Sartre Cookbook.")

Exposition: Writing that makes clear or explains something that might be difficult for the reader to understand; in a play or novel or essay it helps the reader to understand the larger action or subject of the text.

Falling Action: The movement within the story that signals the beginning of trouble or complications for the story or its protagonist (e.g., the point at which Macbeth and his wife commit their first murder).

Fiction: Stories created from the writer's imagination or invented. Novels and short stories are fiction. As novelist Tim O'Brien says, however, just because it didn't happen doesn't mean it isn't true. (See O'Brien's *The Things They Carried*).

Foot: Smallest repeated pattern of stressed and unstressed syllables in a line of verse.

Foreshadowing: Hints of what will come later in the story that the author gives early on.

Free Verse: Does not conform to the traditional rules that govern metrical verse; there is no regular meter or rhyme. Poets using free verse demand that their reader attend to other aspects of the text such as cadence and imagery. Walt Whitman's poetry exemplifies this form.

Genre: Refers to a type of literature specific to its style, form, or content. Examples include mystery novels, epic poems, tragic plays.

Hyperbole: Exaggeration or overstatement of the truth. Holden Caulfield constantly uses this when he describes his own behavior (e.g., lying).

Iambic Pentameter: Since roughly 90% of all verse is written in iambic pentameter it is helpful to carefully define it. An *iamb* is five iambic feet strung together (e.g., ŭpón). Pentameter means that the line has five feet (or ten syllables), which may or may not rhyme as the poet prefers/intends.

Irony: When the writer uses a word or phrase to mean the opposite of its literal or normal meaning. There are three forms of irony commonly used: dramatic, verbal, and situational.

Metaphor: Comparison of two unlike things in which no word of comparison (*like* or *as*) is used, e.g., "the river of life."

Meter: Patterned repetition of stressed and unstressed syllables in a line of poetry.

Mood: Relates to the feeling a text arouses in its reader; can shift between scenes but tends to define a work overall (e.g., the mood of *Macbeth* is ominous or heavy).

Motif: Frequently recurring theme or idea in a work of literature. In Amy Tan's *Kitchen God's Wife*, the motif of secrecy runs throughout the story.

Narrator: Person who tells the story; related to this idea is the extent to which the narrator is "reliable." Also, some narrators know more than others depending on the limits the author has imposed on them; for example, some know only what they "see," while others are privy to every thought and emotion of their character.

Onomatopoeia: Use of words whose sound defines its meaning; examples include *plop, crash,* and *hum.*

Parable: Short story that illustrates a particular belief or moral; Franz Kafka was particularly interested in the use of parables (see *The Castle*).

Parody: Form of literature that mocks a literary work or its style.

Personification: Literary device describing an animal, object, or idea as if it had human characteristics; e.g., "the trees reached toward the sky." Heavily used in poetry but common to fiction, also.

Plot: The "what" of the story: what happens or the action. The plot traditionally contains five elements: exposition, rising action, climax, falling action, and resolution.

Point of View: Perspective from which the story is told. There are several vantage points: first person (e.g., "I grew up in Iowa"), second person (e.g., "When you grow up in Iowa. . . ."), and third person (e.g., "He grew up in Iowa").

Prose: Writing not composed according to the rules and forms that govern poetry.

Protagonist: Main character or hero of a story. (See also *Antagonist.*)

Pun: Word or phrase used in such a way as to imply other possible meanings. Students cannot "get" Shakespeare, for example, if they do not understand and cannot recognize a pun.

Rhetoric: Deliberate use of eloquence to persuade others' feelings and thoughts; the rhetorical elements of a text refer to those aspects of the story that persuade or otherwise guide the response of the readers.

Rhythm: Way in which sound is used in a poem; can be used in an ordered or free manner to create a tone and shape to the text.

Satire: Used to make fun of or ridicule a human vice or weakness or individual failings; classic example is found in George Orwell's *Animal Farm*, which satirizes politics and human nature.

May be copied for classrooom use. Reading Reminders *by Jim Burke (Boynton/Cook, a subsidiary of Reed Elsevier Inc., © 2000).*

Setting: If Plot is the "what," Setting is the "where and when," setting the story in a historical and physical time and space.

Soliloquy: Similar to a dramatic monologue, it is a speech a character delivers while on stage alone. The supreme example is, of course, Hamlet's "To be or not to be," soliloquy.

Sonnet: Poem consisting of 14 lines written in iambic pentameter, the most commonly encountered in high school being the Shakespearean sonnet; there is another type called the Italian or Petrarchan sonnet.

Stanza: From the Italian word for *room*, the word refers to the number of lines a poetic "paragraph" contains: couplet (two-line stanza), triplet, quatrain (four-line stanza), quintet, sestet, septet (seven-line stanza), and octave.

Stereotype: Characters are merely stereotypes when they have no individuality to distinguish them from, for example, historical conceptions of their group. Thus Shylock in *Merchant of Venice* or Jim in *Huck Finn* are sometimes considered little more than stereotypes if not read carefully.

Simile: Compares two unlike things using *as* or *like*. "She stood in front of the altar, shaking like a freshly caught trout" (Maya Angelou, *I Know Why the Caged Bird Sings*).

Structure: Has to do with the form or organization of the text, particularly as it relates to or affects the meaning or action within the story. What purpose is served, for example, by the constant back-and-forth-in-time structure of Bharati Mukherjee's novel *Jasmine*?

Style: How a writer uses words, images, phrases to create a feeling or convey a thought to the reader. It is impossible to discuss some books, such as *Catcher in the Rye*, without examining their style because the style is such a central aspect of the text.

Symbol: Person, place, thing that is, in a text, used to represent something else. As Flannery O'Connor says, however, in *Mystery and Manners*, such symbols must first function as intended (e.g., a wooden leg in one of her stories)

before it can convey a deeper symbolic truth (e.g., about her character's dependence).

Synopsis: Short summary or précis of a story's plot or themes.

Theme: This is the deep structure consisting of the text's ideas and truths, which the writer tries to convey through the action and exposition of the story. Students understand theme when they write "This is a story about alienation," instead of "This is a story about a man who goes to live by himself in the country."

Tone: Similar to Mood, it relates to the overall feeling a story creates in the reader.

Tragedy: Outcome the character could have avoided at any point along the way but, due to certain flaws, chose not to; these errors in judgment lead to their inevitable fall.

Verse: Consists of a metric line of poetry that has some formal structure to it. Used also to distinguish poetry from prose.

Resources

The Concise Oxford Dictionary of Literary Terms, Chris Baldick, Oxford University Press, New York, 1990. An affordable, helpful reference book that has most words you will want to know.

Poetry Handbook: A Dictionary of Terms, Babette Deutsch, Harper Perennial, Fourth Edition, 1974. While the *Oxford* book is helpful as a general reference, you would do better to get this one if you want a book specific to poetry.

The New Princeton Encyclopedia of Poetry and Poetics, Alex Preminger, T. V. F. Brogan, eds., Princeton University Press, 1993. I prefer the Deutsch book but this offers an exhaustive examination of all spheres of poetry and poetics.

Writer's Inc. and *Write for College* (Houghton Mifflin), as part of their encyclopedic resources, both offer a fine little literary and poetic terms section, making them an extremely useful integrated information resource for your classroom.

103 THINGS TO DO BEFORE/DURING/AFTER READING

Pantomime: Scene student chooses or the class calls out to you.

Dramatic monologue for a character in a scene: What are they thinking/feeling at that moment—why?

Dramatic monologue for a character while they are out of the book: Where are they? Why? What are they thinking?

Business Card Book: Write the story in the most compelling way you can on paper the size of a business card.

Postcard: Write to a friend about this book; to the author; to a character in the book; write as if you were the character or author and write to yourself.

Mapmaker: Draw a map of the book's setting.

Moviemaker: Write a one-page "pitch" to a producer explaining why the story would or would not make a great movie.

Trailer: Movie previews always offer a quick sequence of the best moments that make us want to watch it; storyboard or narrate the scenes for your trailer. Focus on verbs.

Billboard: As in the movies, take what seems the most compelling image(s) and create an ad.

Adjective-itis: Pick five adjectives for the book or character(s), and explain how they apply.

Collage: Create an individual or class collage around themes or characters in the book.

Haiku/Limerick: Create one about a character.

Cliff's Notes: Take a chapter and, using Cliff's format, create your own.

Roundtable: Everyone has a chance to talk about what intrigues, bothers, confuses you about the book.

Silent Roundtable: The only rule is the teacher cannot say *anything* during the period allotted for class discussion of a book.

Silent Conversation: A student writes about a story on paper; then passes it to another who responds in writing to what they said; each subsequent respondent "talks" to/about all those before.

Fishbowl: Impromptu or scheduled, 2–4 students sit in the middle of a circle made up of the rest of the class, and talk about a text; the class makes observations about the conversation then rotate individually into the circle.

Movie Review: Write a review of (or discuss) a movie based on a story.

Dear Author: After reading a book, write to the author via the publisher (who always forwards them).

Surf the Net: Prior to, while, or after reading a book, check out the Web and its offerings about the book, its author, or its subject.

Inspirations: Watch a film inspired by a story (e.g., *Franny and Alexander* is inspired by *Hamlet*) and compare/contrast.

Time Line: Create a time line that includes both the events in the novel and historical information of the time. Try using Post-its on a whiteboard or butcher paper!

Mandala: Create a mandala with many levels to connect different aspects of a book, its historical time, and culture.

Transparencies: Annotate a portion of text your teacher has copied to a transparency; use with markers and then get up to present interpretation to class.

Gender-Bender: Rewrite a scene and change the gender of the characters to show how they might act differently (e.g., *Lord of Flies*); can also have roundtable on gender differences.

Picture This: Bring in art related to the book's time or themes; compare, describe, discuss.

Kids' Books: Bring in children's books about related themes and read these aloud to class.

Downgrade: Adapt myths or other stories for a younger audience; make into children's books or dramatic adaptation on video or live.

Draw!: Translate chapters into storyboards and cartoons; draw the most important scene in the chapter and explain its importance and action.

Oprah Book Club: Host a talk show: students play the host, author, and cast of characters; allow questions from the audience.

Fictional Friends: Who of all the characters would you want for a friend? Why? What would you do or talk about together?

State of the Union: The President wants to recommend a book to the nation: tell him one important realization you had while reading this book and why he should recommend it.

Interview Question: When I interview prospective teachers, my first question is always "What are you reading and do you like it?"

Dear Diary: Keep a diary as if you were a character in the story. Write down events that happen during the story and reflect on *how* they affected the character and *why*.

Rosencrantz and Gildenstern: Write a story or journal from the perspective of characters with no real role in the story and show us what they see and think from their perspective.

Improv: Get up in front of class or in fishbowl and be whatever character the class calls out and do whatever they direct. Have fun with it.

What If: Write about or discuss how the story would differ if the characters were something other than they are: a priest, another gender or race, a different age, or social class.

Interrupted Conversations: Pair up and trade off reading through some text; *any time* you have something to say about some aspect of the story, interrupt the reader and discuss, question, argue.

Found Poetry: Take sections of the story and, choosing

carefully, create a found poem; then read these aloud and discuss.

13 Views: Inspired by Stevens's poem "13 Ways of Looking at a Blackbird": each stanza offers a different view of a character or chapter.

Personal Ad: What would a particular character write in a personal ad for the newspaper? After posting on board, discuss.

Holden Meets Hamlet: What would one character (or set of them) in one story say to another if given the chance to talk or correspond? Write a dialogue, skit, or letter.

Character Analysis: Describe a character as a psychologist or recruiting officer might: What are they like? Examples? Why are they like that?

Epistle Poem: Write a poem in the form and voice of a letter: e.g., Phoebe to Holden.

Write Into: Find a "hole" in the story where the character disappears (off camera) for a time and describe what they do when we can't see them.

The Woody Allen: in *Take the Money*, Allen interviews the parents of a man who became a bank robber. Write an imaginary interview with friends and family of a character whom they try to help you understand.

Author Interview: Write an interview or letter in which the character in a story asks the author a series of questions and reflects on how they feel about the way they were "made."

The Kuglemass: Woody Allen wrote a story in which the character can throw any book into a time machine and it takes you inside the book and the era. What would you do, say, if you "traveled" into the story you are reading?

Time Machine: Instead of traveling into the book, write a scene or story in which the character(s) travel out of the book into today.

Biography: Write a biography of one of the characters who most interests you.

Autobiography: Have the character that most interests you write their autobiography of the time before, during, or after the story occurs.

P.S.: After you read the story, write an epilogue in which you explain—using whatever tense and tone the author does—what happened to the character(s) next.

Board Game: Have groups design board games based on stories then play them. This is especially fun and works well with the *Odyssey*.

Life Graph: Using the Life Graph assignment, plot the events in the character's life during the story and evaluate their importance; follow up with a discussion of graphs.

Second Chance: Talk or write about how it would change the story if a certain character had made a different decision earlier in the story (e.g., what if Huck had not run away?)

Poetry Connection: Bring in poems that are thematically related to the story; integrate these into the larger discussion. Use *Poetry Index.*

Reader Response: Pick the most important word/line/image/

object/event in the chapter and explain why you chose it; be sure to support all analysis with examples.

Notes and Quotes: Draw a line down the middle of the page; on one side write down important quotes; on the other comment on and analyze the quotes.

Dear Classmate: Using e-mail or some other means of corresponding, write each other about the book as you read it, having a written conversation about the book.

Convention Introduction: You have been asked to introduce the book's author to a convention of English teachers. What would you say? Write and deliver your speech.

Sing Me a Song: Write a song/ballad about the story, a character, or an event in the book.

Write Your Own: Using the themes in the story, write your own story, creating your own characters and situation. It does not have to relate to the story at all aside from its theme.

Executive Summary: Take a 3×5 card and summarize what happened on one side; on the other, analyze the importance of what happened and the reasons it happened.

Read Aloud: One student starts the reading and goes until they wish to pass; they call on whomever they wish and that person picks up and continues reading for as long as they wish.

Quaker Reading: Like a Quaker meeting, one person stands and reads then sits, and whoever wishes to picks up and reads for as long as they wish . . . and so on.

Pageant of the Masters: In Los Angeles this remarkable event asks groups to "stage" different classical paintings in real life. People would try to do a still life of some scene from a book or play; the class should then discuss what is going on in this human diorama.

Create a Diorama: Create a diorama of a particularly important scene such as the courtroom or Ewells's house in *To Kill a Mockingbird.*

Day in Court: Use the story as the basis for a court trial; students can be witnesses, expert witnesses called to testify, judge, jury, bailiff, reporter—great fun for a couple days.

Censorship Defense: Imagine that the book you are reading has been challenged by a special interest group; students must write a letter defending the book, using specific evidence from the book to support their ideas.

Call for Censorship: In order to better understand all sides of an argument, imagine you are someone who feels this particular book should *not* be read and write a letter in which you argue it should be removed.

Speculation: Based on everything you know now in the story, what do you think will happen and why do you think that?

Questions, Anyone?: Students make a list of a certain number of questions they have about a particular character or aspect of the book; use these as the basis for class discussion.

Newspaper Connection: Have students read the newspapers and magazines to find articles that somehow relate to issues and ideas in the book(s) you are reading; bring in and discuss.

Jigsaw: Organize the class into groups, each one with a specific focus; after a time rotate so that new groups are formed to share what they discussed in their previous group.

Open Mind: Draw an empty head (some people use a bathtub instead) and inside of it draw any symbols or words or images that are bouncing around in the mind of the character of a story; follow it up with writing or discussion to explain and explore responses.

Interrogation: A student must come up before the class and, pretending to be a character or the author, answer questions from the class.

Post-its: If they are using a school book in which they cannot make notes or marks, encourage them to keep a pack of Post-its with them and make notes on these.

Just the Facts, Ma'am: Acting as a reporter, ask the students the basic questions to facilitate a discussion: who, what, where, why, when, how?

SQ3R: When reading a textbook or article, try this strategy: (S)urvey the assigned reading by first skimming through it; then formulate (Q)uestions by turning all chapter headings and subheadings into questions to answer as you read; next (R)ead the assigned section and try to answer those questions you formulated; now (R)ecite the information by turning away from the text as soon as you've finished reading the assigned section and reiterate it in your own words; finally, (R)eview what you read by going back to your questions, the chapter headings, and asking yourself what they are all referring to, what they mean.

Brainstorming/Webbing: Put a character or other word in the middle of a web; have students brainstorm associations while you write them down; then have them make connections between ideas and discuss or writing about them.

Cultural Literacy: Find out what students already know and address what they need to know before reading a story or certain part of a story.

Storyboard: Individually or in groups, create a storyboard for the chapter or story.

Interactive Story: If you have a student who is a computer genius, have them create a multimedia, interactive version of the story.

CyberGuides: Search the Net for virtual tours based on the books you might be studying. Try www.concorde.org.

Tableau: Similar to the Pageant of the Masters, this option asks you to create a still life setting; then someone steps up to touch different characters who come alive and talk from their perspective about the scene.

Audio Books: There are many audio editions of books we teach now available; some are even read by famous stars who turn the book into its own audio performance. Recommend to students with reading difficulties or play portions of them in class.

Sound Off!: Play a video version of a book you are reading—only turn off the sound while students watch it. Have them narrate or discuss or write about what is happening, what the actors are revealing about the story through their gestures. Then compare what you saw with what you read.

Narrate Your Own Reading: Show kids how you read a text by reading it aloud and interrupting yourself to explain how you grapple with it as you go. Model your own thinking process; kids often don't know what it "looks like" to think.

Magnetic Poetry: If working with a poem, enlarge it on a copier or computer and cut all words up into pieces; place in an envelope and have groups create poems from these words; later on discuss using the same words for different texts. Heavier stock paper is ideal.

Venn Diagram: Use a Venn diagram to help you organize your thinking about a text as you read it. Put differences between two books or characters on opposite sides and similarities in the middle.

Write an Essay: Using one of the different rhetorical modes, write an essay in which you make meaningful connections between the text and your own experiences or other texts you have read.

P.O.V.: How would it change the story if you rewrote it from a different point of view (e.g., changed it from first to third person)? Try it!

Daily Edition: Using the novel as the basis for your stories, columns, and editorials, create an newspaper or magazine based on or inspired by the book you are reading.

Read Recursively: On occasion circle back around to the beginning of the chapter or text to keep yourself oriented as to "the big picture." This is especially important if you have questions to answer based on reading.

Oral History: If you are reading a historical text, have students interview people who have some familiarity with that time period or the subject of the book.

Guest Speaker: If you are reading a book that deals with a subject an expert might help students better understand, invite one in. Try the Veterans of Foreign Wars, for example, if reading about war.

Storytelling: After reading a story, pair up with others and tell the story as a group, recalling it in order, piecing it together, and clarifying for each other when one gets lost.

Reciprocal Teaching: A designated student or group reads a section of a text and comes prepared to present or "teach" it to the class; follow up with discussion for clarification.

Make Your Own Test: Have students create their own test or essay questions about the text; this allows them to simultaneously think about the story and prepare for the test on it.

Recasting the Text: Students rewrite a poem as a story, a short story as a poem or play. All rewrites should then be read and discussed so as to understand how the different genres work.

Debates: Students reading controversial texts or novels with debatable subjects such as *1984* should debate the issues.

Literature Circles: Students gather in groups to discuss the text and then report out to the class for full-class discussion.

That Was Then, This Is Now: After reading the text, create a Before/After list to compare the ways in which characters or towns have changed over the course of the story. Follow up with a discussion of reasons.

May be copied for classrooom use. Reading Reminders by Jim Burke (Boynton/Cook, a subsidiary of Reed Elsevier Inc., © 2000).

Dear Sophomores:

The last thing you are thinking about now is reading and writing; you have only the sound of summer months calling in your ears. Still, take a moment to think about what I have to say. You have worked as hard as any class I can remember teaching. That investment in yourself, in your capacity, your potential, in *yourself* is something you WILL WANT TO maintain and nurture. * * *

When I talk about reading this summer, I mean all different types: Web sites, newspapers, magazines, and books. Magazines are great, but they don't usually challenge you as a reader and thus won't make you a better reader. That's why you need to read other parts of the newspaper, more challenging articles and magazines, and books—about anything. For in addition to improving your ability to read, you have dramatically improved your stamina. * * *

Take the attached summer reading list home with you and do your summer reading. Not because you have to or even because it's good for you, which it is. Do it because you know you like to read; everyone in here (with a few rare exceptions) has realized this: that so long as you find something you like to read, you . . . like to read. If you don't know what to read, ask me to mark a title or three on the list before you leave today.

Finally, though it might sound a bit corny, I feel you are always my students once you pass through my class. That means that in the remaining two years you can always come to me for help, for guidance, for space to think, study, or relax. It means my Web site (www. englishcompanion.com) is always there to help you as it is (and I am) able. And it means I will come up to you in the halls in the years ahead and ask you how you are doing (maybe even try to give you a push if you seem to be slacking off!). We are all in this together. * * *

It has been a genuine pleasure to work so hard with all of you. * * * Now finish that final and enjoy your summer. You've earned it.

Mr. Burke

TYPES OF TEXT

TO INFORM
- abstract
- annual report
- ballot
- bibliography
- forms
- job applications
- pager codes
- pager text messages
- précis
- recipe
- report
- tax forms
- bills
- brochures
- catalog
- executive summary
- financial statement
- flyer
- gauges
- index
- instruments
- labels
- manual
- map
- menu
- meters
- minutes
- multimedia encyclopedia
- obituaries
- product labels
- schedule
- statistics
- table of contents
- tables
- want ads

TO PERSUADE
- advertisement
- allegory
- blurbs
- broadsides
- buttons
- campaign documents
- clothing
- editorial
- flag
- gestures
- headlines
- letterhead
- pamphlet
- parable
- proposal

- résumé
- reviews
- signs
- slogans
- television commercial

TO EXPLAIN
- affidavit
- diaries
- journals
- memos
- word problems
- narratives (slave and Indian captivity)
- prospectus
- rubric
- rule
- summary
- textbook
- theory
- time line
- travelogue
- annotated text
- caption
- constitution
- contracts
- dictionary entries
- directions
- law
- memoir
- policy
- school assignment/worksheet
- service agreements
- warranties

MULTIPLE FUNCTIONS
- autobiography
- biography
- business letter
- cartoon
- event program
- chart
- newspaper article
- chat room dialogue
- cover letters
- deposition
- diagram
- dialogues
- e-mail
- essay
- fable
- fairy tale
- film
- flowcharts

- folktale
- hypertexts
- illustration
- instant messages
- lists
- listserv
- logos
- magazine article
- mixed media (e.g., artwork)
- monologue
- montage
- multimedia product
- myth
- names
- newsgroup postings
- novel
- online magazine
- oral storytelling
- painting
- personal letter
- photograph
- play
- poem
- popular magazines
- professional journals
- screen capture
- short story
- song lyric
- speech
- documentary film
- graph
- event program
- symbols
- product packaging
- tattoos
- Web page
- Web site

MISCELLANEOUS
- chapbooks
- eulogy
- graffiti
- history
- icons
- MOO
- MUD
- occasional letter
- sermon
- situations
- television program
- test/examination
- testimony
- tracts

Index